All royalties generated from sales of this book will be paid to Futures Forum Scotland.

Luath Press is an independently owned and managed book publishing company based in Scotland, and is not aligned to any political party or grouping.

Viewpoints is an occasional series exploring issues of current and future relevance.

The contributions to this book are the work of the individual authors. They are neither the views of a particular political party nor the reflection of any ideology. Similarly they are the views of the authors not of any company or organisation that they work for or represent. Their contributions are not to be implied, unless otherwise stated, to their employers or colleagues.

Extract from Edwin Morgan poem 'Open the Doors!' reproduced by kind permission of the Scottish Parliamentary Corporate Body.

D0260198

Agenda for a New Scotland

Visions of Scotland 2020

Introduced and compiled by
KENNY MacASKILL

Luath Press Limited

EDINBURGH

www.luath.co.uk

First Published 2005
Reprinted 2006
Reprinted 2008

The paper used in this book is acid-free, recyclable and biodegradable.
It is made from low-chlorine pulps produced in a low energy,
low-emission manner from renewable forests.

Printed and bound by
Exacta Print, Glasgow

Typeset in 10.5pt Sabon by
3btype.com 0131 658 1763

for Callum and Roddy whose generation will reap the benefit if we succeed and pay the price if we fail.

Acknowledgements

THE THANKS FOR THIS book go firstly to each and every contributor who has allowed the venture to become a reality. In particular, though, I must credit Dr Andrew Cubie who encouraged it and by his participation facilitated it. Also, Susan Deacon MSP who showed political courage in agreeing to step out and above the sectarian swamp of Scottish politics, thus allowing the cross party and no party venture to succeed.

Thanks are also due to Professor David Arter from the School of Scandinavian Studies in Aberdeen who assisted with his encyclopaedic knowledge of Finland and matters Scandic. In addition to Conor O'Riordan the Irish Consul who advised on the Tallaght strategy and lent me his copy of *The Making of the Celtic Tiger*.

As ever, thanks go to Craig Milroy, Euan Lloyd and David Hutchison who assisted throughout and were essential to its accomplishment. Their advice, guidance and comments have been essential from the book's conception to birth.

Also, to my son Callum for his help in drafting biographies and other matters.

Finally, to Karen Newton and Tricia Marwick MSP for support and assistance in this endeavour.

Kenny MacAskill

Contents

Foreword

Rt Hon George Reid MSP
Presiding Officer, the Scottish Parliament

OUR NEW PARLIAMENT SITS at the bottom end of the Royal Mile, where a thousand years of our people's history widens into Holyrood Park, a primeval landscape whose volcanoes shaped Scotland.

Holyrood is a privileged place. Anyone who was anything in Scotland's story has been down the Canongate before us: our early monarchs, Mary Queen of Scots, Bonnie Prince Charlie, Robert Burns and – importantly for all of us who are politicians – the philosophers, economists and practical men of science of the Enlightenment who largely made the modern world.

Enric Miralles has built a parliament in that tradition, which grows out of the land of Scotland. It is not grand, or patrician. It is part of the life of the Canongate, built to facilitate the participative principles on which Holyrood is founded. It is a place designed, Miralles said, for 'conversation', not 'confrontation'.

Agenda for a New Scotland is a contribution to that conversation. Now that we are in our new home, it matches the mood, declared by politicians of all hues, that we must raise our game, think out of the box, and peek over the horizon.

This book asks the right question: now that we have devolution, what do we do with it?

How do we build a sustainable society in Scotland, comfortable with itself at home, and confident of competing in the global marketplace?

As Presiding Officer of the Scottish Parliament I welcome all contributions — Left, Right and Centre — to the debate on where Scotland is going. As we envisage the future, we can shape the policies which we put in place now.

Some of the contributions to this publication may make uncomfortable reading for those raised within rigid party structures. But the men and women of Edinburgh's earlier Enlightenment would hardly have put their stamp on the modern world if they had not challenged the received wisdom of their age.

I commend *Agenda for a New Scotland* to all who believe that our country has a bright future, and who want to play their part in making sure that it happens.

George Reid

Introduction

Romanticism to Realism – Creating a Caledonian Consensus

KENNY MacASKILL

THE CAMPAIGN FOR A Scottish Parliament was ongoing for centuries. Its loss was lamented in prose and its cause championed in print. It was pursued by individuals and parties, conventions and covenants. It was petitioned for, marched in support of and voted upon. Vigils were held for it and referenda about it. Its cause was dear to the hearts of many and its absence broke the hearts of a few. It was sought out of Nationalist sentiment and desired for better governance in a land with a distinct Law, Church and Education. But, at long last it has finally been restored.

May 1999 saw it reconvene after nearly 300 years. A Devolved Legislature with powers ceded through an Act of the Westminster Parliament. But, a Parliament all the same. Recognised from without with powers from within. Placing Scotland once more on the international political scene and allowing once again for national political decision making. Unable to address all issues but able to make a difference in many areas.

Whether it should be a fully sovereign Parliament recognising Scotland's independence or simply a devolved legislature recognising the Scots distinctive identity is still debated and has yet to be finally decided. What is clear though is that this Parliament is here to stay. Its powers may change and its scope may be extended. It will, though, be from and through this Parliament that change will occur and Scotland's future will be decided. No other institution has that right or will take that responsibility. It is for the Scottish Parliament to shape and mould the future of the Scotland. But what is that future to be?

The fight for the restoration of the Institution was not only long but also arduous. Countless difficulties were encountered and many fell by the wayside. The opponents of devolution and the Parliament were many and powerful. Maintaining the struggle meant that the focus was more often on the cause than the outcome. Its achievement as a goal mattered more than its goals upon achievement. The ways to win it were debated but the ways to follow on from the winning were ignored. But, it is here now and what is to be done?

The battle was often waged within rather than without. The hostility and often hatred between those seeking Independence as opposed to Home Rule was great. Oft times it exceeded the enmity between supporters of the Union and those who sought a Parliament of whatever powers. Rancour and disruption plagued attempts to create a consensus for change. Whether it was to be an Independent parliament or Devolved one appeared a higher priority than having one at all. Individuals and parties with a commitment to a Scottish parliament seemed to prefer a fist fight to a common front. Such squabbles are not unique to Scotland. They have scarred other movements and campaigns worldwide and throughout history. Scotland proved to be no different. But, times have moved on and so must attitudes.

Scotland now has its Parliament and within it a multi party democracy representing parties from across the political spectrum. All accept the integrity of the Institution. Even Unionists opposed to Devolution now consider it part of the political landscape. Pro Home Rule parties are in the majority and pro Independence parties represent a substantial part thereof. It is clear that further powers will be devolved. The methodology used to decide what constituted a reserved or devolved matter if not done on a whim and fancy clearly left a lot to be desired. Powers over doctors but not vets is irrational. Devolving justice but not drugs or firearms illogical. Responsibility for Culture but not the media a massive impediment. Some additional powers have already been transferred or are in the process of being so. The devolution of Rail is a substantial boost to the powers and prestige of the Parliament even if it captured little attention. Other powers will doubtless follow whether through political pressure for a Sovereign Parliament or simply for good governance within the United Kingdom. Scotland is on a constitutional journey. The final destination has not been decided but a considerable distance has still to be travelled.

Scotland also now has not just its Parliament but an impressive new Building as its home. Considerable progress has been made since its return. The initial years were uniformly accepted as being disappointing. Delight turned into derision. Mistakes were many and errors abounded. That though is now behind it. There is an acceptance across the political spectrum that politicians 'must raise their game'. They must improve their service to the country and the quality if not quantity of their political output. But, what direction is to be taken, what ideas implemented and what vision outlined?

Scotland has changed but the world has not stood still either. Globalisation of the world economy has happened and the expansion of the European Union has taken place. The competitive threat to Scotland economically from without is significant. The economic statistics confirm that Scotland is underperforming as a country and at the same time being outperformed by other Nations whether in Eastern Europe or South East Asia. That must be a matter of significant concern to all not least the body politic. The Parliament has economic responsibilities as well as a social agenda. A stumbling economy impedes social progress. Action on that and other areas needs taken.

The Scottish tragedy is not that she is doing so badly but that she could do so much better. The under performance has occurred in a land that was an industrial giant despite her size at the beginning of the 20th Century. That in part powered the growth and expansion of the British Empire through her factories and shipyards never mind her people. That has been blessed with numerous talented sons and daughters though not all either stayed or were able to succeed in their native land. Finally, that has been given a substantial natural bounty in North Sea oil and gas.

Despite all those advantages afforded, she has failed to properly capitalise on them. The economic lead and advantage has been overtaken by many and is being caught by more. Throughout all this, Scotland has remained blighted by many social ills and problems. Many of which have their roots in poverty. Nations dealt less favoured hands have played them significantly better in recent years.

That said all is not doom and gloom in this Land. Much has been achieved even if so much more could be done. Many prospered even if some endured penury. There are many areas that highlight not just individual successes but afford a collective feeling of satisfaction. From corporate triumphs to educational prowess – evidence abounds. Perennial doom saying undermines self-confidence and is damaging to the national psyche. It creates a culture of fatalism rather than an acceptance of responsibility. It fosters a climate of blame not an environment for solutions. Scotland can do so much better as a Nation and for its Citizens. The challenge is to achieve that.

Scotland has suffered from the British disease of stop startism and short termism that has plagued both British politics and governance. Governments come and go and as a consequence so do strategy and direction. Key issues are implacably opposed by opposition and key areas repudiated by an incoming administration. The achievement of power unleashes the pent up frustrations felt by an excluded opposition. Change can take place for its own sake as opposed to any improvement in the Nation's well being. That is partly down to the structures of governance in Westminster. The absence of proportional representation creates a winner takes all situation with an uncompromising attitude as a result. Allied to that is a more hostile relationship between Government and Opposition. That has been damaging to the body politic and to the national interest. The new Scottish Parliament is an opportunity to learn from the flaws of Westminster and to follow the successful routes of Scandinavian Nations and our Celtic cousins across the Irish Sea.

Other Nations have chosen not to go down the road of political war. They sought to reach a consensus on core values for the State and agreed strategies by the Government. Matters were debated, discussed but ultimately acted upon and adhered to. Scandinavian Nations benefited from a collective consensus on the role of the state and the rights of the citizen; and the need to balance an entrepreneurial society with a welfare state. There was an accord addressing external problems and meeting internal requirements. An ethos grew up that was accepted and adhered to by a variety of different parties of varying political hues whether in Government or Opposition.

Specific examples can be found in Ireland and Finland. Both are small Nations like Scotland. Similar in size and with similar problems. They are performing well economically and with that success addressing many of the ills within their society. Times, though, were not always so prosperous or harmonious. Both found themselves in the recent past in straitened times. They required to take a long hard look at how they not just addressed Global matters but achieved their society's objectives. They sought to resolve them by working together on particular areas, not continually pulling apart. The solution that they invoked was of creating a political consensus on key areas of concern. It was recognition of the enormity of the problems facing them and the necessity to create a common front for the common wealth.

1987 found the Irish economy in deep trouble and Irish society deeply divided. The outgoing Taoiseach Garret FitzGerald, defeated on the casting vote of the Speaker when commenting on the problems Ireland was facing stated that they 'can only be overcome by an effort of political will involving a commitment and a degree of united effort on the part of all of us in politics. It will not be easy for an opposition to support some of the measures the Government will have to take... yet we will do so. It will not be easy for the Government to take these steps but they must do so.' Recognition of both the enormity of the problems they faced and the requirement for unity in solving them culminated in the 'Tallaght Strategy'. Alan Dukes the Fine Gael and Opposition Leader addressing the Tallaght Chamber of Commerce in September 1987 stated 'it is the role of the Parliamentary Opposition to... redirect Government policy where it diverges from the right track and to oppose Government where it is wrong. In specific terms, that means that when the Government is moving in the right direction, I will not oppose the central thrust of its policy. If it is going in the right direction, I do not believe that it should be deviated from its course, or tripped up on macro economic issues. Any other policy of opposition would amount simply to a cynical exploitation of short-term political opportunities for a political advantage which would inevitably prove to be equally short lived. I will not play that game.' Opposition for the simple sake of it would cease and short-term political advantage would not be sought where it would damage the long-term national interest. It added to and built upon previous accords between Government and Unions, employers and employees on wages and other policies. It initially covered the economy but has been called for in other areas. That strategy is credited by many with being the basis of the 'Celtic Tiger'.

Prior to that accord on the economy a consensus had been reached on the necessity of investing in education. In the 1960s Irish politicians recognised the requirement to prioritise that aspect of Government spending. That step change in seeking an educated Irish workforce allowed for inward investment and economic growth in specialist fields. It was accepted by all Governments of whatever political complexion over the following thirty years. That resulted in the remarkable situation that whilst in 1964 just 1 in 4 seventeen year olds were still in secondary education that figure had risen by 1994 to 83%. As Ray Mac Sharry and Padraic White state in their book *The Making of the Celtic Tiger* 'all Governments from the early sixties on were quick to recognise the potential of education and to invest in the future'. Social Partnerships involving Government, Unions and Employers also afforded a national cohesion and a shared direction even when addressing difficult aspects of pay and other such policy areas.

Finnish society has also faced not just economic but geo-political problems culminating in the term Finlandization entering the political lexicon. That necessitated the creation of an informal political consensus which commenced in the 1960s with a broad-based centre left coalition Government. It has though been renewed in more recent years to address new challenges and other difficulties.

During the period of the Cold War Finland had been partially protected from problematic economic cycles by a regularised trading relationship based on barter with the Soviet Union. At its peak in the early 1980s trade with the USSR amounted to one-fifth of Finland's total. However, an overheating economy in the latter part of that decade coupled with the collapse of the Soviet Union saw Finland's application for membership of the EU coincide with a substantial recession. Unemployment soared to 20% the second worst in the whole of the EU. The Finnish Parliament successfully pressed the Government for a range of scenarios for Finland in 2020 and the unique Parliament Committee for the Future was formed. At the same time Nokia led an electronic and export orientated recovery.

In 1995 a 'rainbow coalition', comprising parties from the former communists through to the Conservatives, generated the consensus for Finnish membership of the EMU and allowed for a series of overarching incomes policy agreements. Finland's strong export performance and moderate incomes policy agreements were supported and underpinned by a consensual political culture of the broad national interest.

Political and civic society in Finland recognised the need to take action and to do so in many instances collectively. It was an acceptance that although short-term measures could be taken long term action was ultimately needed. National plans could thereby not just be developed but implemented. It addressed not just social and economic matters but foreign policy. It secured the political integrity of the Nation, strengthened the economy and allowed for marked social improvement.

It was not rocket science. But, the necessary action by politicians in small lands facing difficulties and seeking to address them. Small Nations have disadvantages in scale and resources but they have huge advantages in the ability to reach a consensus and take decisive action in key areas. It is therefore of no great surprise that the most successful Nations and Regions are of a size akin to Scotland and not that of the global powers.

Lessons must be learned from them. Scotland must follow the successful path of those small Nations. What needs created is not a parliamentary coalition but a political consensus on many areas. It does not mean the abandonment of political parties or the cessation of political debate. They remain a vital part of a parliamentary democracy representing the diversity of views within and of the Nation. There is though recognition that there are matters that transcend individual parties and supersede narrow party interest. There is a national interest in many areas, not least in the economy, that must be allowed to prevail. It necessitates the acceptance of core values and a central vision for the state not across all areas but along some fundamentals. It means the acceptance of a national strategy in the running of the economy and other key areas. Political dissent and debate still take place and lively at that. Challenges and confrontations still occur. However, it must be underpinned by an acceptance of the need to adhere to shared objectives and strategies on critical topics.

Countless sacrifices were made by many over the years to achieve the restoration of the Scottish Parliament. It is the duty of those who now serve in it or who have influence upon it to ensure it lives up to those hopes and expectations. Scottish politics has been marked if not scarred by tribalism whereby Party interests are placed above the National interest. That must change not in all areas but most certainly across key areas.

Scottish politics has suffered not just from an absence of consensus but from the lack of a forum for ideas to flourish in it. The energy dissipated in achieving the restoration seemingly sapping the collective will to outline a vision for the Nation. Ideas have percolated and thoughts have been generated but strategy and consensus has never been addressed or achieved. Debate and discussion about direction is essential. The opportunity now exists to implement some of those ideas and thoughts.

The smart, successful and socially just Scotland that is sought will not be delivered by one Party or Government alone. Nor certainly will it be achieved in one term of office. It will take time. Years, whether of neglect or wasted opportunity ensure that. A New Scotland will not be built in a day. It requires ideas and an accord amongst politicians to deliver them. The time has come for a Scottish Tallaght Strategy whereby ideas and goals can be both agreed upon and delivered. Adhered to by the Government and supported by the opposition. Where short-term political capital is not sought at the expense of long-term national gain.

The New Parliament allows a similar strategy to be devised in Scotland. Economic and social needs dictate that such a strategy needs to be delivered. Many have sought to do so before. They were restricted, though, by the absence of a Parliament to allow such change to occur. The forum afforded and the powers provided by the Parliament were not available in the past but they are available now. It might not have the powers to do everything required but it most certainly can address some of the requirements. The absence of Fiscal Autonomy or representation in Foreign Affairs means that many of the Scandinavian or Irish actions are denied. However, there are still areas of opportunity for concerted and united action. Whether or not the current powers need to be extended, progress can still be made in their absence. And it needs to be. Moreover, it can be an auditorium within which to champion the other changes needed whether legislative, cultural or constitutional. This opportunity must not be passed up. The time has come for Scotland's political leaders to seek solutions not simply apportion blame. The sterile arguments over who caused what and when do not provide the answers for today and will most certainly not do so for tomorrow.

This requires an Executive with vision and an Opposition with courage. It cannot mean simply doing less better or a mantra chant of raising the game. It means new thoughts and updated ideas. It matters not from whence they come but what they can offer. It doesn't mean an end to conflict between parties or conflict amongst politicians. It does mean the creation of new alliances across not just parties but society; around key ideas never mind goals and objectives. The Constitutional relationship will still be debated and fought over. There are those who will never cede the right of Scotland to achieve full Nationhood. Equally, there are others who see no need for secession from the United Kingdom. They can though co-operate for the common good on other areas. There is a responsibility to make things work within the existing Parliament even if a divide remains on its ultimate powers. Co-operating on those areas does not conflict with a continuing divide on the constitutional issue.

The articles that follow are an attempt to create that co-oper-ation and reach that consensus. The authors come from a broad spectrum of Scottish society and have differing views on many issues. This book is neither sponsored by nor is it the property of any one political Party or ideology. It is offered to provide a diver-sity of opinion on a range of topics of significance to our society. Not everyone will agree with all of the sentiments nor do all the contributors necessarily agree with each other. They belong to many parties and to no party: they simply have a vision of where this land of ours could be in a relatively small number of years. 2020 is not that far away and in terms of how Government policy is not just developed but delivered it is short indeed. However the need is great, the competition intense and time is of the essence.

The ideas they have differ both on areas and solutions. Some address economic issues others social, cultural or sporting matters. But each area is of interest and concern to Scotland. Some believe that further constitutional change is needed others do not. For some the change is cultural for others social and economic. There are areas that might be perceived as politically controversial and challenging to current orthodoxy. But, if a Tallaght strategy is to be delivered then such sentiments need said. Other areas are perhaps uncontroversial but have either not been articulated or not been properly heard in a political forum with powers. Now is the time to give their vision a voice.

The restoration of the Scottish Parliament after nearly 300 years imposes obligations on those who serve in it or seek to serve the common good. There can be no greater obligation than to make this land a better land. The slow decline is counter posed with a rapid increase in the ferocity of the competition. The cycle of economic underperformance leading to emigration and social problems needs broken once and for all lest it prove terminal to Scotland's prospects. In any event it's more the failure to deliver from opportunity than the descent into decline that frets and frustrates. This Nation blessed with so much can deliver so much more. Not just for what it does for its own citizens but how it partakes and interacts abroad. Scotland is now once more a participant not just a spectator even if access to seats at all international fora and debate are not available. It can do things as well as say things. It can take actions in its own name.

This is an attempt to see if a national consensus can be created across a broad range of areas; stimulating debate, discussion and dialogue. Moving Scotland on from the romanticism of the past to the construction of a realistic future. Trying to ensure that if an accord can be reached then it can be abided by and adhered to; not for individual gain but the common good. These are visions of how Scotland could be in 2020. Some will falter and some may fail. But, some surely can be the basis of a consensus that lets Scotland be all it can be. Those fortunate enough to be able to influence the New Parliament owe it to those whose sacrifices restored it. In it they have a responsibility to ensure it is used for the betterment of the Nation and future generations of Scots.

Scotland can do so much better and achieve so much more. We can raise the game individually and collectively. For the common weal there must be a Caledonian Consensus.

SECTION I
Scene Setting

From the *Red Paper* to Now

OWEN DUDLEY EDWARDS

The Red Paper on Scotland (ed. Gordon Brown, EUSPB, 1975) is a historical landmark, and like all such landmarks its most obvious use is for posterity to unearth for offen-sive use, either as a sharp or a blunt instrument. Thirty years after, its most obvious use to many is to belabour (rather than beLabour) the Rt Hon the Chancellor of the Exchequer, PC, MP, most obvious Premier-of-the-Future, confronting him with his lost leadership of the Scottish Revolution. To do so is largely a waste of our opportunity, reducing the landmark to a pin-prick, much as though the main interest of Socialism in 1937 was that it happened to be the title of a book published thirty years earlier by the now dying James Ramsay MacDonald.

Whatever place the future may hold for Gordon Brown, whatever place he has won since entering Parliament, are irrelevant to the boy Rector of the University of Edinburgh in 1975 bringing that book together: they can neither add to it nor detract from it. The making of the *Red Paper* is an example, but for Scottish students of the future, not for Scottish statesmen with pasts. It is an indictment of the Chancellor and his colleagues that such students will find it much less easy to draw together the crowd of student printers, journalists, artists, visionairies, cranks, polemicists, votaries, sidekicks, groupies, new-worlders, neo-traditionalists, jokers, zealots, &c, &c, who had brought into being and maintained the Edinburgh University Student Publications Board. The Board is defunct; the publication wing, ultimately branded as Polygon, was sold ten years afterwards to Edinburgh University Press, who resold it over 15 years later to Birlinn; and students today have neither time nor money for such achievement, deprived as they are of their grants, forced into frequently demeaning jobs while getting themselves through their university courses.

It is from that point of view that the *Red Paper* mocks its original maker in his present existence. And it would be easy to denigrate the *Red Paper* itself by making it a convenient stepladder to bring its editor to power while being kicked aside itself. But in fact that makes no sense. A careerist cynic would never have inherited the Publications Board, won the support of its fairly hard-bitten operatives, risked his student career in his confrontations with authority, or above all won the admiration and love given by the contributors and publishing team. Dr Brown has been caricatured in recent years as the 'Iron Chancellor', as a bully or a prima donna; whatever the merit of these judgements (and there may well be none) no such person could have pulled that incessantly arguing mob together. His seriousness of purpose inspired; but his delight in humour, his pleasure in being made fun of, his geniality under affectionate recrimination, his obvious compassion for human suffering, and his clear sense of mission were essential for his success. He may well be the most intelligent Chancellor since Cripps or Dalton; but his leadership and editorship were more reminiscent of St Francis of Assisi or Robin Hood. Writers with vast differences followed his lead in making the landmark, with some of the happiness you might expect from a day with the beggar friars or a night in Sherwood Forest.

We might say that the very achievement of St Francis or Robin Hood was likely to keep them unique; but they did not join governments whose antics had that effect. So the first stark point which comes of turning over the 368 pages of the *Red Paper* is that the thirty years show a disgraceful contrast in the condition of the kind of person who made it. In its existence, it implied a place for youth in shaping the country's future; that landmark is now a tombstone.

The *Red Paper* had many contributors who were not in the Labour Party, but its most obvious political effect lay in converting – or, to be historically accurate, in reconverting – the Labour Party in Scotland to some form of Scottish nationalism. It also confronted the rising Scottish National Party, in the spring tide of its Westminster election surge of 1974, with insistence on eradication of poverty and pursuit of equality as goals never to be postponed.

Gordon Brown had been converted to the unifying of socialism and nationalism when the poet-folklorist Hamish Henderson got him to terms with Gramsci, and fathered a student-led conference on the question, which produced a publication of relevant Gramsci writings in the EUSPB-published *New Edinburgh Review* (now the *Edinburgh Review*). The Labour party in general had shuddered away in 1945 from thoughts of intertwined nationalism and socialism in the desolate aftermath of Nazi Europe. Yet Scottish Labour and Scottish Nationalism drew heavy ideology from common wellsprings and (much more than either admitted) cherished the cults of common gods: Keir Hardie, Jimmy Maxton, RB Cunninghame Graham, Hugh MacDiarmid, CND. Perhaps the most blood-curdling – if unintentional – illustration of this was the SNP delegate giving a party conference speech who thundered 'As for the Labour party, if Keir Hardie were alive today, he would be turning in his grave'.

Gordon Brown and the Labour-linked contributors to the *Red Paper* were (then) firmly on the Left of the Labour party, but the most spectacular convert to emerge in Scottish Labour after the 1975 publication was on the party Right: John Smith. Brown found the going tough in championing the idea of a Scottish parliament. He had given his party the ideological basis for the respectability of Scottish devolution, and the voting swings towards the SNP offered an opportunistic basis, but he learned that many griefs awaited the prophet in his own party. The climate in the English party was even colder, and Scottish devolutionary Labour campaigners found themselves simultaneously denouncing Wilson (or Callaghan) and the SNP. Devolution was not popular in itself; the firmest positions were those of the intransigent Unionists in Labour and Tory ranks (not then including Douglas-Home, Heath, Thatcher, Rifkind, or Ancram), and those Nationalists who opposed the use of any halfway house. The Liberals were traditional supporters of devolution, indeed of federalism all round, but the Liberals were then under the star-crossed leadership of Jeremy Thorpe. The *Scotsman* played a crucial role here. Its own tradition had been fairly firmly Unionist since 1886, when it broke with Gladstone over Irish Home Rule, but it showed some of the most receptive rethinking in or out of party ranks. Brown's personal friends and admirers included its Education editor (and future editor of the Glasgow *Herald*) Henry Reid; the paper's Nationalists acquired the forceful voice of Colin Bell; Neal Ascherson's return to Scotland brought a deeply sensitive and cosmopolitan listener, ready to give positive response to new Scottish ideas, where justified. The paper itself was rapidly changing from an instinctive support for conventional politics to a strong, forceful, well-informed questioning, but a questioning which was constructive and positive rather than merely iconoclastic. The wind of change may have been most powerful in the Arts, whose Editor, Allen Wright, committed the paper to championship of new plays on the Edinburgh Festival Fringe. The *Red Paper* had included an essay by John McGrath, whose leadership of 7:84 Theatre Company had barnstormed Scotland with the great Socialist documentary-comedy-tragedy-history *The Cheviot, the Stag, and the Black Black Oil*, raging against the destruction of the Highlands. McGrath and his associates loudly denounced bourgeois nationalism, and found themselves being cheered to the echo by the bourgeois nationalists. Allen Wright, a Tory, had no personal respect for either Scottish nationalism or Marxist revolution, but he was passionately dedicated to the improvement of Scottish theatre, and Scotland's self-rediscovery flourished on the stage with his benevolent encouragement.

As Allen Wright's case shows, this was a revolution with a sense of humour. Scotland was having its 1960s in the 1970s (a judicious place to have them), and beyond established newspapers there were a variety of irreverent student prints and light-hearted academic confections. Bob Tait (another *Red Paper* contributor) had begun the decade with editorship of *Scottish International*, a far-ranging, free-wheeling challenge to all forms of Scottish conventionalism. Alexander McCall Smith, the future best-selling novelist, was the (Liberal) mastermind directing a hilarious, nationalist weekly Q – *Question* which resulted in Norman Buchan MP taking to epic poetry in reply. But as Buchan's case indicates, however hard the political hitting, many of these figures secretly knew that below their shiftings and flytings lay a common awareness in having

Scotland come back to some self-respect. It was particularly notable in history, where consensus-minded academics of initially British and hence (if they thought about it) Unionist assumptions grew more and more excited in the discovery of Scotland. Their controversies made the heather grow on bare hills, and Scottish history was transformed from sparse outcrops of aridity and kitsch into an inspirational abundance all the more valuable for disputation over what seemed every inch. One very healthy result was that where it had looked as though professional history would be negative, priding itself on destruction of nationalist or socialist myth, the act of writing about Scotland became itself a form of nationalism. False nationalist myths were still most appropriate targets; but even Unionist historians realised that the subject itself asserted the importance of being Scottish. History in Ireland had found itself taught chiefly in protest against official myths. History in Scotland found that it flourished because people were no longer ashamed to discuss the subject. Even here there was a confluence for young historians like Gordon Brown: both Scotland, and labour, were subjects in danger of being written out of history, sidelined, silenced, kicked into kitsch, tokens, or jokes. The 1970s helped bring them out of the cold. To say this is to restate what the *Red Paper* was about.

The *Red Paper* possessed one essential of propaganda: it converted its writers as well as its readers. Tom Nairn, for instance, hymned some of the most forceful cosmopolitanism and funniest ironies of the debate – as well as massive journalism and a philosophical depth indignantly denounced by Norman Buchan; but his massive essay in the *Red Paper* was ferociously critical of nationalism. Yet its logic led him rapidly to identify much that was positive and valuable in Scottish nationalism and to become one of its keenest – never uncritical – votaries. Bob Tait had a comparable change along slightly different routes; so did Jim Sillars. The pursuit of the ideas let loose by the *Red Paper* would send others in different directions: as the years went on, there would be other movements from the SNP to strongly devolutionary wings of Labour. By the end of the 1970s a loose if mutually suspicious alliance of devolutionists emerged.

That 1979 brought the defeat of devolution is common knowledge, and like much common knowledge it is wrong. The thin and inadequate Scottish Assembly ultimately offered by James Callaghan's government was passed in referendum by those Scots who voted. It failed of adoption under an absurd amendment requiring that the referendum be passed by 40% of the total electorate voting 'YES'. This did not mean that Scotland had rejected devolution; it meant that Britain did not know how to administer a referendum, something which the UK's performance in joining the EEC had already made painfully evident. There remains today an English superstition that a referendum is 'undemocratic', a perfect oxymoron; but it has been articulated across the British political landscape, from Sir Keith Joseph to Will Hutton. Nevertheless the achievement in retrospect was a remarkable one. The *Red Paper*, the *Scotsman*, and their personal adherents had had to win popular favour for devolution, a process which not only offended the true believers in Unionism and in Independence, but which was also unknown in British political experience. (That it was alive and well and in operation in Northern Ireland was hardly likely to advance its attractions; however irrationally, it prompted the assumption that Northern Ireland's civil wars were somehow due to devolution. In fact, one of the strongest arguments in favour of Scottish devolution or independence was that their respective votaries were non-violent and anti-violent, thus saving Scotland from the endless drip, stream or cascade of bloodshed in Irish nationalism.) The 'NO' campaign of 1979 was exceptionally disgraceful; Thatcher had reversed her former support for devolution, punished such lieutenants as held true to their beliefs, and simultaneously had Sir Alec Douglas-Home campaign for the 'NO' forces promising stronger measures of devolution under the Tories. Nemesis followed. The election after the Referendum of 1979 resulted in a Thatcher decade which culminated in congratulatory dinners in London and in Edinburgh rejoicing in the denial of devolution to the electorate which had voted for it. The *mentalité* thus exhibited brought home the meaning of devolution in quite a new and acceptable form to the Scottish electorate. Whatever devolution was, it was clear that Thatcher now saw it as anathema. After ten years of her rule, the Scots were therefore ready to welcome it at the first opportunity.

Yet the form in which the Stepmother of Devolution accomplished her own destruction was not merely negative. Her snouting for an invitation to address the General Assembly of the Church of Scotland in 1988 (obtained by her demand for one from her own nominee as Lord High Commissioner) led to the blasphemously-named 'Sermon on the Mound' redolent with all of Thatcher's ideological hatred of welfare, and thence to the desperate need of the Church of Scotland to disassociate themselves from her. Their method was perfect, that of opening their doors to a Constitutional Convention, which committed all political parties except the Tories to much more radical devolution than Callaghan had offered. But what had happened was a very Scottish event, unlike the earlier history of devolution, whose Scottishness (in the *Red Paper* sense) was strong but not obvious. Scotland's identity expresses itself in institutions, of which the Church of Scotland is one (thus making Queen Elizabeth the only human being on the surface of the globe whose religion is legally dictated by her geographical latitude). But the Church of Scotland, whose ministers had been outlawed before they captured the Kirk in 1689, and which had split in 1843 on the issue of their right to choose their ministers, thus claimed a much deeper identity with their people than most state churches could. The Thatcher Government in its historical ignorance attempted to call the Kirk to order when it mooted the Constitutional Convention, by saying that as the State Church it had to do what the State said. The Kirk politely replied that this was, no doubt, sound doctrine for the Church of England, but that Church of Scotland doctrine was the reverse. The Government was supposed to obey the Church. With a pleasing symbolism betokening an end to religious sectarianism, such doctrine was in full harmony also with the teachings of the Kirk's leading rival in numbers, the Roman Catholic Church. All the churches backed devolution, but the Roman Catholic Bishops took the first opportunity after its arrival to declare it had not gone far enough, and Scotland had no need of nuclear submarines (still, regrettably, under Westminster control), while so much poverty abounded. In the process, an old and ugly myth had been destroyed. Despite all the attempts by anachronists to insist on continuing Christian sectarian mutual hostilities, devolution has lined up Catholics and Presbyterians together and encouraged their development of their huge area of common ground instead of crabbing about the small area of doctrinal divisions. The present Cardinal is a vast improvement on his predecessors in this as in many other respects.

These advances are real, if understressed by the media, which on their side have regressed. The great stand of the *Scotsman* for so long gave way to a bitter, partisan hostility to the new Parliament when the newspaper was bought by the brothers Barclay and consigned to the care of Mr Andrew Neil. Thereafter it followed the dictates of a think-tank whose thoughts (if any) remained firmly Tory. It is difficult to think of a more suicidal policy for a newspaper. The *Scotsman* had gently guided itself towards devolution and carried its readers with it during the first uneasy progress of the 1970s; now at the moment of triumph for devolution, with every Tory in a Westminster seat defeated in 1997, on that issue, vanquished by hog, dog, or devil fighting against the Tories – the *Scotsman* went Tory. Toryism by definition was now so Unionist that its reading matter would obviously be a London paper. All the *Scotsman* could do was to use every opportunity to belittle the new Parliament. Even that was hardly helpful to Scottish Toryism which survived only in the Scottish Parliament, by 1999. Today the Scottish Tories desperately try to hope their battle against devolution will be forgotten, and yet their chief voice in the media forever snarls against the existence of a Parliament whose disappearance would once more reduce the Tories to invisibility.

Yet the *Scotsman*, however bent on self-destruction, can have effects in its self-inflicted diseases. Essentially the argument is intended to erode the confidence Scotland was acquiring. The drive to rubbish the Parliament is dangerous, and implicit in it is even greater hatred of independence; the non-Tory Parliamentary Opposition have nothing but contamination to get from such a source,

and however gratifying it may be to pick over the vanities and fol-
lies of the Scottish Executive it is essential not to fall into the death-
trap the *Scotsman* fashions from its own death-throes. Despite the
muster of the vultures, and the economic doomsters, Scotland is in
much stronger political health than England. The obvious instance
here was that exhibited in the European elections. England rushed
madly into the arms of Robert Kilroy-Silk and UKIP, in a climate of
political ignorance and hysteria as disturbing as the later electoral
history of the Weimar Republic. It may be that Kilroy-Silk and
party have both subsequently committed simultaneous *hara-kiri*,
but that does not gainsay that lunacy of having voted for them.
Scotland remained as indifferent to such xenophobia in this European election as in the last. The Scottish experience in relation to
Europe historically differed from the English, and apparently will
continue to do so. Both the English Tories, and English Labour,
have played with Europhobe cultures, and their Scottish counterparts must realise that germ's Scottish victims are most likely such
Typhoid Marys as are fool enough to ingest it. For the rest, both
the *Scotsman* and BBC Scotland seem convinced what that Scots
really require are endless stories of sex-linked crimes, proletfeed à
la Murdoch. The ideal Murdoch state would probably require
politicians to murder babies instead of kissing them.

We return in the end to Gordon Brown, in a curious reversal.
It may be that there might have been no Referendum in 1979
without the *Red Paper* – albeit that there certainly would not have
been one without the Scottish National Party. But whatever the
contradictions among its 28 contributors – and they included
Robin Cook, the abominable No-man of 1979 though not of 1997
– the book as a whole was a ringing affirmation of the existence
of Society, and of a country's responsibilities for its people. While
that country remains unable to raise its own revenue, despite the
promise of the 1997 Referendum (carried by 63% of the voters in
that particular), it remains in a culture of dependency, to suffer
from post-colonialism, Anglophobia, and all sorts of other nasty
things which Dr Gordon Brown in any of his identities past or present is sworn to eradicate. *The Red Paper on Scotland* affirmed

what Gordon Brown's Rectorship had affirmed – that students are entitled to be treated as adults. It seems only reasonable that he should also acknowledge the same status for his country.

SECTION II
A Confident Country

2

Enterprise and Society

DR ANDREW CUBIE, CBE

BEING INVITED BY A politician of any colour to contribute to a book looking at policy issues towards 2020, as opposed to those thought significant for, at the very most, three years is irresistible. I reckon civic society continues to be impatient for a longer view to be part of our political culture. Some of us regard 2020 as long distant – and yet our youngsters at nurseries today will then be pondering which College or University course, vocational or academic, to take or where else to begin work. Many of us will be reflecting then, I fear, about the adequacy of our pension provision, the ability of a proportionately smaller workforce to sustain and increase GDP and what we might have tackled differently 20 or so years before. Whatever our age, whether we are economically active or not, we will have a close interest in the kind of society in which we live, which in turn will be shaped by the global circumstance and our ability to generate wealth within it.

I will not attempt in this brief paper to sketch inadequately how the world order might then be in any detail. My prediction can be no better than anyone else's. However, I fear we are at the portal of a troubled century. The divisions amongst nations will no doubt be of a different kind, but they will be there. History demonstrates this clearly and we show no signs yet as nations of effectively understanding the circumstances or needs of others. There is much talk about doing so, but relationships that are based on parity of esteem are still the exception today. So it will be in 2020. We will continue to be challenged by the clamour of different religions, the impact of different economic achievement and climate change. Floods, drought, hunger, nationalism, regionalism and terrorism will continue to be themes on our screens.

Those writing in Scotland in 1904 for an equivalent publication

could hardly have conceived of the change in world order by 1920 by war, emancipation and disease. So I suspect it will be by 2020 for different reasons. SARS demonstrated in 2003 the potential frailty of public health because worldwide travel is as easy as journeys from Edinburgh to Glasgow in 1904. Yet this is a world today where 90% of the population on our planet have never used a telephone. The country with the greatest divide between the top 5% of the wealthy and the bottom 5% in terms of grinding poverty is now China. In 2020 when China may be the most powerful engine of growth in the world I suspect that division cannot be credible. Thus the emancipation of the next two decades will continue to be a balancing of opportunity amongst widely different groups in communities across the world. I fear also with nationalism alive and well in 2020 we will still as countries continue to spend hugely on defence budgets giving the capacity to wage war powerfully and sadly with even greater killing power than today. These seem eternal threats, but so are some values.

In Scotland and in the UK I am, however, confident that we can rely upon democratic values as part of the bedrock of our society. But, even bedrock can be assailed. There are values, therefore, which need to be enhanced, not just cherished in such a threatening world.

My first conclusion is, therefore, that despite an easy cynicism by those of us not engaged in party politics, we have to make better contributions to the political process. George Reid, as Presiding Officer of the Scottish Parliament, is absolutely right in urging both that we put the cost issues of the Parliament behind us and that we in civic society engage with the institution of the Scottish Parliament – it is a welcoming environment. Thus we must work with it to create an effective organisation which gains respect from a wider community.

I hope Scotland in 15 years time will be a more aspirational community than today. If we cannot have aspirations both for and of our democracy and its manifestation in the Parliament we will be the poorer, both culturally and economically. I offer this regardless of whether the devolution settlement remains as it is, or has changed, as I suspect it shall.

A possible danger to democracy, as we know it, is a waning economy, not fuelled by enterprising spirits. Countries which travel through periods of economic hardship invariably discover extreme leadership an option, inconceivable in days of greater plenty. I know that some regard those who declaim about wealth creation as not fully understanding the social order. Redistribution for some remains a greater priority. I make no apology in continuing to offer the creation of wealth, from relevant 21st Century activity, as another section of the bedrock of a Scotland in 2020. In the 1990s when I was engaged in the development of economic policy for the CBI in Scotland and indeed the UK we returned endlessly to this theme. I like to think our work helped to bring about a cultural shift in attitude of many politicians. Founded upon what we can encourage for tomorrow and deliver thereafter, will determine if we can become a country significantly more economically productive by 2020 than we are today. Creating an enterprising society does again depend on aspiration. Parental aspiration for the next generation, aspiration for each other, employer aspiration for individual businesses and, as already mentioned, political aspiration. If all are in tune we will make our society different.

If we do not work collectively to such longer term goals we will continue to see many of our best, as generations have done before, leave the land of their birth. We can have, and must have, more ranges of worthy initiatives to address such loss, but until we first truly believe we can become an achieving society such initiatives will only be marginally effective.

We have as a country fretted about this for long enough. In some of Tom Devine's recent writing he graphically reminds us of anxieties in the aftermath of the Union of the Parliaments. After 1707 there were deep concerns about the sustainability of Scotland's economy in the then new order, not of the global markets of today, but of the English empire. Whilst Arthur Herman in his book, 'The Scottish Enlightenment – The Scots' Invention of the Modern World', does much to encourage self belief he does so mostly in the context of the achieving Scot overseas who in time took full advantage of the opportunities of empire. Whilst invention does indeed address the 'smart' element of a current mantra, it does not lead to local economic success.

So what has our enterprise given us today?

In a Study of Scotland's Top 100 Companies published by the Royal Bank of Scotland Group in May 2004 there is some troubling detail.

Over half of the top 100 Scottish companies are subsidiaries of parent companies based in other parts of the UK, the US, or continental Europe.

By sector, Banks, Oil and Gas, Electricity and Transport account for 80% of the value added of Scotland's top 100 firms.

Our economy is hugely influenced by the public sector (43% of GDP). However, 14 of the top 20 Scottish firms are linked to the process of privatisation and deregulation. No equivalent business has emerged in the last 10 years.

Scotland's top 100 firms created £40.9 billion of value added in 2002/3 equalling 56% of the Scottish economy of which 70% of that total is contributed by 10 firms.

Beyond this review we also know that not once in the last 25 years has Scottish GDP growth exceeded the UK average of growth.

I could list some of the many reasons advanced for this state of affairs, but will confine myself to very few, as many propositions in this area are prejudiced or very judgmental. However, as noted in the Scottish Executive's Lifelong Learning Strategy for Scotland, published in February 2003, 23% of adult Scots are estimated to have low levels of literacy and numeric skills. Our failure to make the SME sector one seen as awash with opportunity for young graduates has also done us damage. Perhaps also relevant is our approach which encourages employment, rather than self employment or being an employer. I also fear that a lack of employer ambition plays a larger part in our circumstances than we often credit.

I am clear that we will have failed in our generation if a similar review in 2020 emerged with the same outcomes and commentary.

A further conclusion is, therefore, that whilst we properly laud our present merchants of enterprise they are a tiny group amongst the rest of us. By 2020 such a grouping must be at least ten times greater and not so distinct from their peers as today. This would be a hugely important achievement. It would ensure that the profile of contribution from beyond our then top 100 Scottish companies will be different, giving a broader base to the economic output of that society.

We are currently travelling in broadly the right direction for all of this, but we need to add more rigour. Sir John Ward and Jack Perry at Scottish Enterprise are seized of these needs as are others, but we continue to be impeded by boxed thinking. An 'Enterprise Agenda' needs to be developed for Scotland, much as John Ward and I for CBI Scotland did in 1995 in the creation of a Business Agenda for Scotland. Such a step would have at its heart the commitment of leaders from all sectors of the community to such an agenda, rather than the creation of a separate and national initiative. This was achieved in our Business Agenda of a decade ago. Indeed the essence of enterprise is freedom in approach which can flourish in schools, town and country, and privatisation and deregulation, as the Royal Bank of Scotland report demonstrates. A focus on reasons 'to do' as opposed to 'not to do' would be a good national commitment.

Others will write of educational issues in this publication, but in the area of education and lifelong learning opportunities abound for enterprise. I would be disappointed if by 2020 the contribution made to the Scottish economy from teaching and learning was not registering as one of the most significant contributors to the then value added of Scotland's economy.

Sir Walter Scott wrote in reflective mood 'I am a Scotsman; therefore I had to fight my way into the world.' Such a sentiment is even more merited today, but if by 2020 it can be said we have kindled a passion for democratic values in an aspiring, economically successful and fair Scotland we might, in our generation and in our fight, have really got into the world!

3

Scotland's Tipping Point

DR CAROL CRAIG

ON 2ND DECEMBER 2004 over three hundred people crowded into Oran Mor, a renovated kirk now functioning as an arts centre in Glasgow's West End. They were there to listen to what many later declared to be the best speech they had ever heard. Most went away inspired to take action that could be the beginnings of a massive transformation of Scottish culture. The source of the inspiration? Malcolm Gladwell, author of the international best-seller *The Tipping Point*.

Gladwell is a staff writer on *The New Yorker* magazine and his book has been on *Businessweek*'s best-sellers list ever since it appeared in 2000. Given these facts, it is reasonable for anyone privy to this information to expect a groomed, ultra-confident American with a gleaming smile. But no. The man who appeared on the platform and charmed and inspired his Scottish audience was different from the stereotype of the American motivational speaker.

Malcolm Gladwell grew up in Canada to English and Jamaican parents, hence the light brown Afro. He is a slightly built, self-deprecating man who clearly likes his own company. His particular gift as a speaker comes from his ability to tell stories. Stories which anyone can understand: the fall of the Berlin Wall, the rise of radio as a mass medium in the US, the runaway success of the Atkins diet or the tale of Paul Revere who rode out to warn fellow Bostonians that the English were coming. But the power of Gladwell's stories is not that they entertained and held his audience but that they encouraged them to see the world anew and to take action.

Gladwell argues that we tend to see change as something which is not only difficult to achieve but slow and incremental when, in fact, not only does change often happen much more quickly than we anticipate but it also happens in one decisive action – the tipping point. The fall of the Berlin Wall is a good example. Before it was dismantled if anyone had been asked how such an event would come about, they would have predicted that it would have taken years, if not decades, of intricate political negotiations. In reality, it came down rapidly after a mere three months of political protests.

At the heart of Gladwell's analysis is the belief that people are not as independent-minded as we often think and are much more subject to the influence of other people – particularly those in their social circle. Gladwell also argues that people's attitudes and behaviour are conditioned by their surroundings. For example, when an area becomes physically run down it sends out the message 'nobody here gives a damn, so do what you like', hence crime rates soar. And this is why the New York crime wave was turned round by dealing with such apparently trivial things as graffiti and litter. It also shows another of the book's key messages – that small things can make a big difference.

Gladwell's analysis mainly focuses on the spread of what he calls 'social epidemics'. In other words, he is interested in why some ideas take hold and catch on, changing people's behaviour and attitudes, while others don't. He concludes that 'social power' – the influence of others we know – is much more effective in bringing about transformational change than political or economic power. In other words, change is much more likely to be 'bottom up' than 'top down' as people are more open to the influence of friends or colleagues than those in authority. So now you can begin to see why this was such an inspiring message to those gathered at Oran Mor.

Gladwell argues that for transformational change to take place we often need to 'reframe'. In other words we need to start seeing something differently. A contemporary example of a social epidemic caused by reframing is the Atkins diet. It reframed dieting by diverting people's attention from the daunting task of counting calories to the much more simple elimination of a whole category of food. And it is precisely this 'reframing' we need if Scotland is to undergo transformational change. So what is the change in perception we need to bring about?

Until the past year or so the vast majority of Scots keen to see a transformation in Scotland perceived the change they sought as largely political. For many a new, better Scotland would only be brought about by constitutional change. Thus so much energy in Scotland over the past century has been devoted to the home rule/devolution/independence debate.

Party politics has also been the conduit for those seeking other types of changes in Scottish society such as the redistribution of wealth, the regulation of markets or solutions to problems such as landownership. Politics has also been the medium for people involved in the Conservative Party, for example, to resist such changes through the maintenance of the traditional order.

Now there is nothing particularly Scottish about the belief that transformational change is brought about by politicians. Gladwell himself made this point in his speech when he said that people generally overvalue the importance of political and economic power and undervalue the importance of social power. But for a variety of reasons the Scots' view of the world is likely to intensify this over-emphasis on politics. First, since we didn't have our own parliament and political institutions, pre-devolution it was all too easy for us to overvalue the importance of politics and see political change as a panacea. What's more, although we realised the limitations of politics and politicians many Scots tended to believe that the political structures we would create would somehow be different from those in existence elsewhere – hence much of the Utopian daydreaming about the brave new politics of post-devolution Scotland. There is also a proclivity in Scotland to emphasise the collective rather than the individual and this too has made it all too easy for us to assume that transformational change would be brought about from changes in national structures, rather than from changes in our own personal lives.

The confidence issue itself is a good example of this tendency to see everything through the lens of politics. Until recently if confidence was perceived to be a problem for Scots, it was portrayed as a national issue. In other words, it was seen as a by-product of Scotland's relationship with England. The argument being that it was damaging to Scottish self-esteem to be in the shadow of a bigger more powerful, and controlling country, and that only more self-determination could rectify the problem.

My own argument on Scottish confidence is that while it is undoubtedly the case that the relationship with England has cast Scotland in the role of the 'inessential other' and undermined Scottish self-esteem, the barriers to the development of confidence in individual Scots is much more the result of indigenous Scottish values. In other words, many Scots lack confidence at an individual level not primarily as a result of the constitutional relationship with England, but because of the prevailing climate in Scotland. A climate which encourages conformity and a fear of making mistakes and getting 'it' wrong.

The obsession with the importance of power structures seeps into other areas of life. For example, in my own work as a training consultant in education I have found that every tier I have worked with has declined responsibility and passed the issue up to their superiors. So even in a communication or assertiveness skills course, which is essentially about how we express ourselves, pupils will say that they are not 'allowed' to express themselves in an open, assertive way and that I need to do the course with teachers. Teachers tell me that I must do the course with head teachers and head teachers tell me that I must put this case to the education authority. Needless to say the people in the education authority say that this is really an issue for the Scottish Executive as they are ultimately responsible for the culture in education. Interestingly the current Education Minister has been heard wondering why teachers as professionals don't show more initiative and responsibility to sort out problems and stop waiting for something to happen from the top.

It would be stupid of me to argue that there is no merit in the arguments about the importance of politics and power structures. Scotland's relationship with England has damaged confidence. Change does often need to be supported and carried through at a political level – a change in landownership is a case in point. Political will and resources can sometimes affect big changes. Often in organisations, people are not 'allowed' to do certain things.

But if we overestimate the significance of top-down change it will make change much less likely. One of the most dispiriting aspects of the political or top-down approach to change is that it disempowers people and saps them of the drive to take action. For example, if someone believes that Scotland will only change as a result of changes in politics or the actions of politicians then the window of opportunity is only open once every four or five years at election time. What's more, change can only come about if that person's side persuades a majority of voters. And given the nature of democratic politics this is unlikely if it is a big transformational change which is sought. If at work or school someone believes that they are not allowed to do certain things, and that change has to come from the top, then all they can do is wait patiently until the powers that be decide to make the changes. As many psychologists will tell you, thinking you cannot affect change in your life (poor locus of control) often leads not only to stress but also to depression.

So what we need to do is reframe solutions to Scottish problems by using a wide-angled lens which allows us to encompass more areas of life. Let's take it as read that this frame still lets us see that political solutions are often required and resources allocated differently for Scotland to become a better, healthier place to live and work. But the new frame, however, encourages us to divert at least some of our attention from our previous obsession with the outer world of politics, money, consumption and relationships on to other matters. What's more this new frame spotlights the importance of what is happening in the inner world. This is a world not only of personal psychology but also of meaning and spirituality. And it is a world which has attracted very little attention in Scotland in recent years.

So what we need to do is start seeing that many of the changes which would make a difference are attitudinal or psychological. In other words, big transformational change, and a rise in confidence, would come about if we could improve our perceptions, thoughts, feelings and attitudes to self and others so that we become more positive, optimistic, accepting and tolerant of difference. Some of these are small shifts in individual's attitudes and behaviours, but true to Gladwell's thesis if enough people made these changes it would transform Scottish culture.

It is common for Scots confronted with such an argument to ask what this means for poor people living in modern slums. Am I saying that such living conditions are irrelevant? I am not arguing for a moment that a fairer redistribution of wealth is unnecessary or that we should not take action to improve the lot of some of the poorest members of our society. But we are much more likely to find solutions to these problems if we are more positive in our approach. Recent research in the US by the distinguished psychologist Barbara Frederickson has shown that it is when people feel in a positive mood that they are at their most creative and build good relationships with people. So if we want Scotland to become a society which is able to come up with constructive solutions to the many problems which blight our society, feeling better about ourselves and feeling more positive would help us find these solutions.

There is little doubt that a growing number of policy-makers are convinced that significant improvements can only take place in Scotland if both their employees and the people who use their public services begin to see the world differently. Many interesting initiatives on this front have been taking place in Scotland for well over a decade. However, the problem is that this work has been fragmented. In other words, there have been lots of isolated projects, within particular sectors, but the learning has not been discussed or disseminated more widely. Working in this way has also been dispiriting for many of the individuals concerned. They know that what they ultimately seek is a wholesale change in attitudes to self and others in wider Scottish society and they are often unsure of what they can achieve in isolation.

So one of the things we need to do in Scotland is create the sense that there is a coherent movement for change. If those who are already working on the change agenda felt that they were not operating alone, or accompanied by a few like-minded souls in their sector, but forging ahead as part of a broad encompassing social movement, then this would undoubtedly galvanise, energise and motivate people to take action. In other words, if those of us convinced of the need to advance a confidence agenda, to give it a short-hand term, begin to consciously put our weight behind the type of activities needed to advance this agenda would we not reach that tipping point more quickly?

One of the reasons why so many left the Scotland's Tipping Point event at Oran Mor feeling motivated and inspired is that many felt, some for the first time, that they were part of a coherent movement. As the person who had organised the event it was my job as a platform speaker to give a preliminary answer to the question – where is the movement headed or what are we trying to tip?

To answer this question I drew on the widespread experience I've had in the area of attitudinal change in Scotland for the past fifteen years. This experience has convinced me there are lots of Scots who will easily agree that what we need to do in Scotland is create a culture which fosters different attitudes. So what are they?

First, we need to create a cultural climate which encourages more *positive attitudes*. We need more optimism and the expression of positive emotions such as praise, gratitude and appreciation. We need much more emphasis on what's good rather than what's wrong. (Now wouldn't that transform the Scottish press!) If we had more encouragement for such expression not only would we feel better about ourselves but also we would forge better relationships and solve problems more effectively. This is not to suggest for a moment that we should become a nation of unrealistic, and irritating, Pollyannas who are trying to be positive one hundred per cent of the time. Indeed not only is it undesirable to eliminate negative thoughts but it's also impossible: the human brain is designed to think negatively as such thoughts protect us and keep us alert to possible dangers.

Second, we want to create a culture in Scotland which encourages more *confidence* at the national, individual and collective level. And this will happen if we can encourage more feelings of self-worth and self-acceptance as well as instilling individuals with the basic belief that they can achieve their goals.

Third, we want to create a culture which understands and respects *individuality*. Scottish culture, particularly in recent years, has emphasised the importance of the nation, the group or the collective before the individual. Clearly the collective is important and I do not want us to lose sight of our collectivist values which are an inherent strength. However, we need to rebalance our collectivism with a new understanding of the importance of individuality. Scotland will become a better place not because we all think the same way and try to be the same as each other but if we can unleash the power of individuals. We do, however, need to make a distinction between individualism which can easily become the pursuit of the self and its goals with little reference to others, and individuality which is an expression of the differentiated self. We need more empowered, individual selves working not simply to make their own lives better but also to improve the collective.

And this leads on to more *creativity and innovation*, as the fourth item on my wish list for Scotland. In my analysis of Scotland in *The Scots' Crisis of Confidence* I explain why inherent cultural preferences for thinking and intuition have combined to ensure that historically Scotland was an innovative and inventive nation. In certain academic and artistic sectors, Scotland still has a reputation for inventiveness and creativity but for a variety of reasons, including a desire for conformity, our ability to be creative and innovative appears to be compromised if not lost and it is something which we need to reclaim to transform Scottish culture.

The penultimate point on the list of what we need more of in Scotland is *recognition of success*. In recent decades our desire for egalitarianism has ossified into a discomfort with individual achievement. Perhaps as a response to Thatcherism we hunkered down into our collectivist values as a way to mark ourselves out as being different from England and their more materialistic, pro-success values. In other words, our levelling-down egalitarian values intensified and made success for individuals something of a double-edged sword. Of course, we should still believe in the irredeemable worthiness of individuals, encapsulated in Burns's 'a man's a man for a' that' but we need to celebrate the myriad of ways that individuals can express their individuality and their achievements.

The final point on the list is the need for more understanding of the importance of *well-being*. We need to be part of the growing world-wide movement that is beginning to question the importance we place on economic growth and wealth and to put more emphasis on life-satisfaction, happiness and fulfilment. It would be counter-productive for us to give out the message to people that all that matters in life is work, achievement, enterprise and success when in fact for many individuals these things may not lead to a real feeling of fulfillment or enhance their sense of well-being.

The list I've just outlined has not been written on the back of an envelope. It has evolved over many years of discussions with many people living and working in Scotland. But it hasn't been written in tablets of stone either. It is simply an initial attempt to codify the type of attitude change which many people are in their own way trying to bring about in Scotland. Given the Scots' reputation for being disputatious no doubt it will evolve and change over the coming years.

A final reason why many left Oran Mor feeling positive about a new wind of change is that a new Centre for Confidence and Well-being was launched at the event. Its role is not to control the evolving confidence agenda. Rather it is to provide useful resources and maximise the efforts of those already engaged in this area of work by creating a network and opening up channels of communication.

So now you can see why Scotland's Tipping Point was such an inspirational event for those who took part and Malcolm Gladwell, an unlikely but effective, source of inspiration. The challenge for all of us is to make sure that this new social epidemic isn't snuffed out by negativity and 'cannae do' attitudes but spreads throughout Scotland like a virulent, but ultimately benign, infection. An infection which has the capacity to transform Scotland by the year 2020.

Frederickson, B. (2001). The role of positive emotions in Positive Psychology: The broaden-and-build theory of positive emotion. *American Psychologist*, *56*, 218-226.

4

Scotland in the World

RT HON HENRY MCLEISH

Former First Minister of Scotland

'SCOTLAND IN THE WORLD' is not just a glib catch-phrase, a slogan for speech-makers. It is a concept that is vital for our social, economic and political well-being in the 21st Century. We are now at the point where being international, interconnected and interdependent are the paths to success. Our nation has been given a new status and a new role within the UK. After the early years of devolution, we have still not thought through what we do with it – and we also regard it as something narrow, exceptional and complete.

We fail to see how devolution has given Scotland the chance to look at itself in wider contexts. We are not doing enough to re-examine our attitudes and our approach to the UK, Europe and the rest of the world. To do that, and to take advantage of the exciting opportunities presented to us as a nation, we must first change our national mindset and the attitude we present to the world. In his book *How The Scots Invented The Modern World* Arthur Herman wrote: 'Being Scottish turns out to be more than just a matter of nationality or place or origin or clan or even culture. It is also a state of mind, a way of viewing the world and our place in it.'

Herman said we often complain that Scotland's place among nations deserves more exposure than it gets – but these complaints have an ironic, rather than a beseeching tone and we seem to take a perverse pride in being so consistently under-estimated! That must change.

Scotland's self-image is governed by our levels of self-esteem and self-confidence yet our traditional national identity often becomes a reason for complacency and an excuse for not changing. Inside and outside the Scottish Parliament, there is a collective complacency, a lack of awareness and a lack of urgency in addressing the remarkable changes that are taking place around us.

There is much that can be done in the Parliament and Executive and in the country that has nothing to do with the Scotland Act but has a lot to do with aspiration and optimism. Even with the existing powers of the Parliament, we should set higher goals and have more confidence in our ability to act and make a difference.

It is important that we apply a sense of urgency. We forget that while we are drifting into the twenty-first century the rest of the world is moving on; if there ever were any doubts about the need for urgency, a review of our productivity, growth, competitiveness, small business formation, workforce participation rates and entrepreneurship should provide the impetus.

Faced with this paralysis, we need to anchor the debate on the future of devolution and embrace four important factors: devolved federalism within the UK; the new regionalism of Europe; new models of social and civic development in Scandinavia, states of America and elsewhere; and economic restructuring

This new regionalism is an issue of increasing importance to Scotland. We should be thinking 20 years ahead to when there will be a powerful regionalism in Europe and a potentially different United Kingdom with federal devolution. All of this is taking place alongside globalisation, supra-nationalism, political and economic integration in Europe, the transformation of the nation-state and the revolution in information technologies. This is a powerful dynamic which we need first to understand and then prepare for.

Within nation-states and within Europe the idea is growing of the competitive region, so that regions like Scotland would compete for economic advantage in the UK, Europe and globally. Subsidies will have to give way to subsidiarity and redistribution will have to give way to competitiveness. These changes will have profound consequences for Scotland, which we should be identifying now. The present danger is that we are not doing that.

Our current tendency is to be blinkered and to look no further than the United Kingdom. We now have the opportunity to build new alliances and relationships elsewhere in the world. What is needed is a strategic upturn in our aspirations, selling Scotland world-wide and understanding the challenges and opportunities that exist, especially in the US and Europe.

That requires us to free ourselves from the mind-set that all roads lead to, or through, London. Of course, the UK brings us economic, social and political benefits but we can also have our own direct routes to the wider world.

We will also have to ignore the predictable knee-jerk criticism from certain ill-informed and short-sighted sections of the media who will attack the Scottish Executive for 'hi-jacking' UK responsibilities and powers – as well as those at Westminster, sadly including some Scottish MPs, who have always been hostile to devolution and will oppose further powers for Scotland.

For a small nation on the periphery of Europe to become a nation with a leading place in the world requires Scotland to have ambition.

2020 will be the Scottish Parliament's 21st birthday. We must hope that long before that, it will have come of age and will be more mature, more experienced and with a greater grasp of its own destiny and Scotland's destiny. To be a successful nation, we cannot be content to sit back, wait for developments and react. We must look ahead, seize the opportunities and put Scotland in pole position to exploit those opportunities in our national interest.

Where does Scotland want to be in 2020 – in the United Kingdom, in Europe and in the world?

Scotland and the United Kingdom

The nation-state of Great Britain will have to acknowledge and embrace the growing impact of globalisation, supra-nationalism, the enlargement and further integration of the European Union and, in turn, the increasing pressures from the regions and the devolved countries.

We think devolution is exceptional but it is really part of a worldwide process and *we* have to see ourselves as part of a new twenty-first century order, especially the European pattern of 'new regionalism'.

Part of the solution is for the UK, one of the late entrants into devolution and regionalism, to make another significant constitutional shift and adopt a form of devolved federalism. It would also have to mean constitutional safeguards for power-sharing within the United Kingdom and competitive status for each British region.

The recent setback of the government defeat in the referendum on regional assemblies in England was a disappointment but hardly surprising in current circumstances. However, it is inevitable that in 2020 the United Kingdom will have a form of devolved federalism. There will be regional devolution within England complementing Scotland, Wales and Northern Ireland, giving UK a symmetry which it lacks at the moment.

The United Kingdom remains highly centralised and out of step with the emerging Europe and there is an obvious need for a solution to the English dimension. That solution will be about <u>shared</u> power, not devolved power and the UK government will have to think in terms of the regions and nations of the UK.

There will be pressure on Scotland as we face competition from these regions, with the realisation that economic problems cannot all be solved by government in London. The notion of the competitive region in a globalised world has still to take hold.

In all of that, Scotland will play a much greater part – and it is also inevitable that more powers will be devolved to the Scottish Parliament. Our financial regime will have evolved with more control over and responsibility for tax and spending.

In a truly devolved United Kingdom, there must be freedom for the Scottish government to handle external affairs in areas vital to Scotland. Any rigid insistence that foreign affairs and Europe are reserved matters must be met with spirited resistance from Holyrood and St Andrew's House.

Initial post-devolution attempts to increase Scotland's role abroad (particularly in Europe) met with difficulties at Westminster and Whitehall where it was regarded as 'forbidden territory' for the Scottish government. To me, it was no surprise that London would seek to define and protect their responsibility for reserved matters; but, equally, it is the job of Edinburgh to assume responsibilities and powers that apply specifically to Scotland's interests.

There will be a requirement for the UK government to adopt a different viewpoint and to re-think relationships within a new form of Union that embodies a paradox of co-operation and competition. The global and European rule-books will mean more limits on the freedom and ability of the Westminster government to intervene in economic and social problems of any part of Britain.

Within the United Kingdom, there will be keen competition between regions and nations. That kind of competitive regionalism should be encouraged by the UK government as part of a macroeconomic system that allows the regions to develop to their own best advantage. In the end, that will also be to the UK's advantage.

However, we may also want to form alliances with some of these English regions, Wales, Northern Ireland and with the Republic of Ireland in certain areas of economic activity. We are all on the periphery of Europe and by working together we can compete more effectively with other parts of the world – something which is increasingly commonplace in Europe. Put simply, Scotland must open up its economy and society to the outside world.

Scotland and Europe

After the recent enlargement of the European Union, there are 25 member-states. By 2007, Bulgaria and Romania will have acceded; talks with Turkey are scheduled to start in 2005 and could last throughout the second decade of the century; there is the prospect of Norway, Switzerland, Lichtenstein and Iceland seeking membership, plus the countries of the Balkans with Croatia's position already well-advanced; countries which are part of the Commonwealth of Independent States formerly part of the Soviet Union, such as Ukraine, may also seek membership.

All of that could mean a European Union of 40 countries, one-fifth of all the countries in the United Nations, representing the largest single market with the highest GDP in the world. It will also be a Europe where the development of regionalism will parallel enlargement and political and economic integration; the identity of the smaller nations and regions will matter even more and cultural, social and political diversity will be a Europe-wide strength.

Throughout Europe, the new regionalism takes many forms, as in the federal systems in Germany and Austria, the autonomous regions in Spain, the provinces of Italy and in other countries. What they have in common is that, while all are working closely with their national governments, they are also in Europe, building new relationships and alliances.

Cross-border co-operation can be directly established by the regions themselves without any involvement from the national or the supra-national authorities. One example of such a network is the 'Four Motors for Europe' which pulls together Rhone-Alps, Baden-Wurtemberg, Catalonia and Lombardy. There is a real growth in regional consciousness.

In his book *The Regional Challenge in Central and Eastern Europe*, Michael Keating, professor of regional studies of the European Institute in Florence and professor of Scottish politics at the University of Aberdeen, pointed out that as the nation-state loses power to the EU and the regions, it is losing more and more of its importance. It is becoming 'too small for the bigger problems and too big for the smaller problems'.

Already, there are serious questions to be asked about the representation of Scotland in the existing European Union. How can Scotland hold its own in the expanding Europe? How should Scotland participate in UK delegations and policy matters where Scotland has a dominant interest? How should our Parliament participate in and scrutinise legislation emanating from Europe? How can Scotland build closer links with regions, autonomous states and provinces in an increasingly integrated Europe?

An outstanding example of modern federalism working to the benefit of a region and Europe as a whole is 'the Free State of Bavaria'. The Bavarians have a clear idea of their status within the Federal Republic of Germany, while stoutly maintaining their freedom to act on their own behalf. Lest there be any doubt, they have adopted the aphorism of King Ludwig I: 'We want to be Germans and to remain Bavarians.'

They have made a priority of participation in the European policy formulation, especially in relation to preserving Bavarian sovereignty and scope for political action. As the bond of integration tightens, an increasing number of decisions directly affecting them are being taken at EU level. Therefore, they have insisted that in Brussels negotiations, the Federal Government has to consult them and take into account their regional interests.

They have also have built up a network of influence and interest within Europe and aim to gain a place in the prospective markets in America, Asia and Africa through partnerships with California, Quebec, Sao Paulo, the Shandong Province of China and the provinces of Western Cape and Gauteng in South Africa (which includes Pretoria, Johannesburg and Soweto).

In Scotland, we have already embraced the concept of a 'Europe of the regions'. The 'Flanders Agreement' in 2001 opened a new chapter for Scotland in Europe without undermining the United Kingdom because it recognised that the regions of Europe can build their own economic, social and cultural links. It also illustrated that we could push out the boundaries of devolution and need not be constrained in developing our European thinking.

Similarly, in Europe productive alliances can be created with individual regions with which we have much in common, in key manufacturing sectors, financial services, environment, tourism, technology, education, learning and the knowledge industries and creative industries. Scotland has much to contribute, but also much to learn.

On another front 'social' Scotland can benefit from more direct links with Scandinavia and those northern European nations with which we have much in common in our background and history. These are now modernised and increasingly sophisticated nations with the highest quality of life, enlightened and effective policies on health, housing, social services, citizenship and civic pride and innovative approaches to alcohol, drugs and social problems – all of special concern to Scotland – and highly advanced environmental policies, especially in renewable energy technology.

Scotland should also have a distinctive role, along with the United Kingdom, in the development of European policy. As enlargement and integration proceeds, there should be opportunities for Scotland to have a more significant say on matters that are presently the preserve of the United Kingdom government.

In Scotland House in Brussels, which promotes Scotland's governmental and non-governmental interests to the European Union, we have a model of Scottish representation abroad. It provides the vital two-way contact, allowing a wide range of Scottish bodies to access and influence the EU and to receive information and early alerts about European developments.

Why only in Brussels? Scotland House should be replicated in other European capitals and in Eastern Europe, where there is great potential for us in offering assistance but also exploiting opportunities in an emerging market.

Above all, Scotland should set an example to the rest of the UK with a much more pro-active embrace of Europe. Through our Parliament and Executive, we should play a positive pro-Europe role in a referendum on the European constitution and, eventually, the common currency – both of which have long-term implications for Scotland.

Scotland and the world

It is obvious that to promote Scottish tourism and industry, we have to strengthen existing international links and alliances and establish new ones – but we also have to acknowledge that it is important for us to interact with the rest of the world. We have much to learn, markets to develop and influence to win.

Taking our rightful place in the world will lead to rising standards of wellbeing and a better quality of life for our people. But before we take that place, we must have a clear idea of our mission and objectives.

The new global and European context means nation-states like the UK can do less and less in terms of helping the nations and regions and influencing the policies that affect them. It is up to Scotland to help ourselves.

Scotland has played an important role in the world. The presence of the Scottish 'diaspora' around the globe reminds us of that.

This history of world involvement has reflected our traditions of internationalism, humanitarianism, our passion for education and learning and an intense Scottish sentiment that is captured in what can be called 'the Marseillaise of humanity', the Robert Burns song *Is There for Honest Poverty* with its timeless hope 'That man to man the world o'er Shall brithers be for a' that'.

The early 21st Century will see the growth of supra-nationalism in which the world will be comprised mainly of large economic and trading blocs – the Europe Union, the recently formed African Union with its Pan-African Parliament, Latin America, the North American Free Trade Alliance and the Asian-Pacific grouping.

Against that changing background, Scotland will need a strategic over-view, a more distinctive voice and a much sharper focus for existing international activities, looking across departments, recognising and making the most of international opportunities.

Global reach

We have to be prepared to act in countries like India, China, Japan and the United States. These countries, developed and rapidly developing, along with the EU will be drivers of the global economy.

An example is Flanders, a 'federated entity of the federal Kingdom of Belgium' with a population of 5.9 million and its own Flemish Parliament and Government with almost identical devolved powers to Scotland's. It has more than 100 different representatives abroad, including a special diplomatic representative to the United Kingdom with an entirely separate London office for a Flemish Government envoy, the Flanders Export Promotion Agency and a Tourist Office.

Scottish representation in the British embassy in Washington should be developed further in the US and there is no reason why there should not be First Secretary for Scotland representing our interests at British embassies in Beijing, Tokyo and other world capitals. This can only be done on the basis of a deeper understanding of Scotland's needs and the need to use our financial resources wisely; being progressive should also mean being practical.

Selling Scotland

This global network will complement but not duplicate the work of the United Kingdom; instead, it will sell Scotland more directly abroad. Raising our international profile therefore requires a complete overhaul of our overseas outlets for Scottish Enterprise, Scotland International and VisitScotland to provide more coherence, focus and marketing strength. Worldwide, there are over 20 of these outlets, but they are not working as one. A 'Scotland United' approach would achieve a more identifiably Scottish brand.

We should also press the UK government to re-assess the Scottish element of the British Tourist Authority and the British Council and ask the question: What are they doing for Scotland?

American window

In the US, Tartan Day should become America's window on Scotland. It is a handy symbolic description of Scotland, but tradition should be linked to modernity and the content and scope of what is little more than a celebration of 'Scottishness' have to be widened. Tartanalia and tourism should lead on to attention for learning, technology and industry. Cultural exchange is important, but there are greater economic benefits to be had by emphasising our economy, higher education and creative industries.

The UK consulates and embassies across North America, including individual states and Canada, should be mobilised to sell Scotland. And by 2020 there should be other Tartan Days and Tartan Weeks in other countries and other continents.

The knowledge society

In the context of the knowledge society and the information revolution, we need more learning and technology agreements with major players in Europe, North America and the Far East. The partnerships we have begun with California, Virginia and Maryland will help put

Scotland in the forefront of competing for business and establishing links with the best in the world. Some of our universities are already involved in such links but we must go further for the sake of growth, innovation, product development and extension of our national knowledge base.

Scots abroad

The 'diaspora' – our world-wide army of millions of Scots and those of Scots descent who are fiercely patriotic and want to be enlisted to help Scotland – is an under-valued asset. In many parts of America and elsewhere, the Irish community are high-profile, proud of their roots and energetic and active in promoting their ancestral nation's interests.

The Scottish exiles' love of country and pride in their ancestry should be recruited as the Irish have done so successfully in mobilising second- third- and fourth-generation Irish-Americans to present a traditional Irish image, combined with the impression of a modern, progressive and economically successful nation.

Pride and prestige

For Scotland, being connected is absolutely important to encourage the world to visit us. The Scottish Executive's events unit should be given a more prominent role and greater support. Events like the MTV music awards in Edinburgh and the coming 2013 Ryder Cup, with the third largest television audience of all world sporting events, have obvious financial benefits as well as marketing our country's attractions and making a statement about Scotland as a world player. At Hogmanay, Edinburgh – not London – is the focus of the world's attention, along with New York and Sydney. The European Nations football tournament will again be staged in 2020; is it too much to hope that by then the footballing nation of Scotland will have gained the confidence, courage and commitment to make a successful stand-alone bid to be the hosts?

A skilled workforce

Managed migration must remain a priority. Public doubts about immigration should be countered by making the case on the basis of much-needed skills and Scotland's problems of low workforce participation rates, a declining and ageing population. Like Ireland, we should be retaining more young workers, bringing exiled Scots back to their homeland and attracting foreign nationals.

Foreign affairs

In all of this, there is an obvious role for a Department of External Affairs, properly resourced and staffed, with a designated Scottish Cabinet Minister. Titles do not matter; whether it is the Scottish Foreign Office or Scotland Abroad, the mission is more important than the name.

Until now, various piecemeal parts of this portfolio have been combined with other important responsibilities but we should no longer have a part-time approach to Scotland's place in the world. At present, among all his other duties, the First Minister is responsible 'for strategic relationships with the UK government, the European Union and other external relations'.

The Scottish Foreign Minister would create a new momentum on the international front and his department could provide a focal point and resource for all those other organisations in Scotland with international contacts and aspirations.

Challenges and choices

Scotland has been described as a state of mind – and that state of mind has been created by history, culture and religion. We Scots do have a talent for what an Irish writer has called 'begrudgery', a resentment of individual success, an unwillingness to bestow praise and delight in the misfortunes of those who try something new but fail.

There is a 'know-your place' mentality and, for some, being competitive is a dirty word. It is confused with capitalism and confidence is confused with arrogance. It is reinforced by media, whose influence is far-reaching but often strikes a negative chord.

This simply has to change because my experience is that any country effecting change has needed an upbeat national mood to drive it. As a loyal Scot, I would hope that our true mood is far from pessimistic, far from cynical and far from negative.

Without this radical reappraisal of our outlook on the world, Scotland will simply fall further behind in the race for survival in the 21st Century.

A foreign policy journal in the US recently published its annual index of the nations setting the pace in globalisation, based on four factors: economic integration, technological connectivity, personal contact (communications, travel, tourism, telephones) and political engagement. For the third year in a row, Ireland ranked as the most global nation in the world and, with the exceptions of US and Canada, the top ten slots were filled by smaller countries including Finland, Switzerland, Singapore and Denmark.

If Ireland with a population of 3.5 million and other countries with smaller populations can be global players, why are we, with our five million population, not doing better in terms of modernisation and economic achievement? We have the resources, assets and the talent – it is simply a question of attitude.

In setting up its Committee for the Future, the Parliament of Finland admits: 'A fear exists that Finland will succumb to what all of Europe has been criticised for, in relation to America: writing history, looking for old and small-scale problems, and concentrating carefully on their resolution at a time when those who are succeeding are seeking the non-existent in everything, creating new things and trying new approaches even in the context of the old.'

They could have been writing about Scotland ...

It is all-too-easy to blame London when the real fault lies in our lack of ambition. It is all-too-easy to seek simplistic solutions like independence, which will make little sense in the world of 2020.

In the past, Scots have turned blame and finding scapegoats

into an art-form; in 2020, there will be no excuses. The danger is that these become a distraction and create a sterile debate in which we avoid asking the searching questions of ourselves: Why are we not better? How world-class do we want to be? Are we ready for the opportunities that will be presented by a changing world?

With the right answers to those questions, by 2020 Scots can be what they have been throughout the centuries – full citizens of the world.

REFERENCES:

Herman, A. (2001) *How The Scots Invented The Modern World: The True story of How Western Europe's Poorest Nation Created Our World and Everything In It.* New York: Crown Publishers.

Keating, M. (1998) *The Regional Challenge in Central and Eastern Europe.* Cheltenham: Edward Elgar.

5

Activating the Scots Diaspora

JIM MATHER

THE NUMBER OF AMERICANS claiming Scots descent is said to have grown in the last ten years by over 50% and it is surely time that we harnessed and channelled that sense of identity and its accompanying goodwill for Scotland.

This recent phenomenon is further evidence that in spite of undoubted social and economic problems, we live in a lucky country. Not only do we have a landscape, history and culture that inspire others and unlock the imagination but we also have all three to such an extent that the centuries old ties between Scotland and its Diaspora can reconnect even when apparently broken for a generation or more. It is surely time to productively involve the millions of people from that Diaspora together with those many others who simply feel empathy for Scotland, its culture and values and its unique contribution to the modern world.

Of course there are already many Saint Andrew Societies, Caledonian Clubs and Highland Games organisations in existence worldwide and we should build on these structures. I have no negative observations or criticisms of the existing Scots Diaspora organisations. Indeed, I would argue that they are in a state of grace for they have done a great deal to keep the connection with Scotland alive and thoroughly cherished in all corners of the globe where the Scots have settled.

My only criticism is aimed exclusively at ourselves, the people of Scotland. While on an individual basis, we can be charming and welcoming to those who return in search of their roots, we have failed to allow them to be part of Scotland and its future in a structured, permanent and rewarding way. This is a major failure, for it actually has the potential to weaken the link between Scotland

and its Diaspora. It also implicitly rejects and damages what could be an enormous hidden asset and a huge market for Scottish goods and services. Whether this failure was due to a lack of confidence or a certain shyness in the past is irrelevant but it is now clear that this omission has to be remedied. Indeed, such remedial action is patently overdue and we urgently need to allow many millions of well-motivated people of Scots descent to contribute to the development of Scotland.

While we do little more than allow our Scots American and Scots Canadian visitors a chance to indulge in ancestor hunting, our near neighbours across the Irish and North Seas are doing a great deal more. The Irish and the Norwegians have developed innovative and inspiring ways to activate and reward their respective Diaspora and, as a result, they have released a vast reservoir of goodwill for the 'old country'. In Ireland's case they have created an active network in the USA, Canada, Australia, New Zealand, France, Germany, Monaco, London and Japan which in every case adds a special dimension and common denominator to the lives of expatriates, old Irish families and indigenous people with a deep affection for Ireland and all things Irish.

They have created The Ireland Funds, which provide an opportunity for thousands of people of Irish descent across the globe to give, to have fun giving and to respond to the emotional ties to the land of their forefathers.

The American Ireland Fund (AIF) was founded in 1987 by, among others, Sir Anthony O'Reilly, former Irish rugby internationalist, CEO of Heinz and now chairman of Independent News & Media and serial entrepreneur. His personal involvement has been one of the Ireland Funds critical success factors. He has worked with the AIF for almost 30 years and has helped it evolve into one of the world's pre-eminent Diaspora organisations.

Its mission statement, like its founders, has no false modesty or meagre objectives. Instead, it has plotted a course to become the largest worldwide network of people of Irish ancestry and sympathy, and is dedicated to raising funds to support its four central programmes: peace and reconciliation; arts and culture; education;

and community development. There is no doubt that it is comprehensively achieving all of those objectives and more.

The AIF has a board of 70 prominent Irish Americans and plays a leading role in the Ireland Funds worldwide. As the largest part of The Ireland Funds network, it played a major part in the recent 'Hope & History' campaign, which has raised $111m since 1999 alone.

The success of the Ireland Funds in Ireland itself has been based on more than its direct ability to raise funds and support worthy causes. The Taoiseach, Bertie Ahern, recently said, 'The support of the Ireland Funds is converting affection for Ireland worldwide into actual benefit.' His comment is clearly shorthand for the catalytic effect that the Ireland Funds have had on Ireland in terms of

Investment
Trade
Tourism
Migration back to Ireland
Education and student transfers
Improved cultural, social and economic links
The effect of the funded programmes on the lives, attitude and self-esteem of Irish people

However, the key factor that repeatedly motivates the volunteers, donors and professionals who make the Ireland Funds work is the hugely positive impact that their efforts have on ordinary Irish people.

A quick glance at their quarterly magazine *Connect* will readily confirm this claim. Photographs of pensioners, children and young musicians are all ample testament to the organisation's ability to lift hearts, boost self-confidence and hone skills with a portfolio of projects which address social, cultural, educational and economic issues. For me, this makes the strongest and most compelling case possible for Scotland to emulate the success of the Ireland Funds.

This ambition is reasonable and timely after five years of devolution. We have our new parliament in place and a new mood in Scotland. We have international goodwill toward Scotland and a genuine cross party appetite to get this particular job done. I am convinced that the time is right for us to reach out to people of Scots descent all over the world.

I am confident that this statement can and will stand audit. Early conversations with Scots abroad and representatives of Scots Diaspora organisations confirm the truth of this assertion. Both the Irish and Norwegians have generously and openly briefed representatives of the Scottish Parliament's Cross Party Group on the Economy. We have been able to blend the best ideas from two very effective franchise models with no fees or royalties demanded. In other words, we have a road map that is as valuable as any franchise. The Irish and Norwegian advice and experience is detailed and comprehensive and will enable us to avoid many start-up pitfalls. We will 'fast-forward' to a polished and proven operational model in a fraction of the time it would otherwise have taken.

The prospect of increased future affluence appears not to threaten Diaspora-activating initiatives as both the Irish and Norwegians have discovered. Indeed, it is increasingly clear that Diaspora organisations do best when they develop a deliberately positive and optimistic direction, one that is aimed at making the 'old country' as flourishing and vibrant as it can possibly be. It is only then it becomes genuinely credible in its claimed ambition to uphold, maintain and develop cultural traditions and values, cultural differentiation and the national common good.

This confidence doesn't just relate to the short-term implementation phase. The Irish experience has shown that people will give fulsomely, again and again, to deserving and worthy causes in the land of their forebears. The Irish have also established that this phenomenon can be made to flourish even if economic conditions in the 'old country' improve dramatically, as they have done in Ireland.

The Norwegians have blazed a similar trail. The American Norwegian Foundation (ANF) was founded in 2001 with similar long-term objectives to the AIF and the short-term imperative of being able to properly celebrate the 2005 Centenary of Norwegian Independence. However, in achieving that end, they have created an important role model that could be very relevant to Scotland's efforts in America. They have successfully pulled together some 900 separate local organisations in the USA under one umbrella body in support of common objectives.

If we are to match this performance, we need to be confident about our objectives and again our Irish and Norwegian friends have been keen to help. Both are of the opinion that the conditions for creating and developing Diaspora organisations have never been better. Many people in the New World are exceedingly affluent with more money than they need to live a comfortable and satisfying life. They also have a desire to differentiate themselves and reconnect with their ethnic roots. We have been told that we should be bullish about the strength of Scotland's international brand and the extent to which Scots abroad will be willing, in the words of the a leading figure in the Ireland Funds hierarchy, 'to answer to the beat of the ancestral drum'.

This will undoubtedly require leadership, commitment and a great deal of hard work coupled with the humbling realisation that we have never made it easy in the past for members of the Diaspora to play a meaningful and rewarding role in Scotland. There have been worthy attempts by agencies such as Scottish Enterprise, including Friends of Scotland, GlobalScot and Scotland the Brand, to involve people of Scots descent in promoting and assisting Scotland. But my research into the Diaspora activating programmes of other countries has shown that this largely governmental approach is not a model that has succeeded for any other nation. Instead, what has worked elsewhere has been more organic and personal with motivated individuals making events happen and creating an organisation which has grown through contagious optimism and enjoyable social events.

Successful Diaspora organisations share a number of common characteristics:

A worthy, understandable and optimistic cause

A motivated and active board, who show strong and committed leadership by demonstrating their tangible support

A chief executive who is not afraid to ask for money

A cadre of key donors who will support 50% or more of major fund-raising campaigns

A good and steady communication programme that constantly reports back on the difference that the funds are making.

The practical models clearly show how we could emulate our Celtic and Nordic neighbours by activating and motivating the Scots Diaspora. Their example is so straightforward and the portents for Scotland so good that there seem to be almost an obligation that we follow them quickly and to the letter.

The new contacts and connections that have been created and established as a result of the recent Tartan Day (Tartan Week) celebrations in the USA and Canada have proved that there are many millions of Scots Americans and Scots Canadians, who are well disposed toward Scotland and would be very receptive to an opportunity to play a constructive role in Scotland's future.

Looking specifically at the USA, other Diaspora building organisations (Irish, Indian, Arab, Italian, Norwegian and many others) have established and reinforced the fact that many Americans want to involve themselves in the country of their forebears. We can be sure therefore that when we start to revitalise the process of activating our Diaspora in the USA over winter 2004/05 we will find that Scots Americans will respond to the beat of the ancestral drum, especially if it involves them in worthy causes.

At present in the USA there are already a large number of Scots American organisations but few of them are playing a significant long-term direct charitable role in Scotland. Not only is there a gap in the market but we are certain, as with other ethnic groups, that there will also be many individual, high net worth Scots Americans who have a growing latent desire to play a supportive role.

We are only too aware that, while their aspiration is apparent, none of the existing Scots American organisations has yet been able to emulate the scale and effectiveness of the AIF or build links to a Scottish equivalent of The Ireland Funds Dublin hub operation. Our research-based analysis has shown a certain reticence on our part, in the past, to reach out to the Diaspora. What is needed now is a vital catalytic spark from Scotland. We have reached the inescapable conclusion that 'The Scotland Funds' (TSF) needs to be founded to break the logjam and move things forward. This catalytic spark will be the creation of a charity in Scotland that will be the hub of a burgeoning international network of Scots Diaspora organisations, focussing initially on the USA and Canada and the millions of Americans who proudly claim Scots descent.

To achieve that objective, it is clear that we will need to partner with one or more Scots American organisations. This might initially be on a project-by-project basis but obviously it would be in the best interests of all concerned for long-term relationships to be established and formalised in line with the AIF/Ireland Funds model. The success of the Norwegian Americans in bringing their 900 separate organisations under a single banner will make our task a lot less daunting.

Getting such an organisation started and ensuring continued viability would involve support from corporate Scotland. I have no doubt that TSF will be as attractive for domestic corporate sponsorship as the Ireland Funds are. We can draw with confidence on their experience in achieving corporate financial support to cover their administrative costs. The Irish sponsors, some of whom are international companies, can testify to the goodwill and business benefit, domestic and international, resulting from their association with the Ireland Funds. The involvement of Irish corporate sponsors has not only benefited the participating companies but it has also allowed the Ireland Funds to tell Diaspora donors that every cent of their donations benefits specific charitable projects.

For all of those involved in the implementation of TSF: –
The Board and local Boards
The Corporate Sponsors
The Volunteers in Scotland and the US
The Donors
The Recipients and
The people of Scotland
the reward process will be varied but for all concerned, very fulfilling.

The board members will have the genuine prospect of getting

the same buzz that has kept Sir Anthony O'Reilly and his colleagues involved with the Ireland Funds for nearly 30 years. They will have the satisfaction of playing a central role in creating and maintaining a bridge between Scotland and the re-energising masses of people of Scots descent.

The board members will have an important social role in representing TSF at home and abroad thereby widening their personal network of people who are well disposed towards Scotland. This potential for peer-group camaraderie is a motivator that drives other national Diaspora organisations.

Perhaps most importantly, the reward which is most valued by members of the Ireland Funds is the wonderful self-assurance that comes from having heard an important call and answered it.

Corporate Sponsors will have the tangible business advantage of being seen to 'do the right thing' for Scotland and winning increased business and goodwill in the domestic market as a result. This message can also be transmitted to overseas markets and received by those with sympathy for Scotland and its quality brand image and products.

In Ireland, name association with the Ireland Funds is so materially advantageous that the participating companies treat their sponsorship as commercial marketing expenditure rather than as charitable giving. Many of them also go the extra mile and pay for full-page colour advertisements in the AIF quarterly magazine *Connect* which has a worldwide circulation of 45,000.

Individual donors will have the quiet satisfaction of knowing that they are not only improving individual Scottish lives but also helping to make Scotland a more resilient and vibrant country. They will be invited to attend an annual conference in Scotland for donors to TSF and to visit the charitable projects which have received support. This will motivate many donors, who will be keen to see the impact of their donations and refresh their own sense of Scottish identity.

It is clear from the Irish experience that many volunteers and donors find their association with the Ireland Funds to be hugely rewarding. That is not to say that the Irish volunteers and donors are anything less than hard-nosed and objectively professional in 'doing their bit' for Ireland. Board participation at an international, national and local level brings with it, first and foremost, an obligation to raise money for the Funds.

It is becoming increasingly clear that when we channel the power of the Diaspora to the service of Scotland that we also will find, like the Irish, that we have also become more effective, productive and businesslike people in the process. As a result, Scotland will be much more likely to enjoy markedly higher prosperity that, in turn, makes us much better able to enjoy and share our landscape, culture and history with Scots from around the globe.

Perhaps that is what Bertie Ahern really meant when he talked about the impact of the Ireland Funds on his country.

Certainly, that is why I believe we can and must make it happen here. To the extent that by 2020 I would anticipate that we would be:

matching the income currently generated by the Ireland Funds;

have a presence in most developed countries and most states and provinces in the USA and Canada;

generating an increased flow of tourists;

further protecting Scots culture and heritage; and

doing considerable good for Scottish confidence, investment, trade and hence population numbers.

In short making this old country considerably more vibrant but still very much Scotland.

SECTION III
A Vibrant Economy

6

The Economic Development Challenge for 2020

ROBERT CRAWFORD

THE OLD BBC SITCOM had as one of its central characters, a certain Private Frazer, played brilliantly by that wonderful old Scottish character, John Laurie. His catch phrase was 'we are doomed'. As an undertaker Private Frazer had more than a touch of self-interest in such an outcome.

Private Frazer has some kindred spirits amongst sections of the Scottish media who like nothing better than a right good moan about our economic prospects. Perhaps it's a national trait. Or perhaps on their own the Jeremiahs and professional doomsters are also pursuing self-interest. The more they warn of dire consequences and failure the more papers they sell or air-time they receive. There is always a willing ear for bad news.

Whatever the reason or motivation the reality is that there are aspects of Scottish economic life to be concerned about and I will come to some of these presently, but there is also much to be pleased about, especially when one considers the dramatic economic change this country has endured over the last three decades. More particularly there is much to be optimistic about.

The simple truth is that Scotland's economic performance over the last decade or so has been mixed with some sectors and regions, notably cities, powering ahead whilst others have languished. Even the macro-economic data is mixed with some measures showing us global top quartile performers. Yet others suggest we are laggards.

On the debit side there is no denying that our economic growth rate has been disappointing when measured against 'best in class'. For example, between 1964 and 1998 it averaged about 2.1% against the UK's 2.4%. The latter was hardly a stellar performer even by lacklustre European standards with the honourable exception of Ireland where annual GDP growth throughout the 1990s averaged 6.9%.

Strong economic growth is frequently correlated with business level innovation. The latter exhibits itself in many ways including the deployment of processes, people, products, partnerships and management. Very traditional industries such as whisky can be just as innovative and exciting as their high technology brethren. Innovation is different from research and development spend (see below). I doubt if 'Starbucks', spend much on R&D, but they have certainly been innovators in a very traditional field.

The data on international innovation performance is scarce, but within the UK the 'Community Innovation Survey' placed Scotland second bottom of UK regions for company level innovation in a survey undertaken in the early 1990s. I doubt if much has changed in the interim.

Of course, business-level research and development spend is no guarantee of success, either for the company or the host country, but there is no denying that those economies with high levels of R&D spend typically outperform those that don't. Scotland is a relatively poor performer on this measurement. We are in the third quartile of the OECD's league table with a spend of only 0.5 per cent of GDP. This is a really miserable performance (perhaps there's a Private Frazer in even the most Panglossian of us). I believe that many of Scotland's other economic problems are in no small measure connected to underperformance on both innovation and R&D spend.

One manifest outcome of this has been Scotland's productivity performance, so crucial to wealth creation and competitiveness. This has also been unsurprisingly uninspiring for a very long time, frequently growing at less than 1% per annum. What's more concerning though is that those parts of our manufacturing industry which tended to do well in productivity were overwhelmingly foreign owned. This was probably a result of high capital expenditure allied to good skills training. The spate of closures in recent years by foreign multinationals allied to an overall growth of employment in industries with low or hard to measure productivity may in part explain our continuing problems with this metric. But it is far from the whole story. We cannot hide the fact that we under-invest in innovation, research and development and indeed in skills training. All of these are crucial determinants of economic growth in a modern economy.

Meanwhile the public sector, not notably the most innovative or productive part of the economy is growing like Topsy. Even those of us who still believe in key aspects of its remit would probably have to concede that it is way too large and may well be crowding out private sector investment and growth. It is certainly growing at a worrying pace, especially amongst local authorities, which now employ over 315,000 people. The public sector accounts for over 52 per cent of Scottish GDP and about 27 per cent of all jobs.

A large public sector is not of itself a symptom of deep malaise. It generates demand and produces services, notably health and education which are vital to most of us. In addition, it can and frequently does lead the private sector in matters like skills training. Yet the fact remains that the public sector tends to be significantly less efficient and productive than the private and as such a drag on economic growth. Its continuing expansion is not something to be welcomed. (It is reversible though. The Australians managed to reduce their public sector's share of GDP from 32 per cent to 22 per cent between 1987 and 1997).

If this is the debit side there is much to be pleased, if not complacent, about on the credit side of the ledger because on a whole host of indicators Scotland is doing just fine thank-you. True we don't enjoy the growth of Ireland or the Asian Tigers, but we have the lowest level of unemployment for a generation; home and car ownership, foreign holidays and consumer purchasing are all at record levels. Yes, much of this is financed by burgeoning consumer debt. But in that respect we reflect a trend which has been growing in many parts of the world, including countries like the USA and Ireland which boast very robust economies.

At the corporate level there are also real success stories.

A Scottish company, City Refrigeration Holdings was selected by Business Week as Europe's fastest growing in 2004. The Royal Bank of Scotland's growth continues unabated and it is now the world's fifth largest bank. Scottish Power, Scottish and Newcastle, the Weir Group, the Wood Group, Scottish and Southern, First Group and Stagecoach are all fast growing international companies. Whilst Cairn Energy, recent reverses notwithstanding, is one of the brightest stars in the global oil exploration industry.

Scotland was recently selected by 'Foreign Direct Investment Magazine' as the 2004 European Region of the Future. In paying tribute to Scotland's performance it noted:

'Scotland's commitment to long-term development and encouragement to innovation are helping to give it a global profile'.

The article goes onto make specific reference to the creation of the 'Intermediate Technology Institutes' (ITI) specifically designed to tackle the low level of collaborative research in Scotland.

Scotland, as we are often told, is a small open economy. Whilst this does make us vulnerable to the buffeting of global economic storms, it also means that we derive the benefits of having a series of industries including financial services, tourism, whisky, electronics and higher education which have a cosmopolitan outlook on the world. This is potentially a major competitive advantage in an increasingly global economy. If we include exports to the rest of the UK then Scotland is in the first quartile of OECD export earners.

The truth is that the Scottish economy has gone through a very painful and prolonged transition, from a dependency on traditional manufacturing through a period of reliance for job growth in manufacturing on foreign investment, to a position now where we have significant regional 'hot-spots', led by Edinburgh. Alongside these, however, that there are areas of prolonged economic stagnation which never fully recovered from the death of the 'old economy' with all the problems that gives rise to socially, aspirationally and in associated health problems.

The good news is that we have real strengths on which to build. These are primarily intellectual assets and that's a great thing in today's world.

But if we are to improve our productivity through heightened innovation, higher expenditure in R&D and more investment in skills and enhanced management practices then we are going have to be more radical in our policies than hitherto, more determined to stay the course and less given to carping and to listening to the Private Frazers of this world. Above all, the limits of what governments and their agencies can achieve need to be recognised. I fear that at present they are not.

Let's start with economic development support mechanisms which have worked best and draw some conclusions from these. Historically, I am in no doubt that the three most successful of these have been in no particular order: industrial infrastructure, notably the provision of advanced factories and the allied infrastructure needed to support them; the provision of venture capital (VC); and the pursuit of foreign investment. Each had, for the most part, clarity of purpose such as the provision of advanced factory space, winning internationally mobile investments to fill them and VC support for a start-ups. With the exception of VC provision where there was an immature market, there was 'market failure' and/or the unwillingness or inability of the market to meet growing demand.

The 'new town development corporations' were a good example of the provision of factories and infrastructure in advance of the market. What the best of them did was almost a classic example of the 'build it and they will come' philosophy.

The most successful of these were probably East Kilbride and Livingston, at least in part because of their contiguity to Edinburgh and Glasgow respectively. Prior to the creation of Locate In Scotland the 'new towns' were not only providing factories and infrastructure for businesses at a time when the private sector was unwilling to do so on terms and conditions which were acceptable to investors, especially foreign owned multi-nationals, but they also marketed and sold themselves internationally. Their contribution to Scotland's economic development was considerable and may even now not be fully appreciated.

Locate In Scotland (LIS) was established to present a united Scottish front to the world by marketing the country as a premier investment location and thereafter to negotiate with the company concerned. It was hugely successful and alongside the Industrial Development Authority of Ireland was widely regarded as Europe's leading inward investment agency. I have little doubt, and I write this as former director of LIS, that but for Ireland's corporation tax advantage Scotland could have matched Ireland's track record in both the number and quality of foreign investors it attracted. Had that occurred the implications for Scotland's economy would have been profound.

I am certain that 'tax' was the major competitive advantage the IDA had over LIS. And to their credit they used it to great effect. I can recall few occasions when Scotland lost out to Ireland on an investment for reasons other than corporation tax. Never-theless, I am unashamedly an admirer of what Ireland has achieved in economic growth and the transformational role which education, in particular, has played in this process.

Last but not least, there was Scottish Development Finance established by George Mathewson when he was chief executive of the Scottish Development Agency. This made available venture capital at a time when the concept was still in its infancy and there were few other sources, ('3i' comes to mind). In due course it was privatised by Scottish Enterprise and it has continued in its new form to be a successful and adventurous source of risk capital both in Scotland and beyond.

Each of these initiatives had clarity of focus with clear guidelines for success and operated in a market space in which the private sector either did not wish to operate or at least did so only modestly leaving sufficient room for public sector intervention. I would also argue that the latter did so with a private-style orientation, not least of which was a strong competitive ethic. In addition, they were addressing real economic needs set against a backdrop of significant change in the economy as old manufacturing declined. In such a climate there is a real and meaningful role for the public sector. All of these initiatives had real scale and contributed 'step-change' outcomes where success could be readily measured.

Where intervention is less successful is when the national economic development and growth agenda is ignored in favour of some other less specific outcome and/or where it is not obvious that there is either serious market failure or where the nature of the problem trying to be solved is simply too complex for an economic development solution if one assumes, as I do, that absolute focus and clarity are vital to successful outcomes.

For example, the profusion of visitor attraction centres which have spread like a rash across Scotland and the UK over the last decade, sometimes by accessing lottery funding and/or by a combination of public-private capital. These take several forms such as mini-science centres, or themes around an historical event, natural history, geology and so on. Doubtless all of them were very worthy in their own right and of value to their local communities. Some, perhaps the majority, add to the stock of human knowledge and recreation in which case they should be supported from education or sport and culture budgets.

Excellent though they may be they have very little to do with mainstream economic development, notably the productivity and related problems discussed above, and especially the growth agenda. Success is usually measured by the number of visitors they attract which is a sensible metric in itself, but contributes very little if anything to the achievement of growth, especially since most lose money and require ongoing revenue support which is why the private sector has rarely sponsored them without significant amounts of taxpayers 'subsidy'. The Eden Project may not be unique, but it is certainly in a minority.

Frequently the complexities of some socio-economic problems militate against a simple economic development solution. So called 'inclusion' programmes directed towards long term unemployed and/or those individuals and groups which are hugely disadvantaged are usually fingered as being non-core to mainstream economic development and this is true. However, such programmes represent such a small fraction of the spend of the development agencies as to be a sideshow to the real work of the latter. They would be better done by other more appropriate bodies, but by itself their transfer would release few resources to be directed towards more meaningful growth-based activities.

The real distractions which use up large capital sums with uncertain outcomes are the so called 'renewal projects'. The Lanarkshire Enterprise Zone (EZ) can be judged to have been a success. The same cannot be said for its Clydebank and Inverclyde equivalents or in an earlier era the GEAR project in the east end of Glasgow. Dundee EZ was somewhat more successful, but the real transformation of the City was as a result of its knowledge industries and the latter's link to the universities. Therein lies the key.

Other smaller scale failures abound. This is not because of any incompetence on the part of those responsible, far less their commitment which in my experience was always outstanding, but because the multiple issues which lie at the heart of socio-economic decline are simply so complex as to be virtually impossible to resolve without truly massive resources and even then there is no certainty of outcome. As with the visitor attraction centres this will not stop the various agencies in these areas asking for more and more monies to cope with the problems.

Some such investments will succeed because of their location. I suspect that Lanarkshire's success was, in no small measure, connected to its proximity to major population centres in Glasgow and even Edinburgh. In an earlier era this was true of Livingston and East Kilbride and may also explain, in part, why the other 'new towns' were less successful. In a contemporary context one need only look at the spillover benefits Edinburgh has bestowed on south Fife and the Borders to get the point.

Advanced economies are increasingly urban dominated and our cities have created their own hinterland of economic dependency and growth. To ignore this reality is crass and will lead to further claims on scarce resources which will diminish the potential for long-term economic change. There simply isn't enough cash to go round and we should stop pretending that every part of Scotland can get a fair share. Rather we should focus scarce resources on where it will have most impact and this should not be determined by regional allocations, but by opportunity. In other words, we do what successful businesses do by investing in real points of differentiation and core competence. I believe that these are in the science and technology based industries and those businesses with a strong innovative core. Such decisions need not be led by the public sector either. There are many alternative ways of doing so.

The truth is that some, but by no means all, of our universities are the key to long-term success of this economy just as they have been in Massachusetts or Silicon Valley or Cambridge. And the brutal fact is that these can be counted on the fingers of one hand. Some of them have not always recognised or accepted the need to play an integral part in the life of the country. That needs to change and in fairness shows signs of doing so amongst some of them. Most though not all of the key universities are located within our major cities. Therein lies a lesson.

Before I look at some specifics let's not lose sight of the fact that the real determinants of long term economic growth are not the interventions of agencies like Scottish Enterprise or the local authorities, which also have an economic development mandate. It is macro-economic instruments like fiscal policy especially as it affects corporation tax, as Ireland has so ably demonstrated.

In the absence of control over the latter which one assumes isn't imminent, it is vital to concentrate resources on 'scale' projects such as enhancing the research and development capacities of our businesses. Remember the fundamental problem confronting the Scottish economy are low levels of productivity and innovation.

Since this malaise cannot be cured under the existing political settlement via tax incentives it will have to be by other means. And here the development agencies and relevant departments, even under the existing settlement, can make important contributions to economic success.

There is unquestionably a 'demand' failure in Scotland. How else does one explain the chronically low level of research spend? Could it be that too many of our businesses simply don't see the connection between such investment and that of skills and training to ultimate success? It is hard to resist such a conclusion. Of course, many businesses have no need to invest in R&D, but the same cannot be said for investment in innovation and skills. These are fundamental in all businesses from restaurants to software.

There is therefore, a role for the 'bully-pulpit' by government, business leaders and opinion-formers to improve understanding and stimulate demand. This collaborative approach around the core themes necessary for economic success sat alongside the fiscal and educational changes which so transformed Ireland.

Cash based incentives already exist and have recently been altered to make them more appropriate to innovation led projects. But I fear that unless there is a change in the mind-set of our businesses we will not see the productivity advances necessary for economic growth. In any case cash-based schemes are less effective than fiscal stimuli, but that's another story.

One of the major characteristics of highly competitive economies such as Singapore, Ireland, Taiwan, the USA and Canada has been the willingness of governments to engage in long-term, high cost programmes to establish global leadership in key technologies. In the case of some of these countries, like Ireland and Singapore, they have done so with a weaker intellectual infrastructure than Scotland. To those that claim this is picking 'winners' I would respond by saying what on earth do critics think venture capital companies do?

We should fund our universities to enable them to bring the world's leading researchers in key technologies to Scotland even at the expense of diverting funds from other budgets. These individuals will attract like-minded people to work alongside them and students to learn from them. From this starting point we have the potential to build a highly skilled infrastructure of ideas and people which can then be accessed by our Scottish businesses, suitably educated and incentivised, to recognise the potential on their doorstep.

Such intellectual excellence if properly marketed would re-invigorate our foreign investment attraction programmes and allow Scottish Development International to specifically focus on individual companies and technologies which wish to come to Scotland not for grants, far less cheap labour, but because they want and need to access the research and talent available here. There has never been a time when the multi-nationals' R&D departments were more mobile. The more tragic since it doesn't have to be that way.

The advantage of this approach is 'focus' and the ability to have clear benchmarks for success based on the hallmarks of those development programmes that worked best in the past: focus on key technologies where Scotland has serious potential for international competitiveness; focus resources on the latter rather than a disparate attempt to satisfy all constituencies and regions; and focus on outcomes which clearly have an impact on growth. That is the major economic challenge facing this country, just as replacing lost manufacturing via foreign investment jobs was two decades ago.

Such an approach may have serious implications for existing budgets of both the enterprise agencies and departments. And whereas I think our track record is not nearly as bad as the critics would have us believe, there is no denying that it could be better. But unless we recognise the problem we are trying to solve, low economic growth, then we will not use our resources where they most matter.

I have avoided getting into the various other issues frequently discussed such as too rigid planning controls, possibly a barrier to growth, but there many examples of countries with far tighter planning regimes and higher growth and productivity than ours so the matter is more complex than its advocates would have us believe. The same is true for local business rates. I accept that these may be too high and have a detrimental impact on smaller businesses especially, but they are not the real issue and their reduction, however welcome, will have little impact on innovation, skills, good management and ultimately productivity.

So far as transport is concerned, another frequently cited 'barrier to growth', if I had one wish it would be to greatly increase the number of flight connections to key global commercial centres. We have made progress on that front but have a long way to go. This is a real competitive disadvantage.

I haven't dwelt on the 'skills' agenda primarily because it deserves a chapter on its own. Suffice to say that I believe it should remain at the centre of economic development policy-making. One of the most common boasts in the corporate world is that 'people are our greatest asset' (a claim frequently more rhetoric than substance). In the case of most countries (those with vast amounts of extractable resources may be exceptions) this is simply a statement of absolute fact.

I believe that 'skills development' in a very broad sense should include developing social and communication skills and extend into the kind of thing modern industries look for in employees. These skill deficiencies were strongly identified by SE last year in what was the biggest labour market survey of its kind ever undertaken. This certainly doesn't mean that craft and related skills training don't matter. Only that we should recognise that the labour market can change very rapidly (the electronics and semiconductor industries are classic examples) and we should prepare people to understand that some of the key drivers of a modern economy have much to do with a willingness to learn and re-learn communication and social skills and broaden knowledge.

One constantly reads these days about jobs migrating to low-cost locations. Invariably, people associate this with low-cost call centre jobs or volume manufacturing. And this is true, but the real threat is from low cost high skilled research jobs and those with other forms of high value, intellectual content. Skills programmes should be central to economic development. Just as the provision of advance factories or the pursuit of foreign direct investment was in the 1980s and 90s.

In summary. The challenge is how to achieve sustainable higher economic growth given the present constitutional settlement and available economic development resources.

Such resources should be focused on core intellectual assets in the form of our best research universities and those companies predisposed to invest in R&D and/or pursue other forms of innovation. One by-product of this will be a strong orientation to investment in urban centres. This will be politically difficult, but if it doesn't happen we need to recognise that scarce resources will be wasted as the Executive tries to please everyone. Three or four growth nodes across Scotland will do more for the development of their hinterlands than all the rehabilitation and remediation policies with hoped for, but rarely realised outcomes.

The global attraction work of Scottish Development International is already directed towards 'high-value' relationships with corporates and countries. This is appropriate.

Our skills programmes, from the advisory through to the delivery, should be central to our economic development strategy. In fact, Scotland should be recognised as a place with a highly innovative approach to skills. It should be seen as a differentiator and as such will boost national productivity and growth. Unlike the rest of our investment strategy it needs to be national.

Ireland transformed its economic fortunes in a generation. So did Taiwan and Singapore. So can Scotland. You see, we are not 'doomed', however disappointing this may be to latter day Private Fraser's.

Yet neither should we lose sight of the fact that by 2020 our economic growth will depend to a much greater extent than it does now on company level innovation allied to the exploitation of science and technology, from whatever source, and much greater investment in skills investment than is presently the case.

By 2020 countries such as China, India, the Philippines, Russia, Brazil and Argentina will be sources of innovation and knowledge products. In fact, this already happening. Nations like Scotland will require a core of highly differentiated products and services which are themselves knowledge based to compete both with the newly emerging and advanced economies. More accurately, since in reality 'countries' don't compete businesses do, we will need globally innovative businesses steeled for this challenge.

I would like to think that by 2020 Scotland's economic development programmes will focused towards a relatively narrow set of support programmes built around a national consensus that positions the commercialisation of science and technology as our core differentiator, while continuing to recognise the vital contribution of service industries like finance and tourism.

If this comes to pass our country's economy will be dominated by knowledge 'factories' built around, and collaborating closely, with a core of top class universities and colleges. Between them they will attract and retain talent from across the world and will be renowned for intellectual leadership in several disciplines. These will have a support infrastructure and supply-chain including finance and marketing.

The past is not necessarily a predictor of the future. The latter lies in our own hands. We have the competencies the question is do we have the vision, leadership and political courage to make it happen.

7

Working for Scotland

SHONAIG MACPHERSON

WE SHOULD ALL BE in agreement that the number one priority for the Scottish Executive today is to grow the Scottish economy by the introduction of policies that will lead by 2020 and beyond to the creation of more sustainable businesses, the growth of existing businesses and greater participation of all Scots in economic activity. While there are many challenges to overcome in achieving that growth, one of the most taxing challenges is that of our demography. We have a declining birth rate coupled with an ageing population who, some would argue, will not necessarily contribute to the creation of a dynamic economy. The Government Actuary Department recently published population projections using data collected in 2001 by the Census, which project that Scotland's population will fall below 5,000,000 by 2009 and below 4,000,000 by 2041. Due to below replacement fertility rates, decreasing mortality and effectively zero net migration, over 25% of the population will be comprised of persons aged 65 and over, outnumbering those who are aged under 15.[1]

In order to sustain our population and to provide workers for 2020 and beyond we need to contemplate how we can, at one age extreme, raise the birth rate, or halt its decline, and, at the other age extreme, ensure that those members of our society who are over 'normal' retirement age, however defined in these pension challenged times, can continue to participate in economic activity without financial penalty if they wish to do so. While initiatives such as Fresh Talent are welcome measures to boost our workforce, they alone will not be sufficient if we are to prevent economic decline.

The entire debate around families and work, particularly working mothers, is fraught with sensitivities. After all the decision to start a family is absolutely one of personal choice. While women's rights in the workplace are clearly established at law, society remains equivocal about the role of working mothers. The Equal Opportunities Commission's work provides evidence that in certain areas of the business community equality in pay and career prospects has not yet been achieved. From a social perspective, there is ample research to support the belief that the early years of childhood are the most essential in shaping a child's future and maximising children's potential. Many argue that mothers should not work during those early years and in some European countries there are more extensive maternity rights to allow working mothers to spend at least the first 12 months of a child's life with the child without financial penalty. Some European countries have introduced financial rewards in the form of grants payable on the birth of children in an attempt to address falling birth rates. In the United Kingdom some might argue that the Child Trust Fund payments are a similar reward, although not established for that purpose.

If we are to create a more dynamic economy in Scotland, we need to encourage more people to participate in economic activity. This can be achieved by the creation of an environment and society where it is possible for parents but especially women to combine work and family. In any situation it should be a matter of informed choice for the parents of a child whether the mother or father returns to work after the birth and when that return should be. Early returns are driven predominantly by financial need: the increase in the cost of housing alone over recent years being one of the drivers. Much will be dependent on the parents' own personal and family circumstances, including the attitude of their respective employers and the childcare options available to them.

While this is a matter of personal choice, if we really want to improve the birth rate in Scotland, all elements of society, government (central and local), citizens, families, public and private sector organisations and the business community must put the family at the heart of all policy, public services and the community. Scotland has to become a nation where it is easier for work and parenting to be combined for parents, whether single parents or otherwise. While our Governments at Holyrood and Westminster have a key role to play in their respective fields of authority in providing support and infrastructure for families, it is not their task alone to deal with this challenge. We all have a role to play.

While it is far too simplistic to state that the provision of more affordable quality childcare will be sufficient, it is clear that initiatives such as Sure Start Scotland have begun to make a difference. However, there is inadequate provision of affordable quality childcare in Scotland. There is currently only one childcare place for every five children in the United Kingdom. This goes some way to explain the striking finding of the research undertaken by Heather Joshi and Robert Wright as part of the recent Allander Series that in Scotland 71% of childcare is provided through informal networks of neighbours, friends and family. Of even greater significance is that 36% of childcare is provided by grandparents, a statistic which correlates with the percentage of families who received the childcare tax credit in the same period. Only one-sixth of childcare was provided through nurseries and crèches, with one in eight using nannies, au pairs and childminders.

These statistics demonstrate the diversity of childcare provision that is currently in use and required. One of the reasons for the number of parents using informal networks will quite simply be cost. For those on low incomes the cost of formally provided childcare may be a determining factor in parents not returning to work. Other issues include location and availability of suitable provision. Similarly many people who could and would enter into the formal childcare industry as workers will not do so formally due to the low level of wages available to them, the disproportionate burden of income tax on low wages and the potential loss of benefits.

While there will be a continued need to provide quality childcare places and nurseries, it should be recognised that parents' decisions regarding the type of childcare to use on return to work should be a matter of choice without disadvantage. Where parents determine not to use formal nurseries or childcare places they will continue to incur the costs of childcare. In addition to provision of more formal quality childcare places the costs of childcare could be met by the state through vouchers, tax credits for those employing carers directly and payments for family carers. More resource should be made available but the decision of how to provide childcare should be for parents not the State. Why should payment not be made to grandparents or other family members who perform the role of carer for carrying out such duties, especially in rural areas where lack of formal provision is probably compounded by inadequate public transport? If we are to put children and families at the centre of our society then such provision and resource should be available universally: if it were to be, my preference would be to ensure that the majority of resource was targeted at low income families.

The key for me is in ensuring that resources are there for children irrespective of whether or not the child's parents work or not. Our overall aim should be to improve the lot of families. By doing so it is arguable that this will encourage more parents to combine parenting and work. With more childcare options available it is probable that parents would be able to return to work whether full time or part-time, whether with a single employer or multiple employers or they may determine to become self-employed.

It isn't only a question of money although the Equal Opportunities Commission has ample evidence that women have yet to achieve equality in pay, especially working mothers where the Equal Opportunities Commission estimates that more than one-third of the current pay gap arises from the difficulties that women encounter in combining work and parenthood.

We also need to consider how we plan our communities for the future. Historically schools, nurseries and childcare facilities have been adjacent to the home, reflecting a society where women with children did not work but stayed at home as the primary carer for children. It also reflects a society where there is a single employer culture, with the employer being located in close proximity to the home. This is no longer the case as more women have entered into the workforce and with the dispersal of industry causing commuting times to become extended. The community in which home is located is not necessarily the same place as the community in which parents work or where families would choose to access their required public services. Is it reasonable to suggest that nurseries and childcare places might be better suited nearer to the parents' place of work with supporting health care services at hand as well? The growth of City Centre nurseries would seem to suggest that there is some logic in that.

Consideration of an extended year and extended hours for schools are welcome developments. Is there merit in actually moving away from the long summer holiday of 6 plus weeks which is a challenge for the majority of working parents to fill with care arrangements that will benefit and motivate their children? While there are summer camps aplenty for those that can afford them is that really the best option for our children when there is continued criticism that our national skills level is too low. In addition the current right to 13 weeks unpaid parental leave to care for children during the first five years of a child's life could be itself extended to allow parents to cover summer holidays up until the age of 11. How many workers are aware of these rights?

Public transport should be more family friendly with buses and trains that are push chair and young people friendly. More bus routes should consider drop off points at schools and nurseries.

For the majority of those in work their working day continues to be aligned to core business hours of a 09:00 to 17:00 existence. This also holds true for the majority of the public services that we require access to for our children. It would be more efficient for the economy and more convenient for the consumers if such services were to be available outside those hours. Many of the key public services that we all require during our children's early years are available during these core business times at locations usually nearer to our home than our workplace. For many parents, this results in taking holiday or unpaid leave to use such services. It might also be the case that such absences are 'excused' as sick leave. Consideration should be given to extending the hours during which such services are available, perhaps using recent advances in technology to do so. Perhaps there are lessons to be learned from NHS 24 and the increased use of video conferencing. As stated earlier, the location of provision of many of these services needs to be reconsidered. If Community planning is to be truly effective it needs to appreciate that from a planning perspective communities should no longer be restricted to the traditional geographic definition of a community. Recognition of the complex networks that now govern most people's lives needs to be taken into account. If there is to be choice in public services should a citizen be confined to a single location for the provision of such services as an appointment with a GP or Health Visitor or Dentist? Advances in technology and more importantly electronic records management should allow access from any point.

In some industry sectors, working hours patterns are beginning to move away from the traditional core business hours. Some argue that the current right to request flexible working hours available to those with children aged under six or with disabled children should be extended to parents with children aged under sixteen. At present the right is only available to eligible employees. Further the right is not to flexible working hours but instead a right of an employee to request that his or her employer should consider such request seriously. In Scotland the majority of employers are small to medium sized enterprises (SMEs). For many SMEs it would require consideration of the impact of permitting one person to adopt flexible working hours on the entire business enterprise itself, rather than the requestor's ability to perform their role. Others argue that the right ought to be strengthened to become a right to flexible working hours per se. For the reasons stated earlier I believe that this would be difficult for Scottish SME businesses, many of whom already find it difficult to deal with the costs and logistics of compliance with maternity rights provision. However, enlightened employers may be encouraged to introduce flexible working hours themselves as, with an increasingly tight labour market, employers would become an 'employer of choice' by introducing such policies. This may also assist with recruitment and staff retention. In larger corporate entities we are beginning to see flexible benefits packages as employers realise that members of their workforces have differing personal priorities, ranging from car, pension and health insurance. The more advanced also offer time banks or TOIL (time off in lieu) where instead of overtime being paid for, days off in lieu can be earned to deal with the demands of parenting, from doctors or dental appointments to school visits. With the advent of improved technology and broadband there ought to be increased opportunities for flexible working hours and working from home. While initially this will be confined to certain aspects of the service sector it presents many possibilities.

Maternity Rights and Paternity Rights are a major concern to small businesses and can cost them dearly. They argue that the need to train a replacement to act as cover during maternity leave and to keep a position open for returning mothers is expensive; this is further exacerbated when there is a tight labour market. One means of tackling this might be to establish a pool of resource among those who are retired but wish to continue to participate in economic activity who would act as maternity cover without endangering their rights to the state pension as a result of the earnings received during that period. They could also be exempt from income tax where earnings related to provision of maternity or paternity cover for a SME business. Co-ordination of that maternity cover resource could be operated nationally. Provision of suitable cover would be of benefit to employers, reducing costs of recruitment and ensuring that there is minimal disruption to their business.

Research by many organisations including the Institute for Employment Studies[2] has demonstrated that more loyal and committed labour forces are found in businesses that introduce family friendly policies. The requirement for a statutory minimum standard has perhaps been fulfilled but there ought to be flexibility allowing individual businesses to come up with solutions in conjunction with employees to suit their own circumstances. Regulation that stifles economic growth is unacceptable.

I am sure that one of reasons for the recent increase in the number of female owner-managed businesses is the recognition of the difficulties that working mothers face in terms of pay, promotion prospects and combining work with parenting. Many are being established by women who do not have children now but recognise that they might want to have children in the future. It is a question of control and choice. Some use the label 'lifestyle' as a derogatory label for such businesses: perhaps a better label would be 'balanced', permitting informed and self-determined choices between work and family or life. Further support should be made available to encourage more women to set up in business through the continuation of Scottish Enterprise's women into the network programmes and the delivery of enterprise education in schools, colleges and universities.

I hope that by 2020 in Scotland we shall have found the means to ensure that we are maximising our economic potential by providing ample work opportunities for all who wish to participate. In addition I hope that there will be real equality in the workplace for all rather than the few. We should have an environment that does permit parents to combine work and family in a balanced manner, not just for families but for business too. This will require the development of a change in attitude towards work and families. It cannot be achieved solely by the introduction of further regulation that would adversely impact on business. We do now have rights as individuals and it is for individuals, public sector and business to develop through choice a range of options that enables work to be balanced with childcare, recognising the need to personalise options. It is also important to ensure that the older members of our community can also continue to participate in economic activity should they wish to do so, without undue fiscal penalty. It is really a matter of maximising the potential in our people.

[1] Professor Heather Joshi and Professor Robert Wright have provided an excellent analysis of the impact of these statistics in their publication *Starting Life in Scotland in the New Millennium* one of the Allander Series of Lectures.

[2] Family Friendly Employment: the business case – Bevan, Dench, Tamkin and Cummings

8

Developing our Renewables Potential: A Win Win for Scotland

SARAH BOYACK

ONE OF THE MOST striking features of the *Red Paper on Scotland,* 1975[1] was the domination of oil as the energy solution to Scotland's energy needs.

The issue of oil was seen as the economic backbone for an independent Scotland by nationalists and an opportunity to deliver social justice and economic prosperity for the UK as a whole by socialists. The economic impact and social issues generated by the development of oil were seen as important by those contributing to the *Red Paper*, but strikingly there are no references to the wider environmental issues raised by the development of the oil industry. Thirty years ago environmental issues were so detached from the debate in Scottish politics that they did not even rate a footnote.

Sustainable development

Contrast that with today's global challenges, with awareness about transglobal pollution, the reality of long-term damage caused by radioactive fall out from Chernobyl, and the challenge of Climate Change.

We are now at the point where most scientists and governments accept that climate change is happening, although there is disagreement about the extent to which it is unstoppable and whether it is possible to slow it down. The last few years have seen the hottest and wettest summers in a generation, bringing in their wake hugely destructive floods and deaths caused by excessive heat.

Carbon trading is becoming a reality which will be given greater impetus now that Russia has agreed to ratify the Kyoto protocol. The Royal Commission on Environmental Pollution's target of reducing the use of carbon by 60% by 2050 cannot be delivered without radical changes to our energy consumption and our energy generation. We will need to find replacements to gas and coal in the long term. At a recent Royal Society event the audience was meant to be reassured that we have 40 years of UK gas left before we need to worry! Although promoted by some as a clean energy source, decisions on nuclear power remain controversial given the lack of any agreement on how to deal with nuclear waste, global security problems and the financial state of the nuclear industry.

The development of the Scottish Executive's current policy on renewables takes its genesis from the need to think about policy in the round. Not just to think about jobs or environment or social justice, but all three. I believe that the development of policy on renewables will be seen in future as one of the big ideas of the new Scottish Parliament. It is a win-win policy for Scotland – if we seize the opportunity.

Renewables policy development

Several exciting stages can be seen on the route of the development of renewables policy. From the first manifestos for the new Scottish Parliament to the development of the first term Programme for Government and then to the second term Programme for Government with its green thread, more ambitious policy has emerged.

National Planning Policy Guideline NPPG 6 (revised 2000) Renewable Energy Developments[2] set a policy framework for local planning authorities requiring them to take national support for renewables into account when drafting their development plans to identify appropriate locations for renewables and for a policy framework when considering applications for development.

The publication of the Garrad Hassan (2001) report *Scotland's Renewable Resource*[3], commissioned by the Scottish Executive into the opportunities offered by the development of renewables, highlighted just what a huge opportunity awaited Scotland. It revealed a staggering 60 Gigawatt renewable resource in Scotland.

The Executive's response to the UK Government's consultation on Energy Policy, its adoption of an initial target of 18% of electricity from renewables by 2010, and then subsequently increasing the target to 40% by 2020, signalled a step change in Government policy on renewables. The 18% target will be relatively straightforward to achieve, but the 40% target will be a much greater challenge, requiring infrastructure development and rapid expansion of marine and small-scale renewables projects. The establishment of the Forum for Renewable Energy Developments in Scotland was an indication by the Executive that there needed to be an urgent focus on delivery and partnership work with the renewables industry.

The benefits of developing renewables

Writing at the launch of their 20:20 vision on the Future of Renewables in Scotland[4], the Scottish Renewables Forum identified the clear challenges involved in meeting the Scottish Executive's 40% target by the year 2020. 'There will be a need to bring on newer technologies; we will need to manage the grid much more actively, and we will need to ensure that the bulk of the jobs that deliver on these targets are created in Scotland. We also need to give serious consideration of the role of renewables in meeting our future transport and heating needs.'

The most compelling arguments for the development of renewables can be summed up as follows.

We need to develop non-CO_2 energy sources, linked to energy efficiency. A twin track strategy for energy efficiency and renewables could benefit business and consumers. Fuel poverty could be addressed for citizens and lower costs could be good for business competitiveness.

There are major economic prizes to be won – the Danes captured the benefits of developing wind farm technologies. However, we have been able to see manufacturing and employment creation benefits in Scotland through the opening of the Vestas factory in Machrihanish. The challenge is to make Scotland the location for the development of marine technology and production.

We still have the engineering and skills capacity to deliver the manufacturing bases which would be required.

We have the chance to develop cheap energy sources that can be installed by individual householders and businesses whether in urban Scotland or in rural areas.

There is a large degree of political consensus across the Parliament for the development of renewables, although this has nearly been destabilised by the debates over the development of on-shore wind farms. Throughout the Parliament's first five years a combination of Executive leadership, cross party support through the Cross Party Group on Renewable Energy and support from environmental NGOs has enabled a broad coalition to agree on the need to see renewables developed.

My own view is that we need to start with onshore wind because of technological readiness. It is here and it works. There will be challenges, however, in delivering the right decisions on the ground, both in determining which projects should or should not go ahead and what changes need to be made to their design to make them acceptable to our landscape and wildlife interests.

However, it is vital that there is a development of a range of renewables and a direct link made between renewables policy and energy efficiency. Without that, the challenges of the future will become harder – the 40% renewable target will pose bigger challenges and the 60% coming from other energy sources will be even tougher too.

The more energy we use, the more renewables and other conventional sources of energy will be required. The Royal Commission on Environmental Pollution[5] highlighted the cost of failing to reduce our energy consumption in stark terms. 'Unless energy demand is curbed to a significant degree, making substantial reductions in UK emissions would require a massive and environmentally intrusive contribution from renewable sources augmented either by nuclear power or by fossil fuel power stations with large scale capture and isolation of carbon dioxide'. However, we do have the beginnings of a very powerful policy framework for renewables which could make a real difference if allied to a drive towards energy efficiency, backed up by sustained investment in R&D and the promotion of pilot schemes to take new technology from the prototype stage to the commercially acceptable stage.

Offshore wind is being developed in the Solway and Moray Firths. The Talisman project is seen as a showcase for Scottish ambition, and will marry wind technology with Scotland's oil and gas expertise to test out a first generation of deep-water wind turbines, and if successful could grow up to 1,000 mw in size. Marine energy has been developing apace with the new test centre at Orkney and the Pelamis project. The Limpet technology is now working on Islay and could be adopted around our coastline.

The right renewables mix?

The Report on Renewable Energy[6] produced by the Scottish Parliament's Enterprise and Culture Committee in 2004 marked a parliamentary milestone in the debate on Renewables. It represented the first serious parliamentary scrutiny of the issue and generated a great deal of debate amongst MSPs and those giving evidence. In his response to the debate in Parliament, the then Minister, Allan Wilson MSP, announced that there would be extra resources for local planning authorities to enable them to cope better with the assessment of renewables applications. His establishment of a National Forum to engage stakeholders across the economic and environmental interests in dialogue is very welcome.

However, arguably the Committee focused more on the current and emerging big scale renewables, but spent less time debating equally important small-scale technologies. There are a range of established and emerging technologies: solar heating and photovoltaics, mini-wind vanes, geothermal, biomass and combined heat and power schemes. These have the potential to meet needs in both our urban and rural areas, but need a change in attitude from those involved in public procurement, planning decisions and our building standards. They do not require large scale individual developments, but they do have the capacity to deliver CO_2 reductions as part of an integrated framework.

No-one is really against these technologies, but there is a huge amount of scepticism. They don't have the political benefits of the big fix. The building industry does not like new technologies that do not have clear maintenance regimes that householders will readily understand.

I believe there is a real danger however, that we will be left behind. The Netherlands, Japan and Germany are all racing ahead with small-scale renewables. China is committed to training 10,000 African engineers in renewables technology. This technology offers us a potentially exciting mix of energy efficiency and renewables which could be installed in new building developments as well as plugged in to existing properties. The relative costs make them potentially very practical compared with the sorts of money that we spend on installing new kitchens and upgrading bathroom suites.

However, there is the difficulty of knowing where to start and finding skilled people to install these devices. The Scottish Community Household Renewables Initiative (SCHRI) programme has begun to make a real difference as it enables individual householders to gain grant support to install renewables and to crack some of the practical difficulties that need to be resolved if renewables are to become a requirement under Building Standards regulations. In a climate where the power utilities are now telling us that the era of cheap domestic fuel is over, there is a real imperative for government to act.

The extension of eligibility to the SCHRI to include developers is significant because we need the volume builders to become experienced in the opportunities opened up by such technology and to train up the personnel required to deliver them cost effectively. Central government could require social housing developments to incorporate renewables and high levels of energy efficiency designs in all public buildings and social housing and lead by example, stimulating local markets and producers. Local authorities could play a huge role in moving the agenda on. Planning policies locally could be amended to require renewables in domestic and commercial developments.

Local opportunities

Edinburgh and Dundee Councils are already considering the economic and image benefits of being the leading cities in Scotland on environmental quality, with renewables a key part of the strategy. Dundee's Sun City project has seen local companies team up with the Council and Further Education establishments to identify opportunities. Dundee City Council sees branding Dundee as Scotland's Sun City delivering not just economic opportunities but also promoting civic pride and a modern environmentally responsible image for the city. Edinburgh has identified renewable technology to be incorporated in one of its flagship brownfield sites. But it is not just houses and offices which provide opportunities. Schools and hospitals which are built to lifecycle maintenance regimes provide a financial framework which supports the cost efficient incorporation of renewables. The Scottish Executive's Green Procurement Guidelines provide the vehicle to deliver, but there needs to be a clear lead from the Executive that it expects Councils to include renewables in all their public private partnership developments.

In rural Scotland the use of forestry resources locally through wood fuel and district heating technologies would result in a more self sufficient approach to energy use which would provide a sustainable and diversified use of our forestry resource. Small-scale woodland projects could be developed as a result of opportunities arising from reform of the Common Agricultural Policy which could promote financial support for rural diversification.

The way forward

So we are at the point where a great deal of the infrastructure is being developed – although there is a huge amount still needing to be done.

Key challenges are:

- Encouraging embedded generation – that is generation located within the community. This is an issue for individual house-holders wanting to incorporate micro renewables who face extremely tortuous procedures from the electricity companies. The process can add months of delay and significant costs to such projects, and means that householders can miss out on the benefits from installing renewables which trickle power into the grid. We need to see this issue addressed urgently with targets set by the Scottish Executive.

- The development of BETTA (the British Trading & Transmission Arrangements) in ways which will not disbenefit Scottish renewables. The issue is potentially problematic for larger scale renewables and it seems that Scotland will now face higher charges for use of the grid system, as well as more onerous con-ditions. There is a lack of joined up policy here, and we urgently need to find ways to make sure regulation and government policy do not conflict.

- The development of markets for renewables in the domestic and buildings sector is something that can be acted upon now. The Scottish Executive could take a practical lead on this by fol-lowing the Mayor of London's requirement for developers to identify the best type of renewables for new development, be they commercial or residential.

- Decisions need to be taken on the development of the grid to enable new renewables off the north and west coasts to go ahead. The announcement of a Strategic Environmental Assessment of the potential impact of marine renewables will hopefully enable more certainty about the best areas to be targeted for develop-ment. Urgently required upgrades for the grid are expensive and will be time consuming as the optimal routes are chosen. The issue has already generated significant concerns about poten-tial environmental impacts.

We are close to the tipping point where the lessons learnt from pilot studies are incorporated into the mainstream. But we are not there yet.

What are the obstacles? They can be summed up as:

- Risk averse processes that penalise the use of new technologies. A reluctance to build in technology which may be superseded by more efficient models is understandable, but must not be used as a reason not to install renewables at all. More information about relative performance will inform purchasing decisions whether by companies or individuals. The SCHRI should provide validated performance information providing people with some degree of comfort enabling informed decisions.
- Political nervousness about supporting technologies that may be unpopular locally. In particular, onshore wind farm proposals have been identified as problematic, partly because they are visible and partly because there are a significant number of them being proposed across Scotland, with real concerns that need to be addressed on environmental impact, both in landscape and wildlife terms at the detailed design and planning stage. If half the Scottish Executive's target of 40% renewables by 2020 to come from wind farms that would mean something in the region of 70 wind farm rather than the current 200 currently proposed.
- Access to and development of the National Grid for renewables. This will be a critical stumbling block unless the issue is resolved for the medium and long term. Our ambitious targets will simply not be fulfilled if new generation cannot be connected to the grid at a price that is affordable.
- Lack of progress with mainstreaming for micro renewables. There is a major challenge here. SCHRI grants are potentially the way to unlock this block with local authorities taking a lead through green procurement strategies for schools and housing developments.

We need to recreate the universally positive political support for renewables that characterised debate in the first year of the new Parliament. Long-term investment needs long term political support. That means continued political leadership from both the UK and Scottish Government Ministers to provide long-term certainty and correct financial incentives to the renewables industry.

It also means continued work with trade unions, local authorities and local communities to ensure we maximise the potential benefits for job creation, promoting energy efficiency and tackling fuel poverty. Our aspiration should be that if we looked back twenty years from now, we would see the building blocks of the Green Industrial Revolution called for by Tony Blair[7] this year and a decisive shift away from 'business as usual'.

The Scottish Executive's *Green Jobs Strategy*, 2004, is a practical starting point giving a clear lead to the Scottish Enterprise Network to work with business and the Further and Higher Education sectors to put in place the training and investment strategy required to create business opportunities that enable us to work with our environment rather than seeing it as a resource to exploit. But it needs to be followed by similar action right across the public sector.

By 2020 we will need to have made real progress towards a non-carbon economy. That puts the challenge of delivering the 40% renewables target into context. Renewables are not the only answer but they are crucial if Scotland is to develop an environmentally sustainable and economically prosperous future.

[1] Brown, G (ed) (1975) *The Red Paper on Scotland*. Edinburgh: EUSPB

[2] National Planning Policy Guideline NPPG 6 (revised 2000) *Renewable Energy Developments*. Edinburgh: Scottish Executive

[3] Garrad Hassan, (2001) *Scotland's Renewable Resource*. http://www.scotland.gov.uk/library5/environment/SRS2001ExecSumm.pdf

[4] Scottish Renewables Forum (2003) 20:20 *Vision: building Scotland's renewable future*. Glasgow: Scottish Renewables Forum

[5] Royal Commission on Environmental Pollution (2000) 22nd report *Energy – The Changing Climate*. CM 4749 The Stationery Office. http://www.rcep.org.uk/energy.htm

[6] Enterprise and Culture Commission (2004) *Renewable Energy in Scotland*. 6th report second session, Edinburgh: Scottish Parliament.

[7] Tony Blair Speech, 14 September 2004 in London on the 10th Anniversary of the Environment Programme launched by the Prince of Wales.

9

Oil and Gas: Is the barrel half-empty or half-full?

JOHN ALDERSEY-WILLIAMS, JAMES MCCALLUM,
ALLAN MaCASKILL

AS WE REACH THE end of 2004, the UK is passing a milestone in oil and gas production. Although some 30 billion barrels of oil have been produced since the 1960s, estimates suggest that for the first time there may be less left to produce than has been extracted so far. But is the barrel half-empty, or half-full?

For as long as we can remember, the pundits have been predicting the imminent demise of the North Sea oil and gas business, and the supply chain that goes with it. So should we allow these Cassandras to influence our future actions, to give up and go home, or should we look forward with optimism and continue to maintain and develop the skills and economic contribution of the industry to the Scottish and UK economies?

Before debating the future of the industry we must first understand how it has developed over the last 30 years, from its inception in the late sixties to the early years of the 21st Century.

From the early seventies development of the North Sea was the prerogative of Major Oil Companies with deep pockets. The cost of developing a new industry, in a hostile environment was high and only the Majors possessed the capital and skills to develop a virgin basin. These were the companies who built the infrastructure of the North Sea: pipelines and terminals, as well as oil and gas platforms. The North Sea did attract some smaller companies: either joint venture participants supplying risk capital, with little expertise in development and operations, or small exploration companies, hoping to hit the jackpot with a major discovery. But invariably they too would sell to a Major prior to development. As the basin was developed, the supply chain began to evolve in parallel, at first in the form of drilling and service companies with experience in offshore activities in the Gulf of Mexico, and latterly local firms covering many aspects of the supply chain.

This situation continued until the early nineties when the first generation of independent operators arrived on the scene. These companies had been absent previously as they had insufficient capital to invest in the development of the primary infrastructure, but they possessed a lower operating cost base than the Majors. They acquired the infrastructure, taking over mature fields and developing infield and satellite accumulations, which the Majors considered economically marginal or unattractive. However, fuelled by their success, by the end of the decade many of the independents had also become large complex corporations. Although, they were initially more cost effective, commercially innovative and aggressive than the Majors, as they grew, their focus on efficient local operations and marginal opportunities waned in response to apparently easier pickings elsewhere.

Today this evolution has created an opportunity for the emergence of a new generation of small, tertiary operators. These companies have extremely low overheads and specialise in particular niche investments. They use their expertise to manage and mitigate the risks of commercial opportunities deemed uneconomic by the independents. They make use of enabling technology and the existing infrastructure, to further extend the life of fields and maximise recovery. They are cost effective, innovative and aggressive, with deep local knowledge and focus. In general, they are owned and staffed by individuals who served their apprenticeships in the Majors, and who now see the opportunity to benefit more directly in the opportunities they may generate. Tertiary operators are distinct from Joint Venture companies who seek to align themselves with major operators and profit through active portfolio management of small non-operated stakes.

As in so many other things, what happens in the US seems to foreshadow how the rest of the world may evolve. In the US Gulf of Mexico, the same overall pattern of evolution has already been seen. A combination of independents and tertiary operators has succeeded in extending the life of mature fields and developing smaller accumulations that larger operators considered non-commercial. These operators are often at the forefront of the application of new technology and innovative commercial strategies to generate value in their niche areas of focus. Recently this precedent has been noted by the DTI, which is keen to encourage the development of similar companies in the United Kingdom Continental Shelf (UKCS). The introduction of 'promote' licences was specifically aimed at making it easier for small companies to acquire acreage in the UK. The initiative seeks to allow small companies to invest their skills, resources and a small amount of capital to work up development and/or exploration opportunities that are lying fallow.

Given a similar opportunity, we believe that Scottish companies already possess the technical and commercial ingenuity which if applied could maintain a significant indigenous oil and gas business for twenty of thirty more years. Critical to this success will be the continued development of the technology, skills and know-how to find, develop and produce oil and gas in smaller accumulations in one of the most hostile environments in the world. These skills will not only create a vibrant and diverse industry to exploit our indigenous resources, reducing the UK's need to import energy, but also to provide a basis for a strong and thrusting service sector, supplying the world and generating a significant income: proof positive of the concept of a 'smart, successful Scotland'.

It becomes clear that the future development of the North Sea and the maintenance of a successful supply chain in Scotland will depend on three key issues. First the development and implementation of technology to access and develop the remaining resources, second the maintenance of the skills to apply the technology and finally the emergence of a market composed of innovative, aggressive companies with an ongoing appetite for investment.

The industry is currently seeing new levels of activity in response to high oil prices and new, smaller players are starting to emerge. However, it would be wrong to assume that the pace of evolution is sufficient to deliver the transformation that occurred in the Gulf of Mexico. The UKCS still faces several major impediments: the strangling of innovation by existing risk averse operators, premature abandonment of fields and infrastructure and a demographic timebomb with an average workforce age of 49.

If industry and government fail to address these problems, the UK oil and gas business, so critical to the Scottish economy will prematurely wither and die. The skills and experience will be lost and the country will have failed to fully develop a national asset and to grasp a much larger international opportunity that is there for the taking.

The oil and gas industry in the UK stands at a crossroads: the way ahead depends upon whether the key challenges are recognised and properly addressed. Let's indulge in a little futurology, and look back from the perspective of the year 2020 and see how the alternatives might play out.

In the first possible future, we observe a fragmented industry, with a small local supply chain, and very limited export activity. Through the first decade of the 21st Century, the Majors continued to exit the North Sea to explore and develop large field overseas. They retained ownership of their UK infrastructure, but invested little to extend field life and develop new resources. Instead they harvested the assets, using them as cash cows to finance their other activities around the world. Their stranglehold on the infrastructure allowed them to extract large rents from the new generation companies, stifling investment and reducing opportunities.

In response, the independents and the smaller oil companies picked over the remaining acreage. Staffed predominantly by personnel made redundant by the departing Majors, these companies developed specialist expertise and focused on very specific areas and/or types of opportunity. Where in the past capital for drilling had largely come from corporate balance sheets, increasingly private equity from the Venture Capital community funded the drilling activities of these companies. Activity levels fell as less funding was available and a few well-developed technical opportunities chased the limited investment funds.

By the second decade of the Century, the majority of these

smaller companies had exited or simply ceased to exist, mainly as a result of the lack of investment opportunities, but exacerbated by the demographic timebomb having played itself out. Encumbered by the size needed to minimise overhead costs the companies struggled to justify employing new graduates as they could not afford to train new staff to the same expert levels as themselves. There was simply no room for inexperienced staff, who contributed little in the short term.

At the same time, the multinational supply chain companies also left the UK to support the Majors in their international elephant hunting. By 2020 the majority of innovation and development takes place closer to their main markets in West Africa, South America, Middle East and the Former Soviet Union.

An alternative view of the future witnessed government and industry taking a longer and broader view and dealing head-on with the challenges facing the industry.

Once again looking back from 2020, a partnership of industry and government recognised the changing dynamics of the sector. The government ensured that companies either worked their portfolio or divested it. By introducing tax incentives that encouraged companies to invest, they freed up the market to provide opportunities for those companies with a will to invest. Simultaneously the age issue in the offshore oil and gas business was addressed. The recruitment of skilled graduates was encouraged; this significantly reduced the average age of the workforce and allowed the transfer of knowledge from experienced staff developed as the North Sea evolved to the next generation preserving and expanding the wisdom of the sector.

In 2020, the industry is still enjoying the benefits of a liberalisation of the market. This resulted from the development of a new generation of aggressive companies, who invested both in the ageing fields and their infrastructure and in the multiple satellite opportunities surrounding them. The recruitment drive in the first decade of the century, emphasised the overlap in skills between offshore oil and gas and the burgeoning offshore renewables industries, and attracted a new generation of young graduates with a greater environmental awareness. In parallel, innovation around subsea development, deferred decommissioning and the new challenges of offshore wind, wave and tidal energy produced valuable intellectual property, which is sold around the world.

A vibrant supply chain recognising the opportunities represented by the technology needs of offshore energy business – the conventional oil and gas business and the emerging renewables – kept its innovative core in the UK. These companies are now servicing similar offshore markets across the globe.

We have reached a major junction and either future is possible. The opportunity is there for us to grasp. What needs to be done to assure the future of the oil industry and to create significant economic benefit for Scotland? We believe that the prerequisite is a lasting partnership with government and industry, which provides stability for investors and a fair return for the nation. This will require a stable taxation environment that supports investment and promotes a wider access to infrastructure. Government must recognise that the industry can only prosper if the assets and infrastructure are in the right hands i.e. those companies prepared to invest and develop the resources. Government must have the courage to facilitate the transfer of assets and infrastructure from companies that are unwilling to develop and invest to those who are.

For their part industry must harness the all the resources of both the operators and contractor and invest in the development of the remaining potential of the North Sea. Industry must play its role by investing in the talent, the technology, and the infrastructure to maximise the remaining potential of the basin and to create a vibrant export industry.

The window of opportunity is extremely short. In the next three years both government and industry will determine the path we take. In 2020 it will not be acceptable for any of us to look back and say 'it wis nae me, it was him', we will all be implicated in the failure. In a devolved Scotland with such significant resources in both oil and gas and renewable energy it is no longer acceptable to relinquish this responsibility solely to Westminster. The Scottish Executive and DTI must accept that with very large numbers employed in the energy sector maintaining a vibrant energy industry will require leadership and partnership across the legislative boundaries. In conjunction with industry both governments must recognise the importance of the sector and provide support and guidance at ministerial level.

Immediate intervention is required is required if we are to win the prize that is the 30 billion barrels of unproduced hydrocarbon and deliver a long and prosperous future for the UK energy industry, securing many tens of thousands of jobs.

With such potential the authors clearly advocate that the barrel is half-full, maybe even a little more!

10

Transport: Moving Scotland out of first gear

DR IAIN DOCHERTY

I'M SITTING DOWN TO write this chapter on something of an inauspicious date for transport in Scotland. It's 19 November 2004, and the M8 motorway is 40 years old today. Or rather bits of it are, as even after all this time, the major road artery between our two greatest cities remains incomplete, a testament to our almost-but-not-quite approach to delivering the transport system a modern, advanced nation like Scotland deserves.

The piecemeal history of the M8 is a particularly pertinent – and worrying – allegory for the state of Scotland's transport network in general. Parts of the motorway, especially the section through Glasgow, are as impressive an engineering feat as any road in Europe. Other stretches are in a sorry state, having received very little tender loving care since opening four decades ago. Then there's the non-motorway section in Lanarkshire, a critical link in our national infrastructure. It is still nothing more than a patched-up version of the original 'Glasgow and Edinburgh Road', which dates from the 1930s.

Our failure to achieve something that our European neighbours would consider to be only the first building block of a decent national transport network is bad enough. But what really brings home the sheer lack of ambition endemic in our approach to transport is the attitude of our devolved government. Take as an example the reassurances of the Scottish Executive official put up to comment on the M8's mid-life crisis. 'Don't worry,' he said, 'we expect the final upgrade of the missing section to be on the ground in around six years'. Six years? Given the usual slippage in the timetable of anything we try to build, we will be lucky if the M8 is completed before its half century. And that, to be honest, is nowhere near good enough.

The story of the M8 illustrates the greatest single problem that Scotland continues to suffer when it comes to transport. Simply, our system of government seems completely unable to actually deliver the transport infrastructure and services we require. If we are to fulfil the vision of Scotland as a genuinely internationally competitive, creative and socially just country – a vision that inspired many of us to become involved in politics or public policy in the first place – then this failure must be addressed, and addressed quickly.

It's important to note at the outset that the current condition of the M8, and by extension, transport policy-making in Scotland more generally, is no accident. Rather, both are perfectly predictable outcomes of a number of factors, several of which have reinforced each other over many years.

Chief amongst these is the frankly dysfunctional policy-making machinery that we currently find ourselves grappling with. Transport governance in Scotland is in a mess: in large part this is thanks to a series of almost criminal actions, perpetrated by the outgoing Tory government in the 1990s as part of their sinister programme of slash-and-burn of public services. Perhaps worst of these was the abolition of the Regional Councils, implemented out of political spite in an attempt to gerrymander local government, but the lasting effect of which was to destroy important policy-making structures. Added to this were ideological triumphs such as the privatisation of the railways, which might have kept the neo-liberals happy, but have cost the rest of us an absolute fortune whilst doing little or nothing for the actual quality of the services we all rely on.

But let's give the Tories some credit where credit's due. Thatcher, Major, Younger, Lang, Forsyth and co. deliberately set out to bequeath a legacy of institutional change true to their ideological objectives, and they delivered exactly that. The so-called 'disciplines' of the market were introduced to the provision of public services, including transport. One of the first acts was to deregulate and privatise the bus industry. Within months, as bus companies raced each other on the streets, passengers were beginning to turn away for good, utterly confused by bus wars and constantly changing fares and timetables. Then local government was fragmented into neutered, rotten burghs unable to mount a credible challenge to the policies of central government, yet consumed by the need to compete against one another. And so started the fashion for American-style shopping malls, with their massive car parks drawing trade from towns and cities and causing serious environmental damage. To crown it all, the planning system was butchered so that while the car-owning suburbs would flourish, the inner cities would have to learn to fend for themselves with ever-diminishing public transport.

The upshot of all of this is that we're left with a situation approaching every-man-for-himself in local government, which has particularly important ramifications for the ways in which we plan and implement transport policies in Scotland. Each authority now jealously guards its own short-term interest to the detriment of sensible planning as a whole. And don't underestimate the damage this can cause – whilst councils in the west dash to see who can build the most out-of-town retailing the fastest, those in the east stare at each other over the floor of an acrimonious public inquiry trying to come to a sensible decision on road user charging. Given all of this, it's no exaggeration to say that some of our European colleagues (who, after all, are used to actually delivering transport projects) weep at our predicament in Scotland. The only question is whether the tears are those of laughter or embarrassment.

None of this should come as a surprise. Not only was the current situation of internecine warfare between public sector agencies explicitly designed to come about in the name of competitive 'efficiency', but it also suits the civil service, whose dead hand (as ever) lies on the tiller of the policy-making machine. Whilst the current Scottish Executive has made some faltering attempts to patch up the system, imploring organisations to work together in partnership to overcome the worst of the Tories' institutional legacy, central government continues to work in almost hermetically sealed policy silos. Sometimes, the structure of these can be quite comical. What other country in the world would create a government unit dedicated to bus and aviation policy, as Scotland did shortly after devolution?

From the viewpoint of the Sir Humphreys of Victoria Quay, however, such innovations have some clear advantages. This is because the division of transport policy into so many separate, if slightly odd, functional units safeguards the power and influence of the centre. However, it also leaves the goal of 'integrated' transport as far away as ever.

But back to the M8, as there's a final lesson to be learned from its chequered history to date. Let us – for a moment at least – leave alone the question of whether or not road building is an appropriate policy solution in light of the environmental crisis (more of which below). What is certain though is that our inability to see many major transport projects through to completion – whether through prevarication over policy priorities, ineffective delivery mechanisms, or more often, our stop-go mentality when it comes to funding – does nothing to bolster public faith in the ability of government to make things better.

In this sense, the biggest political legacy of the Scottish Executive's failure to complete the M8 (and myriad other transport projects across Scotland) despite having the financial and political capital to do so is the missed opportunity to prove quickly and conclusively that devolution could make a real difference to the quality of government in Scotland. By now, motorists should be reading something different to the faintly ridiculous 'Check Your Fuel' commands that the not inexpensive electronic signs along our principal motorway always seem to display. Imagine if commuters were by now used to this message instead. 'M8 LEFT UNFINISHED BY LONDON FOR 35 YEARS'. 'SCOTTISH PARLIAMENT GETS THE JOB DONE IN UNDER FIVE'. It's not difficult to understand how this kind of real policy delivery might have changed current attitudes to devolution, creating the political climate required if we are to go (much) further.

Although the history of the M8 illustrates perfectly many of the problems inherent in our system of transport policy-making and implementation, none of the above should be read as a call for the Scotland of 20 years' time to reflect the North American model where the car is the almost completely dominant mode of surface transport. Indeed, how we deal with the environmental impacts of our consumption of transport and mobility will be one of the most important and enduring problems that we will have to resolve in the coming years. In other words, the success of transport policy in Scotland over the next two decades or so will be assessed on how well we address the critical issue of making our transport system – and thus our economy and society – more sustainable.

In simple terms, the Scotland of the early devolved period cannot decide how green it wants to be. Whilst there is a wide consensus that we need to improve our environmental performance, when it comes to implementing actual policies that might begin to make such improvements, our political system once again demonstrates it limitations.

The case of what to do about road traffic is critical. We know that we must address the relentless rise in traffic if we are to do anything to reduce our emissions of greenhouse gases. Yet the politics of transport are still too often directed towards ignoring the problem altogether. This ostrich mentality manifests itself in many ways. Perhaps most obvious is the denial that additional taxes or charges on road transport influence traffic levels. Stung by the fuel tax protests, and wary of the power of populist media and local political campaigns against tolling, central government has retreated from the scene, leaving local politicians to make the case, and take the electoral risk.

This is made worse by the simplistic tactics of much of the green lobby. Too often, their approach seems to be to argue for a complete, permanent end to the provision of new infrastructure, particularly roads, as if leaving the M8 unfinished was some kind of carefully crafted, intellectually robust, integrated transport policy. To argue as they do that our transport network should be frozen in time – fossilised, irrespective of whether it is appropriate for current and future economic and social conditions – is exactly the kind of unsophisticated, luddite approach that helps nobody in the long run. Mobility is a very powerful social and economic force, and maintaining it, despite the obvious environmental challenges, will be critical to the health of our society. After all, throughout history, travelling the world has been at the very heart of what makes the Scots an outward-looking people.

The problem with ignoring reality as many 'deep greens' do, of course, is that it catches up with you sooner or later, delivering an almighty slap in the face as it does so. In the modern world of complex economic interdependencies shaped by international markets, Scotland simply cannot afford the luxury of hoping to get away with the low levels of transport investment we've seen in the past. High-quality transport infrastructure is essential for a modern competitive country. The difficult question for governments is not whether to turn off the infrastructure investment tap, but how to ensure we have the necessary connectivity to move around when we need to, whilst minimising the environmental impacts of doing so. This is why other small European countries are spending very significant sums of money on their transport systems in order to safeguard their economic competitiveness and quality of life, and why we will fall further behind if we do not do the same. Price tags such as £375 million for the first phase of a modern tramway in Edinburgh might seem impressive, but compared with the billions being spent in Dublin, Copenhagen, Lisbon, Toulouse or Turin, for example, they are distinctly modest.

Nationalists should not, however, take the failings of both the Scottish Executive and the Green movement as cause to be unduly pleased with themselves. Too often, short-term political realities have obscured the bigger picture when it comes to their approach to transport, especially its impacts on other policy areas such as the environment. Here, two issues are of particular concern. First is the default position in most current nationalist economic policies, which sees the US as the primary inspiration for a more competitive, 'entrepreneurial' independent Scotland of the future. Quite simply, American economic success comes at quite a price, and not just in terms of the extreme wealth differentials and social polarisation that provide the necessary 'incentives' to drive their system. Equally important is the almost complete disregard for the environment that characterises US economic policy, based as it is on complete car dependency, justified in the name of market 'flexibility'. Is a vision of relentless urban sprawl, smog-ridden cities and an obese population that regards walking as an inconvenience to be avoided wherever possible really what we aspire to?

Related to this is a second core policy problem, namely the nationalist hangover of our emotional attachment to oil. There is no doubt that Scotland has suffered massively from the theft and misuse of our oil revenues, nor that they would be an important part of building a prosperous independent nation state in future. But none of this means that we should avoid the hard questions of how we begin to build a more sustainable transport system and economy that does not rely on burning oil to create wealth.

Recent public and political reactions to the rising price of petrol illustrate perfectly the kind of debate that we must move beyond. To be blunt, so what if it's 'oor oil', that we are one of the largest producers of the stuff in the world? Does this give us the right to drive about as much as we like, polluting the planet more as well? Becoming independent means that we will have to assume our full responsibilities as well as rights. Critical to this is the self-reflection required to moderate our behaviour so that we act as respectful members of the international community. An independent Scotland clearly would not want to be in the position of having to abrogate the Kyoto treaty on day one. If the price of fuel has to go up so that more of us walk or take the bus to work as result, then so be it.

Alongside the need to address the global environmental crisis seriously, energy resilience is quickly becoming one of the critical geopolitical questions that will dominate the new century. This will present an independent Scotland with real challenges, and the transport sector may well be first to have to face them. Can we create the kind of economy that would survive a significant oil price shock of the kind experienced in the 1970s? Is it possible to change the whole tenor of the policy debate, to the extent that investments such as electrifying the railways are made in the name of safeguarding the future of our key national infrastructure, rather than avoided because of the economic assumptions of appraisal rules written in – and for – London and the southeast?

Such changes will not be easy to make. First, the inertia that paralyses the policy-making system will have to be overcome some-how. It is likely that this will require pursuing some difficult political choices. Chief amongst these is challenging the orthodoxy that unres-tricted car use in rural areas is somehow more 'essential', and thus defensible, than elsewhere. Then there's the question of whether low cost air travel, which is generating very significant increases in greenhouse emissions, is sustainable in the long term. We might even be forced into thinking long and hard about whether we might have to put up with nuclear power a little longer than we otherwise would like, faced with the difficulties in reducing the impacts of the car, air travel, and other forms of transport dependent on carbon.

Indeed, the very way the word 'independence' is emotionally interpreted sometimes obscures the starkness of the real policy choices that Scotland, like any other sovereign nation state, will have to face in the 21st Century. All too often, independence is seen as a mechanism to solve *current* policy problems in a different, albeit genuinely distinctive, Scottish way. But the real task for an independent Scotland will be to pose wholly new questions, and to engage in the fundamental reforms of the system of government required so that we actually make the transition to a more gen-uinely radical, prosperous and equitable society.

In terms of transport policy, this means shifting the debate away from short-term firefighting, which for decades has masqueraded as a coherent policy response to the twin problems of over-dependence on the car and chronic underinvestment in the alternatives. Instead, we need to create a political culture in which transport policy, as for other areas of government intervention, is focused on a more 'nationalist' agenda about genuine sustainability, which faces up to our international responsibilities, as well as satisfying internal demands. In other words, transport in the Scotland of the future will need to look more like that in Norway or Switzerland, rather than England or the United States.

Even the limited powers of the current devolved Parliament can go a long way to making this a reality. First, we need to accept the requirement to continually invest in our infrastructure, to make sure it meets the needs of our society and economy. Many countries in

Europe, including France, Germany and Switzerland, successfully generated a national consensus on transport over many years that survived several changes of government, and we need to do the same. Already there is the view that transport has 'had its share' under devolution, but to succumb to such a position would be to recreate the stop-go pattern of disjointed investment that has done so much to cripple our transport networks in the past.

Second, we need to be honest enough with ourselves to admit that even the most ambitious levels of infrastructure investment will never provide the kind of transport system that enables us to travel wherever we want, whenever we want. Investment needs to be focused on where it will bring the greatest benefit to the most people. This means that, although particular projects will continue be justified on special local or political grounds from time to time, the priority of a truly integrated transport policy should be on maximising the contribution of the core network, not about the creation of more and more branch lines of questionable economic and social value. Third, we will have to tackle the issue of our dependence on the car. Not give it up, but use it less, and be prepared to pay more for the privilege in light of its undoubted environmental costs.

But let's finish where we started, with the M8. What might it look like in 20 years' time if transport policy moves in the right direction? Hopefully it will be wider, better able to cope with peak demands. It will also be better maintained, and perhaps fully lit by green electricity so as to improve its safety record still further. All of this means that it will have to be tolled, but people will in time recognise this as the cost of reducing congestion and overall traffic levels, thus minimising environmental impacts whilst at the same time providing a better quality of service. Just the sort of road that makes a pleasant change once in a while to taking the new bullet train, in fact.

SECTION IV

A Peoples Democracy

11

A politics of the people

ALEX BELL

---

1 JANUARY 2020 – On a cold, pale morning the year began with an unveiling ceremony at the Donald Dewar statue in Glasgow. Additional figures have been placed next to the bronze figure of Scotland's first First Minister. These symbolise the role of the many people who made possible, what has become known as, the Scottish Model.

The lone statue was an effective symbol of how the old Scotland worked. It was a place of totemic heroes in a divided political landscape. For example, in 2004 the BBC compared Dewar with Nelson Mandela. This embarrassing misjudgement shows how politics and the media had difficulty gaining a sense of perspective. Elevating accomplished politicians into heroic figures revealed insecurity about the worth of the nation's political discourse.

The elevation of Dewar was preceded by the national mourning in 1994 at the death of another Labour leader John Smith. He was buried amongst the ancient kings of Scotland on Iona. Both examples fit the popular narrative of old Scotland, and Labour, as noble causes championed by heroic leaders: besieged by enemies.

In retrospect, this looks immature. The story, boosted by a media largely sympathetic to Labour, was mythical. Like many myths, it required conflict for narrative drive. The noble leaders battled the enemies of the people; the parties fought each other. Devolution was a victory over the hard-line unionists, and begat another war, between nationalists and the soft-line unionists. In reality this amounted to a constant denigration of important issues into petty squabbles.

In the context of the old narrative, raising a statue of a single man seems natural. Only later does it appear different. The cluster that now surrounds Dewar demonstrates a more sophisticated understanding of how this nation has grown up.

In the late 20th Century and early 21st, political models particular to nations emerged. The German model operated roughly from the mid-1950s to the early 21st Century. The Dutch model existed for a similar period. The Irish model dated from the 1980s and the Norwegian model from the 1960s.

The German model was characterised by co-operation between employers and employees, which allowed for industrial change to be moderated by all parties. The Dutch model amounted to social co-operation and tolerance, which allowed society in the Netherlands to grow through major changes in cultural, sexual and gender politics without the conflict experienced by other nations.

The Irish model was one of exceptional economic growth through political consensus, low tax regimes and aggressive Foreign Direct Investment strategies coupled with the benign assistance of the EU. In 2004 the *Economist* magazine judged it the best place in the world to live. Most other measures of good living put Norway at the top of the pile. Its model was based on the use of oil revenues to invest in social infrastructure.

In comparison the achievement of Scotland in the period 1997-2007 was small scale. The nation built a parliament of limited powers. This devolution from Westminster, the UK parliament, did not include fiscal powers beyond a minor variation in the basic rate of tax. Despite the cautious definition of the new parliament in Edinburgh, it was the subject of much interest. Occurring at a time of widespread concern about voter apathy, it was seen by outside observers as an experiment in redefining the public's connection with the political process. This cast Holyrood in the bigger narrative of regionalisation across the European Union.

Within Scotland the reality was less easily read. If anything, the first ten years of devolution damaged the relationship between citizens and the political process, as disillusion with politicians became entrenched in popular opinion. This was mainly due to the lack of obvious policy benefits for Scotland, coupled with popular anger at the cost of the new parliament building. Less obvious, but perhaps significant, was a kind of national psychosis, whereby many Scots found issues which were particular to Scotland intrinsically less serious than UK or global ones. This phenomenon, if true, speaks of a deep insecurity.

Only after 2007 did the Scottish Model we now recognise begin to emerge. This challenged the old idea that individual leaders guiding a large state machine is the only way to improve society. Instead, the Model interpreted Scotland's political evolution as a question of justice for all its citizens, through the empowerment of individuals and the involvement of many in the process of government.

The change came about not because of a great electoral cataclysm. The Holyrood voting system protected Labour's hold on a majority of seats. Rather, the shift in the nation's political zeitgeist, and behaviour, came about from a widely recognised sense that Scotland's people were being short-changed by her politicians.

The Scottish Model was built on two principles. The first was honesty. It was accepted that it did not help the democratic process to endless obscure key issues in partisan debate. The first stage of this honesty was for politicians to collectively recognise Scotland's real problems. In contrast to the cultural issues tackled by early devolution, such as sectarianism and aspects of behaviour that impacted on health, the main problems were identified as economic. Scotland had a poor record in changing the fortunes of those born in the lower economic bracket. This meant those above had little sense of competition for their jobs. Indeed Scotland was a very comfortable place to live if you were middle class, as the lawyers Dewar and Smith would have attested. This comfort zone resulted in low rates of business start-ups or other signs of economic initiative. In turn, this meant the government support of the economy, through the grant from London, looked particularly necessary; how else would a low enterprise nation survive? However the big role played by government money, and public employment, was recognised as distorting the development of the country. Too many bright graduates went into civil service jobs where they were no longer required to think competitively. The ability of those in power to distribute low wage but secure public jobs meant the sense of enterprise in the lower economic strata was also impaired.

This honesty also accepted that the difference between the two ideological enemies, Labour and the SNP, amounted to very little. They both wanted to help the economic growth of the poorest third of the population, and to promote the wealth of the nation as a whole. In the new mood of honesty, the once bitter battle between Unionism and Nationalism was replaced by a discussion about degrees of economic control. If the key issue was how to empower the poorest, then it followed that government itself needed economic empowerment. Holyrood gradually acquired a parity of economic powers with other EU members. This had the effect of attracting a better quality of MSP; the higher the stakes, the bigger the player.

Control over the economy resulted in another tier of empowerment, that of self-confidence. The issue of confidence had been discussed in Scottish politics throughout the 20th Century. Many ruses and fashionable books had attempted to tackle the issue. It would appear that the crucial boost the nation's self-belief needed came from the simple expedient of making it responsible for its fortunes. This had come to be accepted throughout the political classes and the populace at large. As one onlooker at the statue unveiling said: 'You wonder now what all the fuss was about.'

This principle of honesty mirrors the key element in other models, that of consensus. Germany, Ireland and the Netherlands required all sides to come together before their economic booms could begin. The Scottish Model's mood of honesty meant a transparency about where state and private money was spent in the nation. This limited the effect, as witnessed in the other national models, of new wealth clustering around old power.

Politicians realised that if power was to be used honestly, it must be transparent and responsive to citizens. This resulted in the restructuring of decision making. The eight regions from which the list MSPs were elected in the PR ballot used by Holyrood were recognised as separate units. Up until then they had been notional entities to suit the electoral system. The borders of all state and quasi-autonomous bodies were made contiguous with the regional boundaries, to prevent overlaps of accountability. These regions were charged with developing their own plans for development. This meant much greater co-operation between MSPs, councillors and enterprise agencies. Importantly, no new regional tier of government was created. The co-operation did not require additional bureaucracy. In fact as these regional identities gathered momentum, some tiers of government were recognised as unnecessary. An emergent, unwritten principle of the Model was that it was a fallacy that many layers of government improve access – the human voice is lost in the paperwork.

The effect of these regional identities was to create a competitive spirit across the land. Pride was taken in developing original policies. Further, it had the effect of emphasising the difference between the main geographical elements of Scotland. In place of the sameness in food, culture and attitude, regional identities were asserted. In political terms, this also helped the largely rural regions exert themselves over the urban Central Belt, thus correcting a long-held sense of injustice.

These structural changes lead to an attitudinal shift. With power visibly devolved to the region, the sense developed that the leadership of the nation rested on the shoulders of many rather than simply the First Minister. This political empowerment in turn nurtured the idea of individual responsibility. This is often referred to as the Model's 'truth'. When Devolution began it was thought it alone would improve the democratic process, but in fact it required the newly devolved politicians to act and devolve power further for change to occur.

The principle of honesty extended into policy formation. It was marked by an acceptance that policy is complicated. The shift that occurred in the last quarter of the 20th Century, when politicians increasingly avoided ideological arguments in favour of superficial delivery was regretted. As one famous politician said in 2018 'Life is complicated, why should we assume making political sense of it should be easy'. 'Delivery' politics was compared to fast food. It promised a delicious meal without ever explaining where the ingredients came from or how they were prepared. If the effect was a full stomach, it was assumed, that was all that mattered to the voter. This mode of discourse was discredited. The new honesty set out to explain the process of policies as much as their result.

Two things improved policy formation. With the management of the state devolved to the regions, the era of centralised, micro-managed national government ended. Holyrood was able to become a forum of ideas. Secondly, policy debate had been stifled in Scotland as a result of the close financial relationship between government and the non-governmental social sector. Campaigning groups often felt unable to speak out against policy for fear they would lose their funding. The establishment of an independent funding panel ended this so called 'cash censorship'.

This new honesty also allowed Scotland to recognise its policy successes. In the period 1997-2007 the Planning and Mental Health sections of the civil service, for example, had developed enviable strategies. This had been little championed in an era of party political squabbling. Scotland was now able to celebrate and encourage creative policy formation.

It was not simply in Holyrood that honesty and rigour were evident. They were taken as founding principles of the emerging state. Thus the Scottish Model resulted in some of the severest laws punishing corruption, bribery and deception of the public by either state bodies or private agencies. This not only reduced those crimes, and the impact such misdemeanours have on trust, but it fed well into Scotland's image as a 'safe' country, which greatly assisted its financial sector.

The second principle was opportunity. Much as a bystander may wonder 'what all the fuss was about' in the row over Scotland's economic growth, so others look back with mild incredulity at the culture of low enterprise which once existed. Once moribund parts of the country were now active. Businesses were being started. Empty homes inhabited and new ones built. If rigour was the secondary quality to the principle of honesty, then the concept of change became the implicit message of the principle of opportunity. A society almost afraid of change had learnt that it was essential to life.

This new industrious spirit came about in part because of the devolution of power to the regions, coupled to favourable tax regimes. It also benefited from the natural assets of lots of space and clean water; these two qualities had become dramatically more valuable over the course of the opening decades of the 21st Century. It allowed Scotland to attract many wealthy incomers. The fashion for 'community living', whereby village life is prized above urban existence, resulted in dynamic townships throughout the land. This switch to small-scale living also changed Scotland's perverse land ownership patterns. Clinging on to 100,000 acres of wilderness in the name of shooting deer paled besides selling some 200 acre plots off to wealthy individuals wanting to pursue a better life style.

A truth about national models is that they seem to naturally expire after a few decades. The conditions which brought people together are, generally, so successfully resolved that the sense of common purpose withers. Arguably the Scottish Model is in its first flush, dating from 2007. Already there is evidence of how it has changed the political dynamic. One of the first signs of devolution's difference was the emergence of minority parties. The 2007 election was contested by six established parties. In 2020 there are two major parties. These are broader congregations that any party in 2007, and are recognised as such. In simple terms, they represent left and right. This bipartisan split has led to complaints about the lack of choice in Scottish politics.

The question is; how will the nation cope once the Model has run its course? In the new age of honesty and rigour, Scotland's politicians say they have no idea what will happen in 2050, much in the way nobody could know in 2005 what 2020 would be like. All they can do is to try and build a society which is as honest, fair and sustainable. They should be judged on their actions, on the quality of society, and not, as in 2005, on their ability to survive in a world of petty disputes.

As the onlookers move away from the newly unveiled statues, it is as if a crowd is left behind. The new bronze figures almost obscure Dewar altogether. The monument at the top of Glasgow's Buchanan Street is now a monument to many. In the new mood of honesty, the nation must admit its old narrative, of singular heroes beaten in tragic ends, is over. There is a new story to tell, of people coming together to help each other and the end is unknown, but it is not presumed to be miserable. No one person, or party, will determine this tale. It will be told by five million voices, and out of this babble will come one sound, of a nation finally at peace with itself.

12

Education: the Importance of Culture

PROFESSOR LINDSAY PATERSON

SCOTTISH EDUCATION IS IN a state of half-fulfilled radical promise. The revolution that is commonly supposed to have been started in the 1960s – notably with comprehensive secondary schools, with the beginnings of the massive expansion of higher education, and with various sorts of child-centred learning – in fact had its origins much further back, in the great liberal and social democratic modernisations of Scottish traditions that took place in the first half of the century. But despite this longevity, the programme of reform turned defensive under the Conservatives in the 1980s, as supporters of the changes tried to preserve what had been gained against a hostile ideology, and mostly stopped thinking seriously about how the renovated Scottish traditions could be taken further forward in the same radical manner.

So this chapter has as its main purpose the rediscovery of the radical programme to which Scottish education was, by the 1970s, irrevocably but incompletely committed. But simple resurrection can't be all, not only because so much has changed in the meantime, but also because there are now several other claims to radical thought which have gained significant influence. So a subsidiary purpose here is to analyse what Scotland might mean by radicalism: what kinds of reform would be consistent with Scottish traditions?

Achievements

As with most developed national systems of education, the starting point is astonishing expansion. In the 1920s, only one third of young people embarked on secondary courses, and less than one in twenty completed them. By the 1970s, almost all pupils had a chance to benefit from proper secondary schooling, and by the end of the century over two thirds were doing so for a full five years. That expansion is the main reason why we now have an equally remarkable growth of participation in higher education, from one in eight young people half a century ago (and under one in thirty in the 1920s) to one-half today. The meaning of the educational experiences which people have in these transformed institutions may be in dispute – as we will see – but no-one seriously denies that, whatever the problems, this expansion has increased real opportunity massively.

As the century progressed, moreover, Scotland came increasingly to define education for all as requiring education in the same kind of institution for all. There is much less differentiation of types of school now than at any time in the past century and a half, most of the apparent variation being in details rather than fundamentals. Thus the existence of Catholic schools in the public sector may seem controversial in Scotland, but their scope for being different is actually rather small, in that their curriculum is in most respects the same as in other schools, their students sit the same external examinations as everyone else, their teachers are educated in the same universities and trained to mostly the same guidelines as any others, and their programmes of staff development are broadly the same as those on offer to other teachers. Most of the independent schools (proportionately small in any case by international standards) compete with the public sector to do the same things better, not to be fundamentally different; only in a tiny number, such as the Steiner schools, is there a systematically distinct educational philosophy. Scottish secondary schooling provides a common experience also in the sense that it is less socially segregated than the systems in most developed countries.

The same standardisation of institutional type has been operating in higher education as it, too, has expanded. The distinction between older universities and former colleges and central institutions is being eroded by the common funding and policy contexts that have been in place since 1993. Pressure to go further is likely to follow from the merger of the funding councils for further and higher education: it is then likely that there will be slow convergence between higher education institutions and further education colleges.

To critics on the political Right, this standardisation is a denial of choice, but in fact Scottish reform over the past century has been based on the belief that only common institutions can offer true choice to the majority of students. For that majority, there is in fact much more differentiation of learning now than there ever was before the 1960s. Although there were good examples of junior-secondary courses, most of the approximately two thirds of pupils who were on them were condemned to a stultifying programme aimed at inculcating basic skills, vocational competence, and social obedience. Indeed, only for the best students even in the senior-secondary courses was a truly liberating opportunity for intellectual stimulation on offer. These structural constraints in the curriculum were a far more serious denial of choice than any impediments now: the curriculum today is flexible and varied for a far greater proportion of students.

Choice was also restricted because the constraints affected some categories of people more than others – girls more than boys, Catholics more than others, working-class people more than the children of people who themselves had benefited from this system. Inequalities on all these dimensions (and on some new ones, such as in relation to ethnic group) have declined significantly since the 1970s. The wisdom of previous radical thinkers is perhaps best shown here. Structural differentiation that mapped onto constraining social structures was, these radicals believed, bound to reinforce inequalities.

We can also now say that this educational democratisation has become the property of the nation as a whole. All the evidence from repeated social surveys is that a structurally undifferentiated system of schooling is popular, that people believe it to be of acceptable quality and to have brought increasing attention to the needs and wishes of individual students, and that they welcome the resulting expansion of higher education. There is also much evidence that teachers are trusted and respected.

What has gone wrong?

And yet there is dissatisfaction. That might in part be the inevitable discontent which any partially successful revolution engenders, as people's aspirations are encouraged to rise beyond the vision of the first reformers. There is also discontent that is not intrinsically educational, but rather a projection onto education of radical ideas about other areas of social policy. The most notable example would be in relation to social class. Although class differences in educational outcomes have fallen, they have not done so to nearly the extent of other inequalities. The reason is probably that education can't solve the problems resulting from poverty on its own: the only places where class inequalities in education have fallen significantly are countries such as Sweden where there have been much wider and more sustained programmes of state action to eradicate poverty.

But some of the dissatisfaction relates to the character of previous reforms themselves. One is the sense that, in creating opportunity for all, we have ended up imposing impossible amounts of external assessment on all. The objection here is not to the intellectual challenge of examinations, but rather to the educationally harmful effects of too intrusive assessment, and also to the trivialising effects of assessment that is about competence and performance rather than understanding and knowledge.

Even deeper than that is a sense that the expansion has forgotten what it is all for. In this lies the greatest danger of ignoring the motives of previous reformers. The extension of Scottish educational democracy was based on a delicate balance between radicalism as to structures, and caution, even conservatism, as to content. The anger of radical campaigners against a divided secondary education was because it denied working-class people access to general education, to the best that has been thought and said. The democratic intellect was to be at least as much about the intellect as about the access to it; and yet policy since the 1980s has rather neglected the importance of enabling students to engage properly with intellectual difficulty and intellectual worth. Instead policy has approached the problem of motivation by diluting seriousness, by fragmenting difficult programmes of study into modularised segments, and by trying to divert students into intellectually undemanding courses of ostensibly vocational relevance. 'Difficulty', in public debate, is synonymous with 'the basics', as if developing the capacity to read, write and count were the main criteria by which the intellectual seriousness of an education system should be judged.

These tendencies are not overwhelming yet, and are trends in policy more than in practice: many teachers and lecturers, fortunately, do their best to maintain the dignity of their work against such philistinism. But the trivialising tendency sustained for a couple of decades becomes a potent influence, in school policy on the curriculum and assessment, in policy on teacher education and professional development, in the crass utilitarianism of policy on higher education, and in the erosion since the mid-1990s of Scotland's twenty-year attempt to create a community education that would underpin democracy.

The problem here is partly that radical educational thought internationally has come, since the 1960s, to be dominated by the strand of analysis that derives from the French philosopher Pierre Bourdieu and from the highly influential English socio-linguist Basil Bernstein. According to their views (or, more strictly, to the views of their numerous simplifying followers) academic culture is middle class, conveyed in a language that is literally incomprehensible to working-class children. The general education to which previous radicals sought to widen access (in Scotland perhaps more insistently than in most places) was thus itself part of the problem. Add to that the claims that academic culture was inevitably also sexist, racist, exclusively Christian, and (in a Scottish context) anglo-centric, and we have had the conditions over the past couple of decades for a strange convergence between thinking on the Left and the belief on the Right that vocational relevance and economic regeneration were the most important (or even the sole) criteria by which education systems should be judged.

A sort of post-modernist version of multiculturalism then gave spurious intellectual legitimacy to these accounts. If all cultural values are relative and equally legitimate, then why not let students choose anything they want to? The change in radical thought inter-nationally can be summed up by one illustration. Faced with the evidence that working-class students tend to choose vocationally relevant options, the current generation of radicals would conclude that this is wise, ought to be what all students should do, and – as a matter of convenient political fact – allows an alliance to be forged with politicians on the Right who believe that schools and universities foster a hostility to entrepreneurialism. Old radicals, by contrast, would have interpreted working-class choices of this sort as opting for predictability of employment, and as showing that only middle-class students, economically secure, could afford the luxury of general, liberal, non-vocational learning. The solution would then be not the rejection of such programmes, but an attempt to create conditions under which much larger numbers students felt able to risk taking them.

Elements of a renovated radicalism

If that analysis is correct, then the discontent that Scottish educa-tion now faces is due not only to the incompleteness of an earlier revolution, but also to our having stopped thinking about ultimate purposes. At least until the 1950s, Scottish radicals believed in the importance of a general, liberal education. Scottish educational democratisation was motivated by a faith that widening access to that kind of learning would create a more humane, civilised, respect-ful, and outward-looking nation. Many radicals in other countries held similar views, and such views survived and continued to be advanced, although mostly in a minority on the educational Left precisely because of the belief that academic learning was intrinsi-cally middle class. The specifically Scottish tradition of radical thought has tended not to survive in this way, perhaps because it has been too easy here to claim that Scottish culture itself is one of the traditions that was allegedly suppressed by previous programmes.

So, however important the questions of widening access to school and university undoubtedly are, I would suggest that the main problem facing Scottish radicals now is the purpose of educational expansion. I would suggest also that, to understand the expansion which we have inherited, we cannot ignore the motives of previous reformers. If we have a secondary system that is very academic, then that has not arisen by mistake or accident. It is precisely what was deliberately created in order to widen access to worthwhile learning. Our challenge is then not to dilute or abolish that inheritance, but to find ways of enabling effective engagement with it of the multitudes of students now passing through secondary schools and universities.

It would be premature to lay out a programme of educational reform, but what might help a vision of Scottish education in 2020 to evolve is an outline of the principles on which it should be based. The first premise is to insist on the emancipatory potential of intellectual, serious, theoretical and difficult learning. If secondary schools and universities are not about that, then they are barely worth having. 'Relevance' is something we learn with experience, and experience can only be experienced, not taught; we cannot judge relevance unless we have already grasped the principles of a system of understanding. In particular, therefore, vocational courses are not what initial education should be about. They are about training for specific jobs. Where they are not best done on the job itself, learning from the accumulated wisdom of more experienced colleagues (whatever the line of work), they presuppose a body of theoretical knowledge and understanding that ought to be engaged with first. Practice without theory is blind.

If, in the short term, vocational courses might seem attractive as ways of giving some young people employable skills, that should be acceptable to educational radicals only on two grounds. One is that the provision of such programmes is not a substitute for continuing to try to find ways of widening access to general education. The other is that the attractiveness to employers of vocational courses is likely to be temporary, and in any case tenuous in a society where academic credentials continue to be valued by employers for the flexibility of mind that they indicate. Castigating that preference as revealing a bias in recruitment has been another of the common assumptions of Left and Right in recent decades; but perhaps the employers are right to prefer general capacities to specific skills.

Second, since an efficient economic system ought never to be an end in itself, but only the means to such goals as building a fair, democratic and culturally enriching society, an equally important premise has to be that programmes of general liberal education are better at preparing people for life as decent citizens than any other kind of learning. That was something which old radicals understood well. You could make citizens for the new era of mass democracy by equipping them with the cultural capacities which the aristocratic or bourgeois ruling classes had acquired through their schooling. Citizenship was not something to be segregated into discrete programmes, but should permeate many types of study – literature, history, geography, politics, science, religion. The student who learns how to debate the meaning of a poem by Liz Lochhead, or a novel by Alasdair Gray, or a film by Paul Lavery, or to weigh the evidence for and against wind farms or genetic modification, or to understand the reasons why Islam and Christianity have sometimes been in conflict is in fact well prepared for life as a citizen of Scotland.

Third, we need therefore a debate about cultural purposes. This is where new radical thinking is urgently needed. Although I have been arguing that we should recover the old idea that democratising access to a general, liberal education is the only programme that is truly radical, it would not be radical simply to adopt uncritically the content or pedagogical methods that would have constituted such a programme in earlier eras. For example, the culture to which students should now be exposed is certainly not the unitary one that most radicals would have assumed even half a century ago. In Scotland, we inherit ideas from Islam as well as from Christianity, literature by women as well as by men, working-class political ideas as well as middle-class ones, Scottish philosophical thought as well as anglo-saxon. That is easy to assert, and is no more than is common in any serious multiculturalism. The difficulty arises when we have to make selections from a potentially enormous set of curricular options. The guiding principles might be partly the intellectual capacities that we want to be the outcome for students. But it can't be only that, because otherwise there would be little reason not to confine our attention to a fairly conventional canon. There have to be moral, aesthetic and other judgements about the value of particular knowledge, unfashionable though that is at a time when values are supposed to be inherently relative and the curriculum is supposed to be only about developing competences. Only after a thorough public debate could Scotland decide, for example, what the proper place of Islamic theology should be in the curriculum, and what purpose such studies would serve.

None of this prescribes a particular method of teaching or learning. Projects, or cross-curricular themes, or experiential learning, or many of the other ideas that are often associated with learner-centred pedagogy are in fact probably rather more effective at engaging students with truly difficult ideas than less varied kinds of teaching. Radicals must not allow the Right to caricature radical thought as an undifferentiated package. We can agree with conservatives on the importance of cultural knowledge and intellectual difficulty while disagreeing with them about the adequacy of certain styles of teaching. It could be added also that such broad cultural understanding engages much more than the intellect, and so, at its best, has always sought to develop what are now called multiple intelligences. The best teachers of literature, for example, have always understood that there is an emotional aspect to understanding and debating a text.

Fourth, having such cultural enlightenment (however defined) as a goal at some level for potentially everyone requires that nothing is done to undermine the common institutional structures that we have created. These structures are not sufficient for creating a common culture, which is why further reform is needed, but they are necessary. If the Right then raises the question of curricular choice, then we can agree that this is important without abandoning the project. Choice of programme can only be made on the basis of understanding what is rejected as well as what is selected. Students have to have a basis in a broad culture before they are in any position to make properly informed choices. Paradoxical though it may seem, compulsion is in fact the only way to underpin proper freedom. That, further, might be as true at the level of university education as earlier. What should we reasonably expect our graduates to know and be able to do, at an advanced level? Is it sufficient to say that their broad cultural and intellectual preparation has finished at school, or should we expect something more? At the moment, to be frank, we don't even know whether and to what extent existing programmes of higher education are any kind of common basis for citizenship at all.

Conclusions

This essay has obviously been polemical, which is the purpose of this book, and it is not offered as anything more than a preliminary collection of thoughts on these matters. It has been based on the beliefs that Scottish education, for all its strengths, has rather lost its way, but also that the manner in which it has drifted is not at all the one that is frequently asserted in public debate. The problems of over-assessment, or of inadequate educating of the whole child, or of 'standards' are not unreal; but they are symptoms. Underlying them is a lack of serious attention to purpose.

Two generations ago we created common structures of secondary schooling that have democratised access to real learning. But we then stopped thinking about what real learning is. We did that partly because we wanted to reach an accommodation with a Conservative government, and we managed to save the common structures by implicitly agreeing with them to abandon any serious attempt to develop a coherent programme of general, liberal education that would truly match a more democratic age. We also abandoned that aspiration because we accepted the tendentious Leftist claims that such programmes are inevitably culturally biased. There is no reason any longer for the Left to be cowed by the Right, and there is every reason for radicals in a Scottish cultural tradition to accept that broad education can be made available to all. But we have a rather large task ahead in defining what that means in practice.

13

Towards a radically new politics

PROFESSOR JAMES MITCHELL

SCOTTISH DEVOLUTION, as Michael Forsyth frequently maintained, is not just for Christmas. It has been established and circumstances under which devolution would be repealed are difficult to imagine. Fewer and fewer commentators continue to operate as if they are still fighting the 1997 referendum campaign. Yet, supporters of the Scottish Parliament often behave as if devolution is a fragile flower. There has been unnecessary defensiveness about devolution when what is required are two very different attitudes. First, we need a more robust debate on what to do with the tools which devolution has given us including critical commentary on its operation and where we want to go in public policy terms and secondly we need to rekindle the spirit that brought the Parliament into being.

The consensus creating the Parliament

In the years running up to devolution, politics were fairly straight-forward. Two key divisions existed in Scottish politics. The tradi-tional left-right fault-line had dominated much of the twentieth century until a crosscutting fault line emerged in the 1960s. This latter division was on the national question. Those who supported a Scottish Parliament came predominantly from the left but included a fair sprinkling of right-wingers while a large number of traditional left- and right-wingers, notably in the Labour and Conservative Parties, opposed home rule in any shape or form. But Thatcherism changed all that. What gave the cause of a Scottish Parliament its strength and ultimately ensured its establishment was that these two cleavages – on the national question and on class – no longer cut across each other but reinforced one other. The cause of home rule became the cause of a more egalitarian Scotland. There remained much disagreement on what egalitarianism meant, how far it should go, and the institutional form and public policies required to bring it about. Equally, there was disagreement over the nature and extent of home rule. Unity emerged around a negative, anti-Thatcherite message.

But the anti-Thatcherite purpose of home rule meant that efforts concentrated on two objectives: opposing measures deemed to be imposed on Scotland against its will and building a consensus around the case for home rule. Building a consensus around a programme for government was consequently and understandably crowded out. Emphasis on any particular policy endangered what was at times a fragile coalition. If devolution came to be associated in the public mind with support for a ban on smoking in public places or the removal of clause 2A, it would have provoked a backlash in sections of the Scottish electorate. Association with any policy programme would also have undermined the very intention of devolution which was to allow the Scottish people, through a democratically elected Parliament, to determine the policy programme.

The difficulties creating a consensus

Building a consensus around the case for a Scottish Parliament was not easy. While the two main parties, Labour and SNP, were agreed on the need for a Parliament, circumstances prevented much co-operation. This frustrated many who viewed the war between the two parties as damaging to both parties' interests as well as the cause of home rule. New politics commentators bemoaned the lack of co-operation, ignoring the underlying difficulties and good reasons each party had for standing apart. Neither party could see much to be gained from co-operating or aiding its opponents, recognising that the other party was competing for the same votes. In essence the costs of co-operation were potentially great and the benefits uncertain. This was to change in the context of the 1997 referendum campaign. The differences between the lack of co-operation under the Constitutional Convention and the extent of co-operation during the referendum illustrate important differences.

The SNP's decision not to become involved in the Constitutional Convention was roundly condemned at the time as evidence of political sectarianism, of a party acting against the interests of its stated objective. Yet, this was a rational decision at the time and even many of those who disagreed with the decision within the party did so because they believed it would damage the party's electoral position rather than because they believed there was much prospect of directly furthering the cause of a Scottish Parliament through the Convention. There was a legitimate fear that the Convention had a dual purpose and damaging the SNP or at least dissipating its energy was one part. While a case can be made that SNP involvement might have resulted in a policy that was more attractive to the SNP this can only be a matter of speculation. It is unlikely that SNP involvement would have brought home rule any quicker. We may argue endlessly on whether the SNP's decision was the right one but there is little doubt that a rational case against involvement existed at the time.

The fundamental problem with the Convention – as indeed with ideas for an Independence Convention now – was that while the dangers of participation were easy to see the benefits from involvement were not so obvious. When it came to a political cost-benefit analysis, the Convention was not an idea which had much appeal other than in presentational terms. In the event, the Convention did make a significant difference in terms of issues of representation. Without a Convention, it is conceivable that the Parliament would have been elected by the simple plurality voting system and that the number of women elected would have been far fewer. It also served to cement Labour's commitment to devolution. But these were achievements which did not require SNP participation.

The referendum campaign, however, was quite different. Labour and the SNP, along with others, worked together for a Yes/Yes vote. The difference was simple. There were obvious benefits for each party with a clearer common goal which allowed significant differences to continue to exist. The parties were able to work together because the immediate benefits were unambiguous and did not involve either abandoning its core beliefs or aims. That the SNP saw it as a step towards independence while Labour saw devolution as a means of blocking independence did not matter. Both wanted a Scottish Parliament and knew that the referendum result was necessary to achieve this. When a clear objective exists and, crucially, a clear mans of achieving it, co-operation makes sense but in itself some desire for 'new politics' is insufficient grounds for co-operation.

Co-operation between Scotland's two main parties, each competing for the same vote and with different views of Scotland's constitutional future is possible. The questions then arise, what are the circumstances in which co-operation in the future is possible, is it desirable and is it likely? Few commentators today would be willing to offer a positive response to any of these questions. Some have suggested that some combination including the Conservatives with either Labour or the SNP is more likely. Without ignoring major obstacles to co-operation, it is likely that within the next two decades, the referendum experience rather than the Convention experience will prove the model on which Scottish politics develops.

Politics in the absence of co-operation

At first sight, the absence of co-operation between Labour and the SNP since before devolution might have been expected to produce radically different visions of Scotland in the future. With Labour and the SNP freed of the need to co-operate each would be able to head off in a different direction unshackled by the need for compromise. But other than the constitution, the differences between the two parties have been remarkably few. As ever, the public debate has heard emphasis of differences and these have been exaggerated. A noisy battle for the marginal vote has taken place around marginal public policy differences. The 2003 election brought this home powerfully as each party participated in a bidding game; one offering x more schoolteachers while the other proposed x+1.

Neither party produced anything approaching a systematic critique of Scotland's social and economic problems, far less a clear response. Instead, both Labour and the SNP offered platitudes around broad themes or attempted to put a kilt on often equally platitudinous slogans developed elsewhere – moderate left of centre, third way, enterprise and compassion, stakeholder society, and sundry other sound bites obscured as much as they illuminated. In Scotland, as elsewhere, fancy new language has become a substitute for serious policy analysis and prescriptions. At times, post-devolution Scotland appears to have been run by MBAs on speed spewing out slogans, management-speak with a certainty matched only by its vacuousness. Political compasses have been discarded in favour of new gadgets that tell us things we already knew, in language we barely understand. Talk of taking hard decisions abound while difficult issues are evaded.

Scottish electoral politics are intense, competitive but pretty vacuous. This has inspired conservatism, a reluctance to take risks and face up to difficult problems. Added to this is the electoral cycle. Between general elections in the past, local elections and the odd Parliamentary by-election were invested with more national meaning than was healthy. But as in so many other respects, devolution replaced a period of electoral fasting with a period of electoral feasting. Elections now come round frequently, perhaps too frequently. It is a hallmark of democratic politics that parties introduce unpopular but necessary policies soon after being elected to ensure that some mixture of positive outputs and a later emphasis on introducing popular measures help their return to office at the subsequent election. The electoral cycle is as important in public policy as the economic cycle. But when the electoral cycle becomes shorter with important Westminster and Scottish Parliamentary elections every few years this has public policy consequences. What emerges is a reluctance to face up to problems. As problems grow so too does the cost of dealing with them. Whether it is the issue of health reform, economic growth or reform of pensions, putting off means putting up the eventual cost.

In devolved Scotland, we have simultaneously injected a degree of responsibility into our politics by electing a directly elected Parliament but allowed, even encouraged, the development of institutions of semi-detached government. In the health service, government does not directly address the relationship between available resources, demands on services and provision of these services by having a national strategy but allows for incoherence. There never really was a truly British National Health Service but now, in crucial respects, it is difficult to talk of a Scottish National Health Service or, at least, a national health strategy as each health board is left to work out its strategy to triangulate resources, demands and provision.

Sewel Motions, whereby Westminster legislates on devolved matters with the agreement of a majority in the Scottish Parliament, introduced with the understandable intention to allow Scotland to have its cake and eat it, have resulted in government evading difficult issues that ought to be addressed in the Scottish Parliament. A Scottish debate on civil marriages is almost as important as the need to change the law. Process is important especially for the sake of legitimacy. Aspects of Scottish culture are harmful and legislation alone will not change this. Open debate, led by our parliamentarians in Holyrood, forcing us to face up to the uglier and damaging aspects of our culture will start to bring about the changes required. The creeping tendency of the Scottish Government to allow others – either in London or in quangos – to take the hard decisions, and of course the flak, is a renunciation of one of devolution's purposes.

These criticisms may seem an attack on the current Executive but it is difficult to imagine any party in power behaving differently. It is less a function of Labour or the Liberal Democrats being in power than the constipated nature of Scottish politics. Parties are inhibited, government paralysed and the public disenchanted.

Devolution has many purposes. It has fulfilled its democratic function well. There remains a need for progress – especially in ethnic minority representation – but there is much to celebrate. Prior to devolution there was a developing crisis of democratic legitimacy in Scottish politics. This no longer exists. But the democratic component requires to be accompanied by a new responsibility in our politics, a willingness to confront difficult issues. It would be an exaggeration to suggest that we suffer from a risk aversion or leadership crisis but we do suffer from a risk aversion culture. The cacophony of Others following the 2003 election was partly a response to the need for something different but it has done nothing in encouraging the main parties to confront our underlying problems. Nor should we expect these Others to do so. Indeed, the emphasis on local particularisms is part of the problem. Evidence suggests that the rise of Others makes the main parties wary of doing anything that might be necessary but unpopular. Pork barrel politics is unhealthy.

Future prospects?

The evidence pointing towards continued trench warfare between Scotland's two main parties – mowing down opponents, moving the policy debate onwards inch by inch if it all – is obvious. Recent history would lead us to expect more of the same but, as has been noted, there is evidence from the past that change is possible. The crucial factor will be rational self-interest. There is an obvious interest from the electorate's perspective in the two main parties working together to face up to Scotland's social and political problems but that is not the same as the parties' mutual self-interest. One very clear pressure may come from the electorate. It is little wonder that voters drifted off to an assortment of Others in 2003 given the lack of choice from Labour and SNP. The electoral system facilitated this but public disenchantment with the main parties provoked it. The SNP may have been hurt most in 2003 but Labour too was damaged and its long-term decline in Scotland has not been arrested. These parties may opt to change the electoral system to keep the Others out but it seems unlikely that the Others will be seen off completely. The system may be changed to prejudice the interests of the SSP, Greens et al but public disenchantment will win through in one shape or other. If not votes for Others then votes for no-one.

But more positively, the experience of co-operation forced by the electorate failing to give any party overall control has been growing up in local government almost unnoticed, will continue, and it is not inconceivable that Labour and SNP will form administrations up and down Scotland over the next decade and more.

Single transferable vote in local elections will not have the revolutionary impact that some commentators seem to imagine but will change matters gradually. Candidates will have to get used to a new system that encourages them to ask voters identifying with another party to give them a second or third preference. Candidates who fail to do so might find that they cannot get elected.

Within the Scottish Parliament, it was inevitable that Westminster habits have taken hold and that it resembles Westminster in procedures and culture more than any other legislature contrary to some of the more excitable commentary around. But, as Walter Bagehot in *The English Constitution* remarked on the passage of the Great Reform Act, 'A new Constitution does not produce its full effect as long as all its subjects were reared under an old Constitution, as long as its statesmen were trained by that old Constitution. It is not really tested till it comes to be worked by statesmen and among its people neither of whom are guided by a different experience.' While the Parliament was a Westminster creation, few of those within it are entirely creatures of Westminster and many show signs of having little in common with the old system. Over time, we can be fairly certain that politics in Scotland and England will diverge.

Conclusion

Some means is necessary to break out of the risk averse consensus that masquerades as competitive politics with its shrill denunciations and petty point scoring. The solution proposed may seem paradoxical to some, perverse to others. More consensus to break the consensus admittedly seems a strange prescription. But consensus does not mean uniformity. There needs to be acknowledgement that differences exist. Many of these differences probably cut across the parties as much as exist between them. But consensus which simply reinforces all that needs to change would be more damaging than what we have at present. The first stage will have to be debate on where Scotland should be heading – not just constitutionally but socially and economically. Such a debate will not occur openly within either party, at least not yet. Commentators complain at the absence of serious policy debate within the parties and the unwillingness to rock the boat. But simultaneously the same commentators will pounce on any evidence of free thinking as troublemaking or splits. Part of the process will require a more mature media and one with a much more sophisticated understanding of public policy matters and this is likely to emerge over time. Until and unless the media matures, debate will take place privately. Space will be needed in which this debate can take place. Ironically, devolved Scotland – democratic Scotland – will have, already has debates of this sort taking place *in camera*.

Scotland is drifting. Devolution gives us the tools with which we can provide direction to public policy. The national question continues to divide Scotland and its two main parties. But there is much that unites them and within each there are many intelligent people eager to debate openly the needs of Scotland. The spirit which brought the Parliament into being – allowing for a recognition of differences but which identifies common ground needs to be established. Whether these parties like it or not, they are have much in common. Failure to recognise this may result in each sharing the same fate as their support ebbs away to sundry malcontents while an alternative rightist agenda emerges.

But looking to the long-term, there are grounds for optimism. Communities of interests will lead to common action. Co-operation between parties engaged in political trench warfare today will emerge. By 2020, a Labour-SNP coalition will not seem so unlikely as it does today.

14

Changing Scotland in a Changing World

SUSAN DEACON

'What do the people want of the place? They want it to be
filled with thinking persons as open and adventurous as its
architecture.
A nest of fearties is what they do not want.
A symposium of procrastinators is what they do not want.
A phalanx of forelock-tuggers is what they do not want.
And perhaps above all the droopy mantra of 'it wizny me' is
what they do not want.'

Extract from 'Open the Doors!' by Edwin Morgan written for the
Opening of the new Scottish Parliament Building, October 2004

IT WAS, AS ONE commentator put it, a 'gloriously gallus moment'.
And how we all chuckled as Liz Lochhead punched out that poem
from the gallery of the Parliament's Debating Chamber on that
bright autumn day. But beneath the smiles was a self-consciousness
that Scotland's poet laureate had hit close to home. Lack of thinking
and adventure, fear and caution, procrastination, subservience and a
blame culture – Morgan had put his poetic finger on traits which
have become all too evident in both the culture and practice of our
new devolved institutions of governance.

Devolution has delivered considerable achievements, but the
scale and pace of progress has not been that to which many had
aspired. Whether it be in infrastructure development or public service reform, economic growth or social change, it is taking Scotland
too long to do too little.

If our nation is to flourish in a fast moving, globalised world,
we must move forward further and faster. The ultimate test of

devolution and of the Scottish body politic will be our ability to deliver change in a changing world. As Donald Dewar said at the Parliament opening in July 1999, a Scottish Parliament is 'not an end, but a means to greater ends.' If the full potential of devolution is to be fulfilled, we must refocus our efforts on achieving those greater ends.

This will require both a change in mindset and a re-engineering of process.

We must hope that by 2020 there will be a renewed enthusiasm and optimism about Scotland's future and that confidence in and respect for our political institutions will have been restored. But that is only likely to be achieved if devolution is seen to have made a real and positive impact on people's lives. For this to happen, we need *now* to embrace and effect change and to dispense with the caution and inertia which has crept in to our *modus operandus*. After all, the Scotland of 2020 and beyond will be shaped, at least in part, by the decisions and actions taken now.

The time is right to learn from the experience of devolution to date. There is always room for improvement. Indeed, our capacity to reflect openly and honestly on our performance will, in itself, be a measure of our maturity and our worth.

So what might be done differently? Let me be so bold as to offer some suggestions.

There is a need to create more space and to build capacity for more strategic and adventurous thinking in a devolved Scotland. We need to move away from short-term thinking and initiatives and instead map a course for longer-term sustainable change.

Devolution has spawned a hinterland of networks, relationships and forums for debate but such activity is, by its nature ad hoc and often takes place behind closed doors. The Presiding Officer's work to establish a Futures Forum is a welcome initiative, as are the efforts of many of our academic institutions to increase their capacity to address emergent issues in a devolved Scotland. But there is much which could be done to 'join the dots' of all this activity and to forge closer links with the decision making process.

Organisations like the IPPR, Adam Smith Institute, Kings Fund and Joseph Rowntree Foundation have been highly influential in informing and shaping policy at a UK level. We do not yet have the equivalent capacity here in Scotland and we need it. Not that we should simply emulate the models which exist elsewhere – our needs and ways of working are different. But with just a bit of imagination and pump priming we could greatly enhance our own homegrown policy development capacity.

We need also to extend the boundaries of our thinking and debate within the Parliamentary process. Too much Chamber time is dominated by set-piece party political contributions or parochial constituency name checking. Too much time in Parliamentary Committees is spent on considering the views of vested interests and too much advice to Ministers is filtered through the prism of civil servants. Too often the end result is 'lowest common denominator' policy. It is in our gift as Parliamentarians to rebalance those efforts, to exercise a greater independence of thought, to fly a few more kites and to take a few more risks. We should also do more to employ some of the more innovative practices which have been developed, both at home and abroad, to reach out to a wider spectrum of views and experiences.

We – and by that I mean *all* those who participate in or comment upon the political process – need to foster a greater spirit of openness. There is a crying need to get better at 'telling it like it is', for good or ill. At present there is too big a gap between what people say privately and what they are willing to put on public record. Ministers are too inclined to be on the defensive and play it safe, while opposition politicians are too quick to exaggerate problems and to play to the gallery. Many politicians as well as much of civic and corporate Scotland employ a self denying ordinance when in public view, fuelled in part by a fear (real or perceived) of unwelcome or selective media attention or of the potential disapproval or recriminations of political masters. Either way, we will never move forward unless we can break out of this straitjacket and inject a greater degree of candour and reality into our discussions and Parliamentary proceedings.

Political parties have an important role to play in changing this culture. On the vast majority of issues *every* Party votes as a block. The opportunities for free thinking and free voting could be greatly extended without compromising the Executive's programme or the Opposition's role. The Parliament would be the better for it and politics and politicians would be respected all the more.

But extending the boundaries of thinking and debate is only one part of the jigsaw. Analysis needs to be carried through to decision and action. And in this respect the emergent practices of devolution have been found wanting. Procrastination has become almost endemic in certain aspects of the devolved decision making process.

Take, for example, transport and other major infrastructure developments. The reality is that many schemes are being held up, not through a lack of investment or political will, but because of over-engineered, often dysfunctional, process. The combination of protracted consultation, legislation, planning and public sector procurement requirements can be debilitating. It will take the best part of a decade before many vital projects are even approved, let alone constructed. Meanwhile, other countries are getting on with the job of delivering the roads, rail links, trams and charging schemes that we are only talking about. The economic and social consequences of such systemic inertia are obvious.

It is both possible and necessary to streamline this process. For example, in some cases local authorities, the Parliament and the Executive consult the same bodies on the same issue, sometimes even more than once. It doesn't have to be this way. It is within our powers to 'design out' some of this delay and to give greater scope for local delivery agencies to get on with the job.

A radical overhaul of our planning system would be a major step in the right direction. The current system is broken and needs fixed. It is to be hoped that forthcoming changes result in a genuinely streamlined and simplified system and do not simply bolt on yet more consultation and appeal rights to an already protracted and dysfunctional process.

There are many other areas where the pace of change needs to be accelerated. Tackling the chronic shortage of affordable housing is a case in point. It is perhaps worth noting that while the UK

Government was moving forward with the implementation of a range of imaginative solutions to this growing problem, in Scotland we were carrying out a review.

Other areas of vital reform are also in danger of lagging behind. Many parts of the NHS, for example, are becoming almost paralysed in their ability to effect change in a devolved Scotland. Time and again, proposals are sent back to the drawing board, put back out to consultation, referred up then down then up again. And all the while, services become ever less fit for purpose and vital investment is locked up in old buildings and old practices.

The pressure of the electoral cycle has much to answer for. The reality is that Scotland is now in almost permanent election mode with a major election every couple of years. In this context, the traditional tactic – favoured by opposition as well as government parties – of kicking controversial issues and difficult decisions into touch till beyond the next election needs to be declared obsolete. It is a recipe for stagnation on a national scale.

Doing nothing is never a benign act. Indecision breeds uncertainty and that, in itself, affects morale and quality of service and compounds problems such as recruitment and retention as professionals simply vote with their feet and go elsewhere. While it is usually possible to defuse a controversy temporarily with a short term fix or yet another piece of process, delay does not resolve disagreement, it only puts it off for another day, sometimes to come back with an even greater vengeance because expectations have been raised and then not met. We would do well to remember that one of the greatest truisms in politics is that you cannot please all of the people all of the time.

Of course it is necessary to seek to build as broad a consensus as possible for change, and to get better at involving a wide range of interests in the change process. And it is, of course, important to listen. But above all it is imperative to act. Consultation should be a means to an end not an end in itself. Ultimately someone, somewhere, has got to take hard decisions to make change happen.

Consultation has grown into something of an industry since devolution. It is in danger of becoming a proxy for action. At any one time there are several dozen consultations being carried out by the Scottish Executive, not to mention those being undertaken by individual MSP's, Parliamentary Committees, local authorities, NHS Boards or other agencies. Do we seriously believe that this fog of documentation and proposals aids transparency and involvement? And what of the impact on those individuals and organisations who are asked time and time again to submit their views?

We need to revisit and redefine what we mean by 'consultation' and to go back to first principles about what it is that we are trying to achieve. Consultation is not, or at least it should not be, a substitute for clear leadership and direction. We should not expect the public to become strategic planners – the public purse pays people well to do that job. Neither should we think that the conventional methods – thousands of leaflets, impenetrable documents and set-piece public meetings – are effective in reaching out to the vast majority of people.

We need to develop an approach to decision making, service delivery and the management of change which has embedded within it a culture of communication, dialogue and involvement with those who will be affected by decisions rather than a never ending stream of one-off paper based consultations.

There needs too to be a move away from the 'snakes and ladders' approach to policy development which has become commonplace since devolution. Some policy areas have been revisited time and again, with little marked difference in the outcomes on each occasion. Take, for example, the multiple documents and policy processes on family law, the arts and culture or health improvement.

This propensity for constant wheel reinvention needs stemmed. We need to foster a learning culture and to develop a better corporate memory within the body politic. There is absolutely no reason why a change in Minister or of the membership of a Parliamentary Committee – or even a change of Government – should necessarily require a repeat or review of work which has been done before. There needs to be greater momentum so that we constantly move forward in real world terms. Too often we go round in a loop by creating a veneer of 'doing something' while, in truth, adding little value to the outside world.

There needs to be a more dynamic strategic and transparent policy framework within which all concerned can work and plan for the future.

And if change is really to be championed in a devolved Scotland, politicians of all hues need to be challenged to come up with solutions rather than simply oppose those which others propose. Crude oppositionalism and populism have much to answer for in standing in the way of progress and in chipping away at public confidence. It is always easy to be against something, easy to find fault and to criticise, harder to seek solutions and take forward change and yet that, ultimately, is what leadership is all about. It is incumbent upon politicians to do what is right for the longer term not just what is popular in the short term.

Part of the problem is that we have failed to clarify the role of 'the centre' in a devolved Scotland. Though we talk the language of localisation and decentralisation, applaud voluntary endeavour and encourage entrepreneurial spirit, too often our actions militate against those outcomes. We expect Ministers to micro manage problems, Parliament to scrutinise detail and, when things go wrong, we are quick to apportion blame. Funding applications, local plans, project proposals, business cases and the like are held up for months – sometimes years – as Government civil servants cross check, double check, query and question work already done by other agencies. We do much of this in the name of accountability, but the truth is that often we impede progress and foster a climate of risk aversion when that is what we can least afford.

Too often, our stock response to addressing problems or improving standards, particularly in our public services, is to produce legislation, regulation and guidance, to increase inspection or to embark on yet more structural reform. The unintended consequences of this approach can be crippling. Rather than encouraging professionalism and innovation, we are in danger of reinforcing a 'tick box' culture and stifling creativity. Individuals and organisations are, in effect, rewarded for sticking to protocols and procedures rather than achieving results. And with every structural reorganisation, valuable time and energy in delivering improvement is diverted.

The regulatory furniture in our devolved Scotland is now very cluttered. There is a strong case for rationalising the number of bodies responsible for regulation, audit and inspection and for simplifying and reducing the sheer volume of regulatory and statutory requirements. The hoops and hurdles now required to be gone through by care providers, for example, or even by local youth group organisers are now quite excessive. There is little point in having gold plated standards and monitoring if the net result is a reduction in provision.

The scrutiny process too needs to be refined to reduce quantity while improving quality. The avalanche of parliamentary questions, correspondence, consultations and inquiries which devolution has spawned has placed considerable demands on many individuals and organisations. This has an opportunity cost in terms of the time and energy which could be directed to other activities – not least the delivery of improvements in the very areas under examination.

Scotland's devolved government and Parliament ought to be concerned with strategic leadership not operational interference. National politicians have a vital role to play in mapping a direction of travel, establishing strategic priorities, setting national standards, allocating resources and promoting improvement, but detailed prescription and operational intervention should be the place of last resort.

As national politicians we should do more to hold public bodies to account for their outputs and achievements, rather than pour over the detail of inputs and internal operation. If there is one thing that we need at every level, in our public services, businesses, in voluntary organisations and communities – it is good leadership and strong management. We will neither attract nor develop sufficient individuals with these capabilities if we are constantly breathing down their necks. It is time to 'let the flowers bloom', not in a *laissez faire* sense, but by recrafting an approach to government and governance which is about supporting and enabling rather than instructing and questioning.

This thinking is not new and such approaches are being advocated and tested elsewhere in the UK and across the world. The exciting thing is that Scotland is uniquely well placed to develop such an approach should we choose to do so. We are a small country, with a broad basis of agreement on key aspects of social and economic policy. The scope for us to develop a more 'bottom up' approach to change and to forge powerful partnerships for progress is considerable. There is enormous potential to create networks, build relationships and, in so doing establish trust between the key agencies and individuals who will effect change.

But for this to be effective, those who are charged with the task of effecting change need to be given support, not have the feet kicked from under them when the going gets rough. The reality is that getting results means taking some risks.

Last, but by no means least, if we are serious about taking Scotland forward then the machinery of government must be up to the job. The roots of much of the inertia and caution, not to mention failures of policy implementation, which we have witnessed in the early years of devolution are to be found in a Civil Service which is not yet fit for purpose. The need for wholesale reform of the Civil Service cannot be understated. Indeed, there will be little prospect of achieving the kinds of changes and improvements discussed above unless such a change takes place.

The fact is that too much of the prevailing civil service culture and practice is the product of a bygone age. In a modern, devolved Scotland, civil servants need to be skilled in the management of people and projects, not just paper and policy. There is a crying need for greater specialisation rather than the constant rotation of talented generalists. A great many more Scottish Executive civil servants – especially those around the top table – need to be drawn from a wider pool. Not just from business, as is often suggested, but also from those with a track record of managing change in, for example, local authorities, the NHS and the voluntary sector.

It will take more than a few incremental changes or external secondments to bring about the transformation which is necessary. A major programme of organisational change is required within our civil service and that, above all else, should be taken forward as a matter of urgency.

SECTION V
A Just and Fair Society

15

Prospects for Scotland's Health and Healthcare

PROFESSOR SIR DAVID CARTER MD FRCSEd FRSE

Scotland's health – some bad news

SCOTLAND'S POOR HEALTH RECORD is well known. Despite dramatic improvements in life expectancy we lag behind other Western European countries, including England. Recent estimates are that a girl born in Scotland in 2000 might expect to live for 78.7 years, 57.5 of them free of limiting longstanding illness and 67.2 of them in a state of health that is self-assessed as good or fairly good. Estimates for boys are 73.3, 54.5 and 64.6 years respectively. Demographic trends suggest that by 2021 there will have been a 15% fall in the number of children aged under 16, a 29% rise in the number of people aged 60-74, and a 30% rise in those aged over 75. These trends clearly have important implications for health service provision.

It cannot be assumed that life expectancy will continue to drift upwards. Even if it does, there are worrying indications that *healthy* life expectancy may not increase. Much will depend on whether life circumstances and lifestyles improve. Although overall smoking levels have edged downwards, we enter the 21st Century with 30% of adults smoking and the highest level of female smokers (32%) in Western Europe. No less than 22% of our adult female population is obese. Small wonder that diabetes is an increasing problem and that we languish at the wrong end of the Western European league table for mortality from coronary heart disease and cancer.

The income gap between rich and poor in our society is growing rather than narrowing and large numbers of Scots still live in appalling socio-economic circumstances. Scottish women in the most deprived population quintile can expect 11.1 fewer years of healthy life (on self assessment) than those in the least deprived quintile. For men the difference is 4.8 years. In our largest city, Glasgow, some 50% of the population live in postcode sectors classified as 6 or 7 (i.e. the most deprived) on the Carstairs-Morris index of deprivation[1]. Clearly, deprivation is not confined to Glasgow, or for that matter to our towns and cities, but over half of the one million people who live in the 15 UK parliamentary constituencies with the highest rates of premature mortality are in nine Scottish constituencies, many of them in Glasgow. In Shettleston for example, the chances of dying before the age of 65 are 2.3 times the national average.

We live in a country on the same latitude as Labrador and our winters cannot be described as hospitable. However, Iceland, Sweden and Norway have some of the highest life expectancies in Europe so that living in cold northern climes is not necessarily bad for you. This is not to say that living in damp, ill-heated homes is conducive to good health – clearly it is not, particularly when those homes are full of tobacco smoke and in areas of high unemployment, vandalism and crime.

Scotland's health – some less bad news

Let us not get too mired in gloom. Life expectancy in Scotland *has* improved markedly, and we sit in the better half of the European league table for a number of health indicators. Since 1980 our infant mortality rate has more than halved and premature mortality from coronary heart disease has almost halved. Survival rates for many types of cancer continue to improve, although falling levels of coronary heart disease may increase the cancer burden as more people 'live long enough' to develop cancer.

The importance of smoking cannot be overemphasised. It is not just the danger of getting lung cancer. Smoking increases the risk of developing other forms of cancer, obstructive airways disease, coronary heart disease, stroke and peripheral vascular disease. It is now certain that the risks extend to those in the vicinity who do not smoke themselves (passive smoking), to the unborn child, and to aspects of reproductive health. Reduction in smoking levels is undoubtedly the single most important public health measure available and it is heartening that Scotland has now signalled its intention to ban smoking in enclosed public places.

The turn of the century has seen a refreshing willingness on the part of the Scottish Executive to acknowledge the importance of life circumstances and health inequality. A particularly encouraging sign has been to implement the Arbuthnott report (*Fair Shares for All*) and allow for deprivation in the allocation of Health board funding. Deprivation cannot be addressed by NHS agencies working alone; there must be concerted action and enlightened partnership involving City Councils, housing agencies, social services, academic interests and above all, the people themselves. We should be encouraged by the decision to fund the Glasgow Centre for Population Health and its multi-agency approach to understanding, preventing and eradicating deprivation-associated ill health.

Populations are most likely to benefit from health improvement initiatives when they are fully engaged and involved from the outset and not simply on the receiving end of well-intentioned rhetoric and exhortation. The final Wanless Report of 2004 (*Securing Good Health for the Whole Population*) with its 'slow uptake', 'steady state' and 'fully engaged' scenarios (according to the degree of public engagement) was primarily concerned with England but has valuable read across to Scotland. 'Individuals are ultimately responsible for their own and their children's health... People need to be supported more actively to make better decisions about their own health and welfare... A NHS capable of facilitating a 'fully engaged' population will need to shift its focus from a national sickness service, which treats disease, to a National Health Service, which focuses on preventing it... The key threats to our future health such as smoking, obesity and health inequalities need to be tackled now.'

Scotland as a small country – size matters

It is undoubtedly easier to organise and administer health services for a population of 5 million than 50 million. We have a devolved Parliament (housed in a building to be proud of) and health is a devolved issue. We are in control of our own 'health destiny' and can even vary the rate of income tax raised by 3%. At the same time, our small country is often denied the economy of scale available south of the border. We need to guard against talking ourselves down, making a religion of self-criticism and becoming too parochial in outlook.

Scotland's traditional regard for its health services, universities and medical schools has provided it with a more robust NHS infrastructure, higher staffing levels and greater health expenditure than other parts of the UK. However, the fact that Scotland entered the 21st Century spending 22% more *per capita* on health than England can hardly be a source of satisfaction to English MPs and we can anticipate increasing impatience with the failure of the Barnett formula to bring about convergence.

Scotland also has more robust databases and can link registries to explore relationships between heath status, longevity, socio-economic data, disease incidence and treatment, and survival rates. There is a tradition of audit, evidence-based medicine and publication of health outcomes. For our size, we have punched consistently above our weight in biomedical research. And yet, are we sufficiently courageous to invest heavily in what some may see as high-risk controversial areas such as embryonic stem cell research or population genetics. Timing is critical and today's slight advantage can so easily become yesterday's missed opportunity in the drive to develop and sustain internationally competitive centres of excellence.

Health and politics

Sadly, health is now fully politicised. The UK political system (or maybe it's the politicians we elect) regards health as a football to be kicked for short-term party political advantage. Cross-party

Select Committees provide one method of reaching higher ground, but there have been few signs that MSPs find it easy to put aside party politics in a concerted drive to improve Scotland's health. Our media often seem more concerned with negative and at times hostile 'shock-horror' reporting than informed debate.

Today's Minister is held accountable for the latest health statistics, regardless of how long the underlying factors have been in play. After all, captains in the Royal Navy are court-martialled if their ship runs aground, even if they were asleep in their bunk at the time. Why should the Minister not take full responsibility for each and every blemish in service performance?

One thing is clear to me – Ministers have short shelf lives. In general, they are well-intentioned human beings who enter office with high aspirations and a determination to make a difference. But health and health services are complex and cannot be improved overnight. The oil tanker takes a long time to come round – and sometimes sails blithely on regardless. Fashions come and go – command and control gives way to the internal market, fund holding general practices move from being flavour of the month to yesterday's big idea, Trust hospitals enter the scene and are then dismissed.

How is the Scottish Executive Health Department best organised? Are we to retain a Minister of Health and Community Care with responsibility for health and health services, or are we to create a separate Public Health portfolio? To my mind a separate Minister for Public Health would send the wrong signal about the role of the 'main' Health Minister in health improvement and health promotion. Combination of responsibility for health and social services in one portfolio is attractive in theory but experience elsewhere has not been encouraging. I can see real virtue in delegating responsibility for day-to-day health service delivery to an agency so that the Minister is free to concentrate on health improvement. Sadly, I fear that party politics and our media will prevent any experimentation with this model.

In his thoughtful analysis of the post-devolution divergence of UK health systems, Scott Greer[2] sees Scotland as having backed *professionalism* by aligning the organisation with the existing structure of medicine. England incidentally, is thought to have bet on *markets* in which independent Trusts, rather like private firms, will contract with each other for care while some 30 regulatory organisations ensure quality. I have no doubt that we have put our money on the right horse!

Organisation of services – the quest for quality

Do we need to retain 15 Health boards that serve populations ranging from 20,000 to just under one million? Try telling the people of Orkney that they are to be 'submerged' in a Health board based in Inverness (or Aberdeen), or the people of Dumfries and Galloway that they are now part of Greater Glasgow. I see the importance of retaining local ownership and decision-making, even though small boards are denied critical mass when it comes to delivering some services. For specialist services such as heart surgery or cancer treatment, Scotland often divides most readily into a 4 (+1) model in which supra-regional services are based on large teaching hospital centres in Aberdeen, Dundee, Edinburgh and Glasgow. Inverness and its hinterland is often seen to need special consideration and accounts for the (+1). At the end of the day, I would retain 15 Health boards provided that we have systems (and mindsets) that encourage collaboration in supra-regional planning groups and managed clinical networks. Just because NHS funds flow 'vertically' to Health boards they must not become trapped unproductively in silos.

While I do not mourn the passing of the 'internal market' in Scotland, I was saddened to see the dissolution of Trusts signalled in the 2003 White Paper, *Partnership for Care*. At the same time I was encouraged by much of the rhetoric (...patients and national standards as drivers of change, empowerment of clinical staff, explicit rejection of command and control, distrust of structural change, and disinterest in change for change's sake...). My regard for the Trust system as a means of delivering focused, locally owned and accountable services does not mean that if I became Minister of Health tomorrow I would embark instantly on yet another reorganisation. At all costs we must avoid change for its own sake and reject the instinct to tinker with the organogram as a substitute for reasoned progress. The troops in the trenches have become cynical and enured to constant organisational change and demotivated by it – they long for a period of stability.

Scotland is rightly committed to equity of access to services. However, this cannot mean that every specialised service is available around the clock in every acute hospital. Yes of course, local access is desirable and convenient but it must never at the expense of service quality or safety.

For some highly specialised small-volume services such as liver transplantation, concentration of resources on one site is the only way to achieve economy of scale, maintain expertise and sustain critical mass. More open to debate are specialist services where caseloads justifies multiple sites, but not to the extent of providing the service in every acute hospital. For example, peripheral vascular surgical units need to have a critical mass of skilled personnel if they are to deal with life-threatening emergencies such as ruptured aortic aneurysm at any time of day or night. But how many such units can Glasgow justify? How should such services be provided in Fife or the Borders?

The pressure to 'protect my local hospital' and all of its services is a fact of modern life. The public does not take kindly to loss of local services and politicians need to get re-elected – remember Kidderminster! As the NHS Scotland edges towards (and for the moment backs away from) an unavoidable round of service review and rationalisation we can expect to see more public clamour and media outrage, political opportunism, and pressure on Ministers to retain an unsustainable *status quo*.

The real determinants of acute service provision are disarmingly straightforward. Is there sufficient expertise to deliver a service of appropriately high quality? Is there a critical mass of trained staff to sustain an emergency rota? Is the volume of activity sufficient to maintain specialist skills and good outcomes? Yes of course the service needs to be affordable and cost effective, and yes the tyranny of distance needs to be taken into account. But when all is said and done, can Perth and Dundee both maintain a fully staffed neonatal intensive care unit? Can Stirling and Falkirk (or Dunfermline and Kirkcaldy for that matter) each maintain a full rack of services at a separation of some 15 miles? Should the Borders General Hospital develop a specialist service for the occasional management of complex vascular emergencies?

The European Working Time Directive (EWTD) is now having a profound impact on emergency services. Even if infinite funding was available, we simply do not have the work force to run complex rotas on multiple sites for every specialty. Hard decisions have to be made with emphasis on quality, safety and sustainability. Such decisions require political courage and there is an onus on politicians, professionals and the public to put aside parochialism in an objective appraisal for what is best for the population as a whole.

Managed clinical networks (MCNs) offer a promising way forward and figure prominently in the 2003 White Paper. MCNs allow the totality of resource available to a region to be used to provide the best and most equitable service for that population. They comprise linked groups of health professionals and organisations (from primary, secondary and tertiary care as need be) working in co-ordinated fashion across traditional boundaries to provide integrated services of high quality. Some aspects of these services may have to be concentrated centrally whereas others can be delivered locally. For example, patients with breast cancer in South-East Scotland should not need to travel to Edinburgh for every aspect of diagnosis and treatment provided their local hospital can sustain a high quality service that meets the standards defined by NHS Quality Improvement Scotland (NHS QIS). However, they may well need to travel to Edinburgh for radiotherapy or complex breast reconstruction surgery. The MCN concept is based on pragmatism – one size will not fit all – and some services may be better provided in more traditional ways. Above all, MCNs are intended to improve services for patients rather than save money or provide convenient ways of working for staff.

Public funding and the NHS

I applaud the recent determination to spend a greater proportion of GDP on health. It seems near miraculous to me that the NHS survived as well as it did on miserly funding and derisory capital investment. At the same time, it is naïve to expect that a few years of increased spending can rectify years of neglect. Some 70% of funds are needed to pay the workforce and this demand is set to increase with acknowledgement of the need for more doctors and nurses, increasingly specialised services, introduction of new contracts, and implementation of the EWTD.

The scenarios used in the 2004 Wanless Report provide sensible stalking horses for health spending. Total UK health spending (public and private) is seen as rising from some 7.7% of GDP in 2002-03 to around 9.5% by 2007-08. In the 'slow uptake' scenario spending then rises to 12.5% by 2022-23, as opposed to 11.1% and 10.6% in the 'solid progress' and 'fully engaged' scenarios respectively. Clearly there is much at stake here and full engagement of our population in health improvement will be the crucial determinant.

It has become almost fashionable to question the sustainability of a NHS paid for by public taxation and look enviously over the fence at alternatives such as social insurance, managed care and increased privatisation. However, the NHS in Scotland has served us well; it is not broken and does not need to be thrown away. Respected outside commentators such as Sheila Leatherman and Don Berwick[3] see the NHS as second to none in its ambition and capacity to serve the health of the public. They contrast our open and comprehensive attempts to improve health care with US efforts that remain mired in debate about pricing and reimbursement, commercial secrecy, timidity in admitting to quality issues, and continued tolerance of the 'national shame' of over 40 million uninsured Americans. The WHO Report 2000[4] ranked the UK 18th out of 191 countries in healthcare system performance. Not as good as France perhaps, but much better than the United States which spends 40% more per head than Britain but ranked 37th largely because its system is so inequitable. Leatherman and Berwick do not wear rose-tinted spectacles – they recognise our need to improve performance, emphasise learning over regulation, and depoliticise health and healthcare.

My commitment to the NHS does not preclude pragmatic occasional use of the private sector to relieve waiting pressures in respect of say, coronary arterial surgery or hip replacement. I also see great virtue in Diagnostic and Treatment Centres (DTCs), as highlighted in the 1997 Acute Services Review, but see no need for them to be provided from outwith the NHS.

The changing nature of healthcare

Recent experience with emerging diseases such as HIV-AIDS, SARS and variant Creutzfeld-Jakob disease tells us that by 2020, other new diseases will have arrived on the scene. Infecting agents will continue to evolve, hospital-acquired infection will remain a big problem, and antibiotic resistance will be a profound concern as the trickle of new antibiotics from industry slows. More hopefully, immunisation will extend to the prevention of more infectious diseases and to some cancers. MMR will have regained public trust despite the probability that media-driven scares and 'scandals' will be as common as ever. Screening for diseases such as cancer will be more effective and extensive, and advances in genomics will allow more accurate prediction of individual risk of developing disease. The same advances will make drug treatment safer and more effective by tailoring it to the individual and/or infecting organisms (pharmacogenomics). Prophylactic treatment will be more widely available for those with a genetic make-up that predisposes to disease.

Healthcare in 2020 will be radically different. Government will finally have cracked the problems surrounding IT modernisation and bulky hand-written case notes will be a distant memory. 'E-health' will provide electronic medical records, information systems and booking systems; and patients will hold their own health record. DTCs will be an important feature of the NHS landscape; they will be large and few in number (if they are to function efficiently) but patients will be happy to travel to them (perhaps they will even have car parks and bus links). Clinical performance and patient safety will have improved but NHS QIS will still be there to monitor standards and drive them ever higher. Stem cell technology will have revolutionised the diagnosis and treatment of Parkinson's disease and diabetes, and will shortly transform organ replacement. Ortho-paedics will flourish as the ageing population fracture their bones and need joint replacement. MCNs will thrive.

Primary care will still be the bedrock of a vibrant publicly funded NHS and at least 90% of patients contacts will still take place in that sector. The new GP contract may well have improved service quality and primary care will play a much fuller role in health promotion and improvement. The traditional bond between patient and GP will have diminished as will the prospect of receiving out-of-hours services from a doctor that one knows. NHS Direct and NHS 24 will have gone from strength to strength.

Multidisciplinary teams will be the norm and traditional boundaries between professions will have been greatly eroded. Most doctors will be women and the last bastion of male chauvinism (surgery) will have fallen. Training and work patterns will be more flexible. Matrons will be back in fashion after a period in the wilderness; most of them will be men.

The burden of chronic debilitating diseases will not have shrunk but better treatments will be available and more use will be made of expert patients. Diabetes and dementia will be of particular concern. Coronary heart disease will still be a significant problem but will occur later in life and seldom require surgery. Premature deaths from cancer will have fallen markedly and there will be new 'magic bullets' for some cancers. The cancer burden will increase as people live longer but survival rates for many common cancers (e.g. breast and colorectal cancer) will have improved. There will have been relatively little improvement in survival from cancer of the lung, oesophagus or pancreas but lung cancer incidence will have fallen given that less than 20% of Scots will smoke. Deprivation will not have gone away but the health inequality gap will at last have begun to narrow. The public may not yet be 'fully engaged' in health promotion and improvement.

None of us are particularly blessed when it comes to reading the runes or gazing into the crystal ball. However of two things I am certain. Health and healthcare will continue to occupy centre stage in 2020 and we will still have a great deal to do in the drive for improved health!

[1] The Carstairs and Morris index was originally developed in the 1980s using 1981 census data. It employs four indicators (overcrowding in private households, male unemployment, head of household in social class 4 or 5, and lack of a car) to assign postcode sectors to categories ranging from 1 (very low deprivation) to 7 (very high deprivation).

[2] Greer, S. (2003) 'Four way bet: how devolution has led to four different models for the NHS'. QMW Public Policy Seminars, The Constitution Unit UCL.

[3] Leatherman, S. and Berwick, D.N. (2000) 'The NHS through American eyes'. BMJ 321: 1545-6

[4] World Health Organisation (2000) The WHO report 2000: health systems performance. Geneva: WHO

16

From Hovels to Houses, But Now Let's Have Some Quality

DR DOUGLAS ROBERTSON

HOUSING IS A PRODUCT of income and wealth. Put simply, the rich are well healed and well housed, the poor are not. Fredrick Engels came to this conclusion in 1846, and it is still as true today. So if you wish to influence the nature and quality of housing in Scotland, then the crucial lever to pull is that of wealth distribution. Holyrood, given its lack of fiscal competence, is consequently hamstrung. But it is not inept.

Given that housing itself is a critical measure of wealth, there is scope for the Parliament to have an influence, by using housing and consumer policies not only to change the nature and quality of housing provision, but also to contribute to altering the current pattern of wealth distribution. Clearly, focussing on fiscal reform would provide us with a better range of options and be a more productive approach, but we can only work with the tools provided.

Scotland is better housed than it has ever been, as the most recent Scottish House Condition Survey highlights[1]. That said, the measure of quality, the tolerable standard, set some forty years ago, merely distinguishes between houses that require immediate demolition, and those that could hold out for a few more years. While in relative terms, the housing we currently reside in is a marked improvement on the slums and hovels grudgingly offered by landlords, whether urban or rural: they fail to measure up well against our northern European neighbours. Internal space standards, quality of finish, provision of amenities, quality of environment, nature of neighbourhood facilities and transport linkages are all distinctly poorer. We pay a high price for our housing, and not just in financial terms.

Undoubtedly, the public sector played the key role in the immediate post-war period, through tackling severe overcrowding. It also created worker settlements in the six new towns, and via the now defunct Scottish Special Housing Association. Eventually it got back to tackling slum housing, having touched on this task in the late 1930s, through the questionable use of high rise and system built construction, before leaving this challenging task to newly emergent housing associations dedicated to eradicating tenement slums. The public sector was less successful in providing housing for those who did not conform to the idealised nuclear family or those with a specific special need. Again it was the growing housing association movement who met these challenges.

Public sector housing, reflecting Scotland's municipal and socialist traditions, was primarily a vehicle for public sector construction interests. Once built, the public sector proved less than successful at managing its utilitarian product. When public sector construction halted, abruptly in the mid 1970s, powerful construction interests merely remodelled themselves into inefficient, unaccountable and, not surprisingly, expensive maintenance operations, which served their own, rather than the tenant's interests. Nowhere is this better illustrated than with the much lauded Glasgow housing stock transfer, where the City Council's direct labour organisation was gifted a five year maintenance contact by the new operators, worth some £270 million annually.

Council housing has also suffered from being the 'cash cow' for local government. Although legally the council's housing revenue account is 'ring fenced', so that cash cannot be moved from council funds to subsidise council housing, or vice versa, sundry departments make block charges against this account. Such general charging thus subsidises other Council functions, whether administration, legal services, parks or cleansing. Further, the HRA traditionally pays for homelessness, despite the fact that everyone, and not just council tenants can, and do draw on these services. Interestingly, where councils have opted to transfer their entire housing stock, they retain homelessness as a dedicated Social Work service. So the old criticism that council housing was subsidised by ratepayers could not have been further from the truth. Rather, it has long been tenants who have unwittingly subsidised councils.

Given the recent and rapid polarisation of council housing into a welfare sector – for those who cannot compete within the private market – this practice becomes even more perverse. Bloated rents are now underwritten by Housing Benefit. The justification that this is acceptable, because it's the government that pays, and not the tenants, conveniently ignores the fact that these high rents act to trap the poor into council housing. Those in low paid employment cannot afford these rents, thus ensuring an increasingly welfare dependent and poor council house population. So, although Scotland's housing conditions have improved, this has been achieved at a personal cost for many.

The cost to Scotland, as a society has also been very high. This nation, to its shame, still has some of the worst housing conditions in Europe. It is no longer the mean nineteenth century 'single ends', but rather the dour, bleak public sector solutions to that original slum problem. A walk, or drive from Springburn, out past Barmulloch into Greater Easterhouse, and back through the East End reveals a housing and social scandal of enormous proportions, ignored by politicians and polite society alike. Other towns, especially those in west central Scotland, as well as all of Scotland's cities have neighbourhoods which mirror this social and personal calamity, but none comes close to matching the scale and intensity of Glasgow's multiple problems. This is also where the bulk of Scotland's prison population comes from.

Periodically, a damming set of official statistics about premature death, chronic illness, high unemployment or appalling educational attainment pricks the conscience of both *The Herald* and *The Scotsman's* readership. But after a suitably moralising editorial, it's straight back too the real task of selling adverting space in lifestyle sections. Rapid de-industrialisation explains much of Glasgow's misery, but the crassness and cynicism of so much public policy has exacerbated what was already an awful situation.

Here is the legacy of four decades of expensive public interventions, dreamed up by successive Scottish administrations. These linguistically crafted initiatives, offered up in the form of humiliating competitions, are then rolled out, publicised and then prioritised for strictly defined time periods. These wastelands on which these seeds are thrown, were not created by the pernicious activities of capitalist exploiters, but rather the consequence of the 'bread and butter' activities which sustain the not insignificant and ultimately parasitic 'poverty industry'. The prime example of these failings was, undoubtedly, the Glasgow stock transfer.

Writing off a billion pound housing debt was of great benefit to Glasgow, and retaining all the jobs in a swollen bureaucracy, an added bonus, especially to a political party with strong ties to public sector unions. But crucially, whether the city's tenants will see a lasting benefit – rather than the short term spending bonanza we are currently witnessing – through the provision of high quality, well designed, sustainable houses set within attractive and connected neighbourhoods, suitable for the 21st Century is still highly debatable. The real danger is that this new landlord, like its predecessor before it, will continue to be the problem, not the solution.

The private sector, for long the pariah of 'socialist' housing policies, also made a very significant contribution to improving Scotland's housing conditions. From being a small and marginal part of the Scottish housing system, dedicated to meeting the requirements of the wealthy elite, it has, from the late 1960s, become the tenure of choice for nearly two thirds of the population. Its growth has come from new construction, through the creation of large and ever expanding suburban housing estates, built by speculative developers. Again, the quality of what has been produced has been questionable, especially, but certainly not exclusively, at the budget end of the market. Far too many suburban estates look the worse for wear, although it has to be said they never looked that good in the first place. Perhaps, in a relatively short space of time, they could find themselves being the new slums. The real problem here is that speculative builders secure their profits through enhanced land values, rather than via the 'housing product'. Consumers of speculative housing have always been shortchanged.

The latest off the shelf offerings, those tall thin boxes, merely encourage another relatively quick house move. This does not bode well for the future, especially given their physical remoteness and total car dependency. What are the other housing choices? Renting from the public sector has not been possible, given the dominance of 'needs based' allocations systems, declining quality and high rents, relative to mortgage costs. The real killer is, of course, the stigma that now hangs over council housing. Private renting has long been similarly stigmatised, a niche market acceptable only to elderly single men, students, those just out of university and people needing a bolt hole during a relationship breakdown. Owning has long been a housing necessity, rather than a choice. Add to this a fiscal system, long dedicated to enhancing owner occupation's appeal through generous tax treatment, and until quite recently, an effective subsidisation, via mortgage interest tax relief, then its little wonder owning became so popular.

New construction has not been the sole driver in the growth of Scottish home ownership: transfers from both the public and private rented stock have made just as valuable contributions. Given the failings and exploitation of the public sector, it is little surprise that when tenants were offered the opportunity to purchase, with a deep discount, they jumped at the chance. Not only did this prove to be markedly cheaper than renting, but it also provided – in most, but not all cases – a significant capital asset to pass on. The faster and greater the polarisation of the social rented sector, the steeper the rent rises. Then, those that could afford to - those in work – quickly bought out their homes. Allocation policies, which had long ensured that the 'best' tenants ended up in the 'best' housing, helped greatly in facilitating this tenure switch.

A similar pattern of tenure change had occurred earlier, from the 1950s onwards. With increasing personal affluence, more people were able to service new mortgage products. Hence, landlords could now offload property which, since the introduction of rent restrictions in 1916, had failed to deliver profits, and consequently, had missed out on investment. So poor quality rented housing delivered a capital sum to landlords, keen to disinvest. At the same time, the State offered generous grants to these new homeowners so they could improve their homes. Had landlords been able to make a reasonable return, through rent increases and more equitable tax

treatment in comparison to other businesses, then basic maintenance and improvements would have been viable. Other countries
managed, through regulation coupled with fiscal support, to
ensure private renting played a role in mass housing. If this been
the case here, then the State would not have been obliged to fund
comprehensive clearance and associated new housing programmes. The cost of renovation grant work on those houses that
avoided clearance would also have been avoided. Instead, what we
are left with is a small private rented sector, a large proportion of
which is effectively part of the owner occupied sector, seeking to
benefit from capital appreciation, rather than the income stream
of rents, given the recent poor performance of pension funds and
other investment products. Pluralism is not a feature of our housing
system, or our housing history; it's time it was.

Private landlords in Scotland have always received a very bad
press, and often rightly so. But the caricature of the immoral
exploiter of the working class demands some revision. We need to
acknowledge that the landlords' financial circumstances were largely
determined by long-standing public policy ambitions. Interestingly,
when the most vociferous critics of landlord exploiters, socialist
councillors, failed to invest in their own housing stock, because
they did not have enough income from rents, they never saw the
irony, or double standards of their position. And then let's not forget
that housing policy throughout the immediate post-war period was
all about keeping rents low, so that inward investing manufacturing businesses could pay low wages. As Engels observed, housing
conditions are a direct function of the capitalist system.

Overall, a combination of long lasting rent control, increasing
and justified public health demands, coupled with a municipal desire
to wipe out private renting in favour of their own direct provision,
ensured money continued to flow out from renting, increasing the
need for more public investment. Private renting became the housing
of last resort.

Unfortunately, the current failure of the public sector mirrors
closely the failures of private renting. Council housing is now the
tenure of last resort. The overt favouring of owner occupation, by

successive governments, now ensures that sector is in high demand, even by those who can barely afford it. It is now council housing, in places like Arbroath, Brechin and Dundee down to Paisley, Kilmarnock and Dumbarton, which lies empty, neglected and abandoned. But again Glasgow in terms of sheer scale, stands out. In some instances, housing built as a solution to the slum problem has itself, in just over three decades, become a slum. In addition, housing refurbished in the last ten years, is now being cleared away. This represents a massive waste of resources, and given the scale of recent investments, the actual cash sums involved are considerable.

It was often said that the reason the Danes, Swedes, Norwegians, Dutch and Germans had better housing than us was that they invested more in it in the first place. Now it might well be the case that we have invested far more, in total, and are still left with the poorest of quality. Glasgow's council housing, despite its billion-pound mortgage debt, was worth less than nothing, given its need for investment: a truly damming indictment. The fact no one chooses to see it as such is truly breathtaking. But then, this was just housing for the poor, and the Glaswegian poor at that.

Scottish housing does have a profound 'Groundhog Day' quality about it. Avoidable delays in tackling the initial slum problem ensured that much improvable stock was allowed deteriorate into atrocious slums, leaving far too many people to suffer the indignity of living in squalid housing. We have now allowed the exact same thing to happen all over again, within the public sector. Policy has long favoured one tenure above all others with major repercussions and significant costs; personal, financial and environmental. Our public culture of always trying to do things on the cheap has proved shortsighted. Housing demands vision, creativity, real joined-up thinking and a proper commitment to quality. Scottish housing policy has failed to demonstrate these attributes. Housing quality, for example, has always been the 'fag end', rather than the driver of housing agendas. What this revisionist analysis of Scottish housing reveals is that powerful vested interests, and especially those of housing producers and their professional functionaries, have for too long been dominant.

The real task is to openly challenge these narrow sectional interests, and redress the balance, so that the consumers of housing are put in the driving seat. This can only be achieved by supporting an overtly consumerist agenda, in both the private and public sectors. We also need to introduce greater plurality in housing provision, because offering different housing choices is an essential part of supporting our different life stages. To do this we need to introduce a greater degree of competition between tenures, and at the same time incentivise distinct quality and sustainability goals. There is also a need to examine the local governance of local space, to ensure local people are given a more direct say in how their neighbourhood is managed.

Given the dominance of owner occupation, let's start here. Although housing is likely to be the most expensive purchase we make, it is shocking to discover you have fewer rights when buying a house than when buying a fridge or a washing machine. While housing has become a mass market, rather than a specialist niche, its 'modus operandi' has remained almost unaltered. Rather than trying to enhance the position of purchasers, the system is still tied into the quaint (but for all the professionals involved in housing transactions, very useful) safety net of 'caveat emptor', or buyer beware.

Solicitors largely control every aspect of the property market. They not only undertake the legal work of conveyancing, but uniquely within a Scottish context, often provide estate agency services. Solicitors' property centres, as the Monopolies and Mergers Commission reported were effectively *'a monopoly, but one which operated in the public interest'*. Many also offer mortgage advice and facilities. All the relevant consumer information about the property is not available when the property is marketed. Surveys are not surveys, merely lender valuations, and a recent report[1] found that most are useless when making a judgement about the actual physical condition of the property. The speed of the selling process, and the limitations of information, ensure bids are too often made by the heart, rather than the head. The unique blind bidding system is a disgrace, in any market context, and is open to abuse.

To change this unacceptable system we need to introduce a sell-ers' pack, covering all legal and technical information, at the point of sale, thus enhancing the consumers' position through limiting the scope of 'caveat emptor'. We should make it a legal requirement that all bids are submitted to a public office, charged with displaying the top bid submitted, with a 48 hour window for other bidders to adjust their offers if they wished. This would introduce a chal-lenge to the offers over lottery, so beloved by those on a commis-sion fee. Such an arrangement has operated for years in Northern Ireland. Both changes would introduce much needed transparency into the house buying system, a critical necessity to enhance con-sumer power within any market.

Within rented housing, why is it that the relationship between tenant and landlord is legally governed by tenancy, rather than con-sumer law? Is it that as a tenant, you are a lesser form of consumer and, consequently, not eligible to have the housing services you purchase, governed by laws that demand people receive what they pay for? Do we not need to up the ante here, and set down service quality targets that hold landlords to account? There are important lessons to be learned here from France, where tenants – whether public or private sector – have their rights enshrined in consumer protection laws, and where tenant interests are collectively repre-sented to ensure there is a proper counter balance to producer interests. Ensuring a less socially polarised and, consequently, wel-fare dependent rented sector is also critical in this regard.

What is unfortunately termed 'social rented housing' should be capable of housing a wider range of people, and to do this 'needs based' allocations system should be dumped. What is portrayed as an equitable solution, merely creates social ghettoes and sump estates. Allowing more people to access this housing would transform the sector's mode of operation, and tenants' expectations. In relation to social mix, the time is also right to kill off the right to buy, at discount, but to allow sales at the full market price.

This rented sector also needs investment: the ten-year pegging of new public investment by New Labour has been a disgrace. Only through investment in new stock can we start to offer alternatives to the owner occupied and private rented sectors. An enhanced level of investment should also allow a scale of development that brings about real change. It would also allow the building industry to engage in long term planning and develop new products. It also needs to modernise its Dickensian working practices, so that multi-skilling and creative thinking are a reality, thus increasing the quality of the housing produced, while reducing its cost.

Housing associations should be allowed to compete directly with private builders, to ensure more and better homes are produced. The fact that a speculative builder can make £3 million, for one year's work, suggests there are significant inefficiencies within the system. Allowing housing associations to build for sale would help introduce innovation and better design into what is an architecturally challenged and moribund private housing industry. Profits could then be recycled back into their renting business, and this would also encourage more socially mixed developments.

Quality has to be the key policy ambition. When we talk about building in quality, this needs to involve urban design, encompassing community facilities and transport in a long term and strategic manner. There's also no point in investing in housing that was thrown up in the 1950s or 1960s. The real challenge now is to create new housing within an attractive, supportive and socially mixed range of distinctive neighbourhoods that offer a long term and stable housing option.

Inextricably linked to quality is the issue of sustainability. There's a need for urban intensification, rather than allowing ever-expanding suburban growth. That's not to say suburban solutions do not have their place, but only when tied into rapid transit public transport infrastructure. We must plan to reduce car usage. With the expansion of intensification, we need to produce excellent amenities that can be shared by all residents. This in turn will demand a proper system of flat management, an issue that both the recent Title Conditions and Law of the Tenement Acts shied away from. Legal remedies must meet the aspirations of residents actually living in multi-owned property, rather than the ambitions of a small group of eminent property lawyers. Such urban intensification could also bring with it a desire to have a rural retreat, through the development of holiday huts, as is a common feature of Nordic living.

Housing neighbourhoods are the building blocks of our society, so lets make sure their foundations are strong. Only by having a locally focussed governance regime, building on from residents associations, can local government services be truly subjected to service level agreements and consumer monitoring. Enhancing the role of consumers should never be viewed as an individual activity, as there is a collective dimension that is equally as important.

How the wider environment, including local schools and a range of other facilities, are designed, maintained and managed, has traditionally been a local authority competence. But as local government has stopped being local, the current arrangements need reviewing. A useful model, in this regard, is provided by locally based housing associations, which have introduced a form of community governance which engages with, and often carries out tasks previously the remit of councils. Creating more equitable relationships between local neighbourhoods, their communities and local councils will be crucial to shaping the nature of a whole range of social, cultural, political and economic opportunities. Change the housing and you will help change our society.

But we still cannot ignore the fact that poverty and housing is inextricably linked, as Engels noted so long ago. If you really want to improve housing, you really need to tackle the gross inequalities of wealth distribution. Doing it the other way round is more indirect, and consequently limited in scope. The Parliament could, however, re-introduce a proper local property tax. Or, better still, a land value tax, which would help reduce the over consumption of housing by the wealthy, and draw valuable resources back into communities. But to properly redistribute wealth the Parliament needs fiscal powers, and more crucially the political will. In an ideal world, housing should be taxed, as a consumption good, on an equitable basis, and the income generated used to support a range of initiatives that enhance the quality of our society. Introducing a capital gains tax, on property would also depress the housing market, allowing resources to flow to more productive parts of the economy, rather than propping up lender profits. Given the long-standing iniquities of wealth within Scottish society this would represent a massive challenge. But we need to be up for that challenge, because for too long Scotland, and Glasgow in particular, has tried to satisfy itself by tackling the symptoms, but never causes, of poverty.

Twenty years from now the Parliament could have made a significant contribution to improving the quality of housing in Scotland. It should also have become better at seeing the linkages between housing and other areas of public policy, especially transport, governance and environmental issues. It might also be well down the road to understanding that vested interests rarely concern themselves with the public good. If it really made an effort its housing policy could have started redressing the critical issue of income distribution and wealth. So there are no shortage of issues to be addressed, and opportunities presented, but as yet, it is unclear whether the political will or imagination exists to confront them.

---

[1] DTZ Pieda Consulting (2002) *Research on the Scottish House Buying and Selling Process*. Edinburgh: Scottish Executive.

17

Social Work: Change for the Future

DUNCAN MACAULAY

SOCIAL WORK IS A profession that I am extremely proud to be a part of.

To live in a country that aspires to the social inclusion of all of its citizens is to live in a country that must hold the values of social work at its very core. The political and societal hopes for the future here in Scotland are clearly bound to the concept of our society being all-embracing. Since devolution, our country is in the strange position of being a nation at once ancient and yet also fledgling. The question for our future is whether we can again be a great nation. What will it mean to be 'great', and what part will social work have to play in our brave new future?

Gandhi wrote that a nation's greatness could be measured by the quality of the lives of its poorest citizens. If Scotland is to aspire to greatness as a nation, I believe we must adopt this measure. How we as a country provide for the poor and vulnerable amongst us must be the real test of our aspiration for social inclusion for all.

Historically, social work has been central to social inclusion: tackling poverty and deprivation and assisting community regeneration. Today, it seems that the values of social work have become the values of government. Our ideals have become its ideals – our language, its language. Our profession has, in many senses, never been nearer to the centre of government, or more important to our nation. Today, as a country, we spend nearly £2bn[1] each year on social work. More than 275,000[2] adults receive a social work service. Yet most people only hear of social work when a tragedy makes the headlines. It is quite right that tragic mistakes should be publicised but we must report these rare occurrences responsibly. Our country relies on its social care workforce and demoralising such a crucial group makes recruitment harder, leads to existing workers being over-stretched, and, through this, may contribute to more mistakes in the future.

What will the role of social work be in Scotland in 2020? I would love to think that there will be no role at all, that there will be no social problems, but 2020 is just 15 years away and Utopia, I fear, lies a little further off. No doubt in 2020 social work will be doing what it does best: working with those who for one reason or another are excluded or pushed to the margins of our society. But it will be doing it differently and, I believe, doing it better.

To do that, we as a society and as a profession need to change. Luckily, the very essence of social work is change. Effecting positive changes in people's lives is what we are called to this profession to do. I believe that as a profession we have a record of successfully delivering change and that is why I am confident that we can make the changes required to equip us to deliver world-class services to the people of Scotland in 2020 and beyond.

Evidence from the recent past supports my confidence. 15 years ago the Secretaries of State for Health, Social Security, Wales and Scotland presented to parliament a White Paper called *Caring for People: Community Care in the Next Decade and Beyond*. This paper announced a radical shift in the way that community care was to be delivered and resulted in the NHS and Community Care Act 1990. That Act transformed social work services; introducing the quasi-market and the purchaser/provider split. This is not the place to debate the merits or otherwise of that Act. Rather, it should be noted that social work has successfully delivered the major changes required of us over the last 15 years.

The Danish physicist Niels Bohr said, "Prediction is a very difficult thing – especially about the future". However, some things can be predicted – as a nation we are getting older. In the year 2020, and the following ten years, the children of the 60s will be in their 60s, and the aspirations of those coming to an older age will have changed considerably. The welfare society will no longer meet these aspirations and our nation will need to grasp the concept of wellbeing for all its citizens if those in political power wish to remain there. An ageing population and the concomitant need for appropriate social work services is an issue common to developed countries. The US Bureau of Labor Statistics[3] is predicting that in the year 2020 the US will need 70,000 social workers just specialising in the care of the elderly! The population of Paisley is 70,000. You couldn't even fit them all in Murrayfield stadium.

In Scotland, the population is falling but older people make up a growing proportion of that population. The General Register Office for Scotland is predicting that by 2020 the population of Scotland will be under 5 million but the number of those who have reached pensionable age will be more than 1 million and the number aged over 75 will be more than half a million. Our best predictions suggest that 30%, or 150,000, of those people will have regular or continuous care needs and the services they will demand will be different from those provided today.

A greater proportion of our people will live in cities and large towns with fewer and fewer of us in more remote areas. Not only will this be likely to bring an increase in the urban poverty we see in our major centres of population; it will also provide logistical challenges in providing modern services over large, sparsely populated areas.

One exciting change is that there will be a greater ethnic mix and greater cultural diversity in Scotland in 2020 than ever before. We must be absolutely clear that racism can have no place in our country. One of the great challenges we face in the coming years will be to extend a welcome to other cultures. Social work has a key role to play in fostering a climate where racism is not tolerated.

A colleague of mine working in a London Borough told me that there are over 50 first languages spoken in their primary schools. As Scotland becomes ever more culturally diverse, we in social work will have to adapt the way we work.

Scotland's poor health is well recorded. We cannot escape the fact that we have one of the worst health records in the developed world. In the 2001 census, 20% of Scotland's population identified themselves as having a long-term illness, a long-term health problem or a disability. The services demanded by people with disabilities have changed almost beyond recognition and need to go on changing if we are serious when we talk about social inclusion.

In my career in social work, I have been constantly impressed by my colleagues; the people who make our profession what it is. What causes me to be so impressed? In our workforce we have a highly valued resource. Our workforce has exceptional talent and is committed to continually developing its professionalism. Our practitioners are competent in their work and their achievements continue to inspire us.

Nevertheless, recruitment and retention have become more and more challenging. Recently, a group of social work academics wrote a passionate manifesto for our profession, calling for a return to prominence of the values they felt had been squeezed out of the profession by a culture of 'marketisation and managerialism'[4]. They noted that,

> 'It is still the case that that people enter social work not to be care-managers or rationers of services or dispensers of community punishment but rather to make a positive con-tribution to the lives of poor and oppressed people. If it is the widening gap between promise and reality that breeds much of the current anger and frustration amongst social workers, it is also the awareness that social work could be much more than it is at present that leads many of us to hang on in there[5].'

They correctly diagnose the motivation of our workforce but the manifesto gazes fondly into the past instead of looking to the future. The quasi-market and the need to be effective managers may not have been part of the equation when social work began as an organised profession but they are now and they will remain so. Crucially though, the requirements of modern service delivery and the values that underpin social work are not mutually exclusive. Does our profession need to reinvigorate itself? Yes. Can it be much more than it is at present? Yes. Will it achieve this by a return to former practices? No. What is required is the assimilation of modern professional skills without the loss of our traditional strengths. Changes are already underway to help us to achieve this.

The Scottish Social Services Council and in particular its mission to drive up professional standards is as welcome as it is overdue. The social care workforce numbers more than 118,000 in Scotland today. By 2020 it will be larger still. The need to regulate this workforce and to ensure standards of service is clear and is a massive task.

Through the use of Scottish Vocational Qualifications, Scotland will have a trained social care workforce. This workforce will be registered with the Scottish Social Services Council. The register will be open to public scrutiny.

The title 'Social Worker' will be legally protected. Social work will be a graduate profession – those wishing to become social workers will need to have earned a degree. This is a crucial step in raising standards.

The profession, like any other, requires leadership. Currently, in each Local Authority, this leadership is vested in the role of the Chief Social Work Officer. The 21st Century Social Work Review group currently reviewing our profession is considering the future of this role. Whether the role remains as it is currently constituted or changes, one thing is clear: the profession of social work needs to be led by professional social workers.

The challenge for social work is to ensure that Scotland has a social care workforce that is well-trained, professional, regulated and fit to deliver modern services to those who most need them and that this is built upon a continuing espousal of traditional social work values.

The Social Work (Scotland) Act 1968 was amended by the Local Government (Scotland) Act 1994 to the effect that Local Authorities were no longer required to have a unitary Social Work Department but instead could design their service departments to fit local needs. This has allowed reorganisation of our services to become something of a norm, but there is a danger that reorganisation has become an end in itself or something carried out because it is easier than making real improvements to services. The Institute for Public Policy Research[6] has pointed out that 'structural reform is not a panacea' and that 'anyone who believes that transforming social care is simply about changing its structures will be sadly disappointed'.

For staff the danger is reorganisation fatigue.

'I was to learn later in life that we tend to meet any new situation by reorganising; and a wonderful method it can be for creating the illusion of progress while producing confusion, inefficiency, and demoralisation'.

When this quote, commonly (and mistakenly) attributed to Petronius, starts to appear on office walls, the effects of reorganisation on staff can be quickly inferred. Yet, strangely, if we are to be more effective in the year 2020, I am proposing that the service need to change in the following ways.

We need to ensure that staff are involved in designing the changes and that all changes are demonstrably linked to improvements in outcomes for service users.

The Disability Movement has epitomised the growth of user-led organisations. Collective advocacy, political lobbying and user-empowerment have been powerful catalysts for changes to both service delivery and legislation. Some see these movements as challenging the traditional authority of professional social work. I prefer to see these movements as the fruits of a social work profession that has fostered independence rather than dependence amongst those it has worked with; that has contributed to the growing confidence of marginalised groups; and that has helped them to find their voice. If users' expectations for services are now higher than before, our profession and those of us who live in this country should celebrate the fact that our service users are demanding equal treatment as equal citizens. Inevitably, these raised expectations and increased demands will bring social work into conflict with user groups because budgets will not rise in line with users' expectations. There are two challenges for social work here. The first is ensuring that our services are as efficient as possible, ensuring that we wring every penny of service from every pound of our budget. The second is to explaining what service levels can be achieved with existing budgets and campaigning for increases where we can evidence the improvements extra money will bring.

Traditional models of service delivery have been led by the professionals. There is much talk of new models of user-led services. More realistic is to think that services and policies of the future need to be designed in partnership.

Users are best placed to know what they need – that has always been at the heart of social work assessments, often the difficulty has been encouraging users to engage in the assessment process.

Professionals are best placed to determine how assessed needs can be met by creatively using existing resources. I firmly believe that our profession will be enhanced if professional social workers readily accept that part of their role requires them to act as gatekeeper to services. This involves tough decisions because we cannot afford to meet everyone's needs in the way they wish. We cannot hide from these decisions by saying that we did not get involved in social work to be a rationer of services. We cannot excuse ourselves from helping people because resources are not infinite.

Those who run our country need to hear what level of resources is realistically required to provide modern services that promote social inclusion. But in order for them to respond positively, they need to be confident that our profession has the expertise to deliver improvements that represent value for money.

To return to Gandhi: 'The future depends on what we do in the present'. We have a marvellous opportunity to shape the future of our services. Social work can lead this country in the integration and inclusion of all its citizens. In return, our society needs help to understand the work we do, and through that understanding come to value, praise and celebrate the work we do on their behalf. I hope, above all other things for the future of my profession, our country learns to hold my colleagues in the highest regard.

[1] http://www.scotland.gov.uk/stats/bulletins/00344-09.asp

[2] Estimate

[3] The National Institute for Aging (1987) *Personnel for health needs of the elderly through 2020*. NIH Publication Number 87-2950

[4] Jones et al (2004) *Social work and social justice: a manifesto for a new engaged practice*. http://liv.ac.uk/sspsw/manifesto/Manifesto.htm

[5] Ibid

[6] Kendall, L. and Harker, L. (eds.) (2002) *From Welfare to Wellbeing: the future of social care*. London: The Institute for Public Policy Research

18

Equality: The politics of poverty

DAVID DONNISON

The politics of poverty

WHEN THE ENGLISH – never the Scots – chose Margaret Thatcher and her Party to govern them, they soon realised that this was not to be the usual, reassuring, tidying-up, Conservative regime. These were ideological reactionaries who understood, at gut level, that to bring about the complete change of course they had in mind they had to ban discussion of problems that previous governments, Labour and Conservative, had worried about, and refuse even to meet the people who wanted to talk about them. Keith Joseph, Thatcher's principal guru, had written a book that denied there was any such thing as poverty in Britain. It was inequality that the poverty lobby were on about, and that was not a problem but a solution – for idleness and incompetence.(1) Within days of his appointment I attended a meeting with Patrick Jenkin, Thatcher's first Secretary of State for Social Security, and his top officials. They told him that the Child Poverty Action Group – Britain's most authoritative spokesmen for the poverty lobby – were asking, as usual, for a meeting with the new head of the Department mainly responsible for poverty policies. 'Who are they?' asked Jenkin; and, when they told him, he said: 'Crickets in the field! No reason why I should see them.'(2) Those of us who had an obsession about the injustice of poverty in a rich country – gained, in my case, from years of talking with the poorest people in Britain – had to spend eighteen more years under a government that prohibited its officials from talking about it.

So when, in 1997, we elected a Government that was prepared to talk about poverty again, and was soon promising to do something about it, a long nightmare ended. Thanks to academics like

John Hills and David Piachaud who had refused to be censored, and to Richard Best and the Rowntree Foundation who backed them (3), the new Government was armed with much of the knowledge it needed to start work on the problem.

But when Britain's establishment and the chattering classes to whom they listen have not discussed an issue for eighteen years, a lot of catch-up learning has to be done. The problems have moved on; a new story has to be told about them and about the society we are trying to create. Scotland can play an important part in that task.

In London, New Labour started by going back to old ideas about poverty; treacherous ideas. Viewed in this way, poverty is apt to become – and when conservatives return to power undoubtedly will become – laden with blame. The problems are located 'out there', among 'the poor'; and solutions will be found by taxing the rest of us – 'hard-working families' – without greatly disturbing our lives. Thus it was that Blair's Government began, not by listening to the poor themselves, but by setting up task forces and 'czars' to deal with drugs, truancy, teenage pregnancy and the like – confident that they knew what the problems were, and that they would be solved by changing the behaviour of the poor. (They have now learnt better.)

This philosophy shapes the whole politics of poverty and the responses of the poor themselves. People mobilise to fight for their rights as women, as ethnic and religious minorities, as people with particular disabilities, as lone parents, lesbians and gays; but it's much harder to mobilise a rainbow coalition of the poorest people – and when we try, their best leaders constantly desert them by getting jobs and becoming non-poor. Meanwhile women and the minorities who mobilise more successfully end up fighting for more of the top jobs and privileges in an unjust society, not for an end to injustice itself.

Equality: the new agenda

But a new story about society that defines our problems and goals in a different way is slowly taking shape. If we ask each of the more militant groups what they want, their varied answers have one common feature. They want to be treated with respect – a respect equal to that accorded to any other group in our country. Together, they want a more equal society.

That is a much more threatening prospect to a lot of people in the mainstream. It brings all of us into the policy agenda. Britain is now more unequal than most of its European neighbours, not because of the dire poverty of our poorest people but because of the runaway increase in incomes and wealth secured by our richest people. (4) Changing that is going to disturb powerful folk. Once we define the nation's problem not as poverty but as inequality, then everyone who selects people for jobs, awards pay increases, allocates hospital beds, or admits students to universities and colleges has to ask themselves whether they are part of the problem or part of the solution. These are dangerous questions: better opportunities for poor children to enter the best schools and universities will restrict the opportunities of families who now expect to win these places. Better opportunities for gypsy travellers to find legitimate stopping places provoke hostile responses from the neighbours. So we have to have a convincing story to tell which explains why movement towards a more equal society, if wisely managed, benefits everyone.

These are some of the points to make in that story. The great majority of crimes committed in this country are offences against property – theft, burglary and the like. When unemployment falls and low wages rise, these offences decline; we all benefit. When people with physical disabilities win easier access to housing and public buildings, and more user-friendly designs within these buildings, they have won a victory for all of us. Before we are through, most of us will be disabled to some degree, or caring for loved ones who are disabled. If you are reluctant to concede equal rights and respect to gays and lesbians, bear in mind that your own children and grandchildren may one day be among those who will be grateful for those things. Think too of all the benefits that people in the mainstream have gained from the work of previously impoverished but now increasingly successful minorities; the Asian pharmacists and doctors, the African nurses, sportsmen and transport staff, and the delightful music, the delicious cuisine and colourful clothing created by such groups. It was always thus: we owe many of the most heart-warming things about Glasgow to Irish, Jewish, Italian and other migrants of previous generations. Last summer a secondary school in Drumchapel won the cricketing competition that takes place all across Glasgow and Lanarkshire. An unlikely place to find cricket champions? Every boy in the team was the son of an asylum seeker.

If all this sounds too like liberal, middle-class romanticism, let's recognise that there are poor whites who benefit less from the contributions of immigrants, who fear competition for their jobs and homes, and who nurture (wildly unfounded) illusions about the benefits that newcomers are given. (5) That is why I began by saying that progress towards equality has to be wisely managed. It must also be led by politicians who are prepared to say these things – to tell the new story about our society.

There is hard, demographic evidence – Richard Wilkinson and Michael Marmott are among those who provide it (6) – that in more equal societies people tend to be healthier and to live longer than in more unequal societies at a similar stage of economic development. Even their drivers are safer and their criminals less likely to draw guns.

The idea that the rich are healthier than the poor is not new. But the better health and life expectancy of more equal societies are not confined to their poorest citizens; they reach up to affect more than half the population. 'Inequality', the Inland Revenue could justifiably print across our tax returns, 'damages your health'. (6)

I am not suggesting there is a simple, direct, causal link between equality and all these good things. Income distribution and life expectancy are both indicators or 'proxies', linked in many ways to factors that together help to create a happier, healthier society. 'Social capital', the concept some people have coined to explain these patterns, has been dismissed by others as merely a metaphor (7). It may nevertheless be a useful metaphor which should remind us that it's time western societies broke off their long, uncritical love affair with economic growth. Growth is fine for the rich. But, unless it works in equalising ways, it is likely to damage the rest of us.

What can Scotland do?

If that is the kind of story that egalitarians have to tell, what lessons can we learn from it? And how should they be applied in Scotland during the next fifteen years? My purpose here is not to offer a political programme but to ask the kinds of questions this story poses, and to suggest that Scotland can help to find the right answers to them.

Much that the Westminster Government is doing to get people back to work, to shift the distribution of benefits and tax burdens, to raise minimum wages and to improve schools in hard-pressed areas – the whole Gordon Brown agenda – is moving Britain in equalising directions (8). The Government never talks about equality for fear of frightening the horses; but the trend is clear. Even the statistics they use to measure reductions in poverty (which is defined as living on an income less than 60 per cent of the national average) are really measures of inequality. What can Scotland add to this momentum?

The Executive and Parliament have made an encouraging start. It's not perfection – why are the ethnic minorities unrepresented? – but it's a good beginning. Power is more accessible. We see much more of our Ministers than the English see of theirs, and they stay on after making a speech to talk with the people. Poverty Alliance delegates – not voluntary agency bureaucrats but people who actually experience poverty – choose half the agendas at meetings where Ministers and their officials talk with them about inclusion policies. Its Petitions Committee provides real opportunities for the public to contribute to the work of Parliament; and the building itself is a world-class example of what a people's parliament should be.

What more do we want? Being less panicky than Blair's team

about the Murdoch press and the tabloids, our leaders should talk more frankly about inequality than their counterparts down south. If they can take on the Catholic Church and its wealthy supporters over Section 28 (2A in Scotland) when New Labour at Westminster funked that, they should go further to inform and educate their people, telling them what a fairer Scotland could be like. John Hills' latest study (9) shows that average citizens know pretty well how much workers like themselves get paid, but greatly under-estimate what their bosses get. Another recent report by Karen Wren shows the Scots tend greatly to exaggerate the amount of help given to asylum seekers. (10) In Sweden, where official documents (which include tax returns) are all open to public inspection, everyone knows what their neighbours earn. If we had an equally mature attitude to these things we could compare the rewards of people at the top and bottom of each organisation, recognise that their wages all come out of the same kitty, and ensure that representatives of all grades play a part in deciding how the money is divided. (They would understand that professors may be worth more to a university and senior executives may be worth more to a firm than their security men and canteen staff – but how much more is a question worth discussing.)

The wages of less skilled workers depend heavily on the scarcity of labour at the bottom end of the labour market. If there's a queue of people waiting for your job, you can't get too stroppy about your pay. So getting more people back into work – particularly on Clydeside, in Dundee and the former coalfields – has to be a top priority. A buoyant economy will also need to offer more jobs for young graduates. We have succeeded in creating a huge higher education 'industry', but far too many of its graduates have to leave Scotland to start on their careers, or stay at home and do work that wastes their talent and training.

Child care suited to the needs of children and their parents, and better schools – particularly in neighbourhoods where the educational task is hardest – are other urgent priorities. The demand for nutritious, free school meals for all children should not be brushed aside just because it first came from Tommy Sheridan.

In every service – in the private sector too – we need to fix in professional minds the idea that we have to listen to, and learn from, the people who are to be served. Scotland has a strong tradition of community-based services: the Glasgow housing co-operatives built on that, and we are beginning to apply the same principals in other fields. Take a look at the New Gorbals, now being created after many years of disastrous public building that destroyed communities and provoked a massive flight of good people from this area. The creation of human-scale streets with human-scale shops, the provision of small public green spaces, play areas and private gardens, the mixing of tenanted and owner-occupied housing – indistinguishable from each other because all are of good quality – these are what Gorbals people asked for in long and lively meetings with Mike Galloway, first Director of the project, and his colleagues who worked from an office in the area that was open to the public. Together, they set standards, to be seen elsewhere in Scotland too, that should become the norm for our public service professions.

I could extend this list of things we should be doing, but these may be sufficient to show the directions we should take. To what destination? How far along this egalitarian route should we go? No sensible person expects complete equality in a world where there will always be differences in talent, energy and luck. But when is a society equal enough? Put this question to academics and they tend to disappear into a maze of definitions and paradoxes leading to paralysis by analysis. There is a simple answer to it. We shall be equal enough when different social classes, income groups and ethnic groups have similar life chances – similar chances of a healthy start in life, of getting an education that takes them as far as they are capable of going, of finding a partner and raising healthy children, and similar life expectancies. It can be done; the Scandinavians have already made a great deal of progress in that direction.

So what should Scotland look like in 2020? Class differences and ethnic differences in life chances, and differences in the pay and status of men and women should all be reduced, with all the implications for education, health care, and housing that follow from that statement. The range of incomes from top to bottom of the social hierarchy should be a matter for well-informed and critical discussion. All the main groups in Scottish society should be well represented in our Parliament and the corridors of power. We shall then no longer be talking about creating a 'classless society' – any more than we would seek a raceless or genderless society. We will have created an open, plural community in which different groups can be proud of their own traditions, their own contributions to Scotland, and know that those are respected by other groups. And we shall still be offering shelter to asylum seekers, whether they excel at cricket or something else.

Notes

[1] Keith Joseph and Jonathan Sumption, *Equality*, London, John Murray; 1979.

[2] The meeting (but not these words) appears in David Donnison, *The Politics of Poverty*, Oxford, Martin Robertson, 1982; page 164 et seq.

[3] For example, Joseph Rowntree Foundation, *Inquiry into Income and Wealth*, York, Joseph Rowntree Foundation, 1995.

[4] John Hills, *Inequality and the State*, Oxford University Press, 2004.

[5] Karen Wren, *Building Bridges: Local Responses to the Resettlement of Asylum Seekers in Glasgow*, Glasgow, Scottish Centre for Research on Social Justice, Glasgow University, 2004; page 38 et seq.

[6] M.G. Marmot and R.G. Wilkinson, *The Social Determinants of Health*, Oxford University Press, 1999.

[7] Richard Wilkinson, *Unhealthy Societies*, London, Routledge, 1996.

[8] Ray Pahl in Donald Robertson Memorial Lecture, Glasgow University, November 2004.

[9] Guy Palmer, Jane Carr and Peter Kenway, *Monitoring Poverty and Social Exclusion in Scotland 2004*, York, Joseph Rowntree Foundation, 2004.

[10] John Hills, *Inequality and the State,* Oxford University Press, 2004; page 34.

[11] Karen Wren, op. cit.; page 38.

19

Crime and Justice

ROGER HOUCHIN

IN A FAMOUS PASSAGE on the social functions of crime and criminal justice, Emile Durkheim, in 1895, wrote 'Imagine a community of saints in a perfect and exemplary monastery. In it crime, as such, will be unknown but faults that appear venial to the ordinary person will arouse the same scandal as does normal crime in ordinary consciences ... Thus crime is necessary. It is linked to the basic conditions of social life...'. Crime, he was arguing is inherent in social life: it is an unavoidable and necessary element of all social organisation.

The identification and prosecution of crime has functions for social life that complement those of religion. In describing their gods societies idealise their identity – their construction of their gods expresses their understanding of who they are, what they strive for and the values that bind them. In creating crimes societies establish a threshold of behaviours which, if practised, identify the perpetrators as not of them. Crime identifies, to use the term coined by Cohen, 'folk devils'.

Crimes are behaviours of symbolic meaning stronger, then, than those that are simply unwanted, inappropriate, disabling or inept. Such behaviours, whose disadvantage is often largely felt by the actor, can be addressed through programmes of education, social counselling or training and public health.

Crimes are behaviours of symbolic meaning stronger, even, than many failures to observe conventions or regulations or even many behaviours causing specific harms to individuals. Restitution for such behaviours can be ordered through processes of civil and private law. The role of any such orders by a court is not to punish but to compensate for the breach or the harm. Where there is a victim, the compensation is typically ordered to be made to the person harmed.

Crimes are breaches of norms or acts inflicting harm of such symbolic meaning that they are held to offend not primarily the victim, but the normative basis of the society itself. The response is primarily punitive: its purpose is not to grant remedy to the person harmed; it is a symbolic act communicating that the person who committed it, in doing so, put himself beyond the bounds of those shared values that bind the society together. (This picture, it is recognised, while its application may seem straightforward when applied to simple societies is considerably muddied if we try to apply it as it stands to complex and diverse societies, such as our own)

The response of society to crimes is similarly symbolic: the state responds by inflicting on the offender one or more of a range of harms from which, for others, it is one of its core responsibilities to give protection. If we look at the history of criminal justice we find punishments of inflicting pain, injury and mutilation; confiscation of property; enforced work; suspension of the protection of the law; ritualised shaming; banishment; deprivation of liberty; deprivation of life.

In all but a rump of states, shamefully led by some of the United States of America, killing is no longer used as a sanction for criminal acts. Confiscation of property, in the form of the imposition of monetary fines, is the most widely used sanction in Scotland – used in about 60% of cases in which a punishment is awarded – but it is little developed. In many circumstances in which fines are imposed the distinction between the criminal fine and a civil penalty is marginal.

Each of the other forms of punishment now finds elegant transformation in that multi-purpose social institution of the early 19th Century, the prison. In inventing the modern prison, the early Victorians concentrated into one penal technology all the sanctions that, throughout history, society had devised for its miscreants. It is a place of exile. It is a place of shame. It deprives its inmates of the enjoyment of their property. It takes away their liberty. It exposes them to danger and, in that powerful but archaic term found in the literature, to moral contagion.

Only in our very recent history and then only because of the sanctimony that governments feel able to express through international institutions has society's natural tendency to place its inmates outside the law and, in the name of 'lesser eligibility' – a doctrine that those subject to criminal sanction should enjoy conditions no more salubrious than those available to the most deprived in our communities –, to sustain levels of degradation and dehumanisation that only international supervision of the rights of all men to be treated as human beings has challenged. Only by offering to each nation the possibility of interfering in the business of others – through binding international treaties and supervision – have we been able to find a process by which some formal humanity has been brought to the conditions into which we have been prepared to cast our folk devils in the name of justice.

And the elegance of the prison as a response to crime goes beyond that. When the modern prison system was established in Scotland in the 1839 Prisons Act it was possible to ascribe to it a new social purpose. Not only did it allow all our available sanctions to be efficiently imposed in one sentence; not only was it the 'punishment and repression crime'. The 1839 Act also gave to the prison the purpose of 'reformation of criminals'. While the punitive content of imprisonment has remained virtually unchanged since then, we have seen a succession ways of conceptualising prisons reformatory ambitions. Penitence, correction, discipline, training, education, counselling, groupwork, psychological intervention are some of the policy banners under which the prison system has sought to pursue its reformatory goal. Chaplains, psychiatrists, social workers, personal prison officers, officer instructors, teachers, forensic psychologists – each group has had its day as the champions of personal change in prisoners. The reason that none has persisted is that none has been successful. The prison system does not work as an institution with a role in reducing levels of offending in society.

Imprisonment is the core sanction for those crimes that the courts feel merit that spectrum of sanctions that fulfil the social purpose of criminal justice – to mark those behaviours that are beyond the boundaries of what the society stands for – and where imprisonment fails, criminal justice fails.

It is for those reasons that, whereas the wish expressed in

Cathy Jamieson's recent policy paper 'Supporting Safer, Stronger Communities, Scotland's Criminal Justice Plan' to reduce the number of people sent to prison is to be welcomed, the cocktail of reforms that she proposes is fundamentally unsatisfactory. It is, of course, true that the courts are archaic and inefficient, that police performance in solving crimes is lamentable and that there is very poor co-ordination of response between the various agencies that might work constructively with those who come before the courts, but tinkering with the organisation of the existing institutions isn't going to have significant impact – a conclusion recognised, presumably, by an Executive that, while professing its aim to reduce the prisoner population, is investing heavily in providing more prisoner places.

Criminal justice, and imprisonment on which it relies so heavily, is failing not because its institutions are performing poorly; it is failing because we have been seduced by the elegance of the possibility that an institution that conveniently is able to parcel up such a full set of sanctions might also, by virtue of its having a captive clientele, be able to tackle the symptoms of our complex and insecure society.

In 1839, parliament wished to 'punish crime', now we punish criminals. And we punish them in the name of their reformation. Pursuing the joint aims of punishment and reformation we express the policy hubris that it may be in our power to 'manage offenders' – this segment of our society to whom we ascribe a perpetual label emphasising their separateness while purporting to wish to integrate them into our communities.

The mantra of the Executive's policy in this area is 'Reducing Re-offending'. Despite the rhetoric about diversion and alternatives to imprisonment the core tool deployed in this task is the prison. The default outcome of an arrest for crime is no diversion and non-use of the alternatives. That default outcome may relatively infrequently occur, but it is the constant shadow at the end of the line. The institution that shames, that exiles, that deprives, that disadvantages holds the central role in reform and re-inclusion, in welcoming those who have committed crimes back into participating and contributing membership of our society. By

2020 we need rather more explicit recognition of the lack of realism of that dependence.

At the beginning of this discussion I set up a distinction between unwanted behaviours to which we respond by offers of help and development, unwanted behaviours that trigger an order for restitution and unwanted behaviours of symbolic meaning to which we respond by rejection. It is, of course, for any society to decide into which of those three categories it wishes to place any acts. Suicide and homosexuality are behaviours that 50 years ago were criminal. We now view them quite differently. Drug misuse in the Netherlands is treated as a public health problem whereas we wage war on it with the toolbox of criminal justice. The parodying of people from other ethnic origins was until recently a widespread public entertainment; it could now be prosecuted.

Too frequently in our current discourse we consider that if the behaviour that we are considering causes widespread or publicised offence our response should be to resort to the approach that most strongly signals our disapproval. Too seldom do we hesitate to consider whether it might not be more effective to focus on a requirement for restitution or on working with the person whose behaviour gives offence to help them resolve any underlying problems. In doing so we forget that the primary purpose and the clear consequence of resort to criminal justice is to emphasise our abhorrence at the behaviour and our rejection of the person, a purpose and a consequence that lessens the probability of that person's successful re-integration back into the community as a contributing member.

It is and it will remain necessary to accept that outcome in some circumstances: our need to signal abhorrence outweighs our wish – or our capability – to reform, but, if criminal justice is to disencumber itself of the routine and fruitless burden that it now carries we have to be as parsimonious as we can in its deployment. If we are really interested in reducing offending then we should start to explore every avenue available to us to remove behaviours from the ambit of criminal justice and deal with them in ways that will be less likely to increase the probability of continued criminality.

Before turning to discuss some areas in which I feel progress could be made, I should like to turn from abstract speculation to empirical description and in so doing show that what reflection suggests must be the case is, in fact, what happens.

I had the opportunity in 2003 to look at the social origins of those members of our communities who were, on June 30th, the night that I collected my data, in Scottish prisons. The results were simultaneously both as one might expect and arrestingly dramatic.

I calculated imprisonment rates for segments of the overall population defined by gender, age and the level of deprivation of the community in which they gave their home address. The imprisonment rates I calculated varied from 10 per 100,000 for all women in Scotland to 3,427 per 100,000 for 23 year old men from the 27 local government wards that scored over 70 on the Scottish Index of Multiple Deprivation[1].

I clustered local government wards according to 10 integer intervals against the Multiple Index and calculated the imprisonment rate for each cluster and found a near absolute correspondence – throughout the entire range between the level of deprivation of communities and the rate of imprisonment of those who live there. Whereas 4 out of every 100,000 men from those communities with scores less than 10 were in prison on that night, there were 953 out of every 100,000 from our most deprived communities (SIMD = >70).

I found that 25% of the total prisoner population of slightly more of 6,000 came from just 53 of the 1,222 local government wards and that 50% came from just 155 wards.

I found that there were 269 wards from which there was no-one in prison.

That is, I found that the impact of the criminal justice process in Scotland is concentrated on a very particular segment of the population. It is focused on men. It is focused on young men. And it is focused on young men already excluded from normal benefits of decent housing, decent health, decent education and employment opportunities. That general conclusion might not be surprising. The extent of the skew, however, has to cause considered reflection.

A simple explanation is that these young men are, in the expression of our First Minister, 'neds' and what has to happen first and foremost to 'neds' is to get them off the streets. But if, as I found, 1 in 9 of the young men from our most deprived areas are going to find themselves in prison during their 23rd year, we have to consider whether we wish to continue to aggravate the problem with which we are faced by indulging our need to express our abhorrence at their behaviour in defiance of the evidence that in so doing we are simply confirming and compounding their existing multiple exclusion. And not only are we doing that, but by prioritising the punishment of this group we are aggravating the disadvantage and exclusion that will already be being felt by any children for whom, by the age of 23, they may be responsible.

I would argue also that much as we may dislike the lawless and often violent and self-destructive pattern of these young men's lives, it is not their behaviour that most affronts the important values that we would want to characterise Scottish life. They people an underworld from which it may be comforting for the rest of us, through the operation of the criminal justice system, to distance ourselves. Their values may seem atavistic. We may be irritated, affronted and some of us harmed by their behaviour, but it is marginal to the life of the great majority of us. The capacity of older, more influential people to act in ways that cause harm more profoundly offensive is far greater but seldom touched by criminal law.

What then might be achieved by the year 2020 to rescue us from the present drift into increasing, and increasingly extravagant and ineffective, attempts to repress crime? I would suggest that three developments might be pursued.

The first derives directly from the argument developed at the start of this discussion. We should seek to reduce the range of unwanted behaviours to which we choose to respond through processes of criminal justice.

To achieve this, we should prompt now a debate as to what are the forms of unwanted behaviour in respect of which we are prepared to risk the dangers of a predominantly expressive, denunciatory response. We should ask what are the values that the Scottish people hold sacrosanct and for breach of which we would be prepared to sanction the offender to the extent that we recognise that this will be likely to blight the rest of their life and render their contributing participation in community life less likely in the future.

We should be clear that any decisions we take in this area are of the utmost seriousness and we should seek to restrict the range of behaviours that falls within this ambit to the minimum. I would suggest that the guarantees of respect for individual rights such as are expressed in the European Convention on Human Rights, especially where behaviours impact adversely on the enjoyment by many of the rights to which we are committed, could provide a set of principles against which we could test whether specific behaviours justify a criminal justice response.

Whether ECHR would be the best such set of principles I am not sure. But I am clear that there should be principles against which proposals to create crimes should be assessed. It is because any behaviour can now become a candidate for statutory denunciation in a criminal justice act that we have seen the reckless creation of new crimes in the recent past. It should no longer be sufficient that there is a public outcry against a form of behaviour for it to be criminalised and contribute to the clutter of the processes of punishment.

We should also review the range of behaviours that presently constitute crimes against the principles that are developed and move out of the ambit of the criminal law all those that do not satisfy the criteria. That does not mean that we should tolerate these behaviours. To the contrary, it means that we should prioritise reducing their occurrence above denunciation of their commission. To achieve this we would develop ways of responding to them that give restitution to those suffering harm and we would focus on the underlying causes. We know what those underlying causes are. There are many pockets of young men in Scotland with no legitimate stake in the wider society in which they live.

I have argued that an inevitable and indeed intended consequence of criminal prosecution is the estrangement of the person convicted from their community. In expressing its abhorrence for a person's behaviour society rejects the person. The purpose may be to express abhorrence at the act. How we give expression to that abhorrence will decide the consequential extent of the exclusion of the person. It is the processes of criminal justice that will communicate to the person the extent to which the denunciation of their behaviour extends to denunciation of them as a person. It is the processes of criminal justice that more or less criminalise the person.

Unless we are prepared to imprison criminals and 'throw away the key' it is in no-one's interest to associate continuing exclusion with a punishment any more than is inevitable. I would suggest that we should review carefully the operation of our criminal justice processes and seek to reduce those aspects of practice that compound the exclusion that cannot be avoided.

Each process from arrest, to trial, to prison sentence, to supervised release should signal, 'Though we abhor what you have done, we recognise you as a member of our community who is valued and we look forward to seeing you return, on completion of your punishment, to your position as a contributing and benefiting member of your community'.

That is a tall order. What is achievable in the immediate future, is an examination of the practices of the police, prosecution, courts, prison service, social work departments against the principle that albeit that the person may have committed abhorrent acts they remain members of the public with all the respect due to them as human beings as we would expect for ourselves. We should abandon talk of 'offender management'. We do not want to create 'offenders'. We want to recruit participating and benefiting members of our communities.

Finally, we should take steps to give more authority and resource to communities to respond to unwanted behaviours that damage their quality of life.

As I have developed above, criminal law should not extend beyond behaviours that give flagrant offence to the core values of the Scottish people. The prosecution of crime, therefore, is properly a state function. But the lawless, self-destructive, disorderly and violent lifestyles that result at present in the great majority of prison sentences are symptoms of the inability of our social organisation to offer meaningful and engaging roles to significant and very specific minorities in our communities.

This exclusion from participation in fulfilling roles lies behind the patterns of behaviours that now fill our prisons. I am suggesting that there is both an ethical duty to those whose exclusion from such roles leads to the behaviours that we now punish and a strong interest on the part of all of us, rather than responding to their behaviour primarily by expressing our abhorrence of it, rather to prioritise its resolution.

The debate, as I see it, is quite simple. Is our primary interest to express our outrage at these behaviours we don't like by prosecuting them under the criminal law in the knowledge that doing so we will be ineffective in reducing the levels of such behaviour? Or is our interest in reducing offending? If it is the latter, three things should happen. Responsibility for responding to the problems should be removed from the remote institutions of the state and returned to the communities where the behaviour occurs. Those communities should be given the authority and the resources to tackle their own problems. Secondly, the responsibility of those whose behaviour gives offence for the harm they cause should be marked not by punishment but by processes of restitution, developed within civil and private law. Thirdly, investment should be available to tackle the causes of the problem. We know that half the prisoner population comes from a small number of acutely deprived communities. Unless we are prepared to eradicate the inequities in the distribution of the benefits of membership of our society and life in conformity with its laws, we have to expect that these excluded minorities will develop cultures that, while offering the benefits of alternative memberships to those who are otherwise marginalised, are threats and nuisances to the rest of us.

My agenda for the development of criminal justice between now and 2020, then, has 3 core elements:

Develop a set of principles against which to assess whether specific unwanted behaviours should be treated as crimes or would better be responded to by more constructive measures. As a consequence greatly reduce the ambit of criminal law and shift its emphasis away from petty offending, rooted in social exclusion, to behaviours that deeply offend the core values of the Scottish people.

Review the processes of criminal justice with a view to minimising the long-term socially disabling consequences of a criminal conviction

Invest more authority and resource in our communities to allow them to tackle the underlying social causes of lawless behaviour and to develop locally relevant means for those whose behaviour gives offence to make amends to those who suffer the consequences.

[1] The Scottish Index of Multiple Deprivation (SIMD) was first produced in 2003. It assessed each of the 1,222 local government electoral wards in Scotland against 5 multiple indices of deprivation: *Income Deprivation; Employment Deprivation; Health Deprivation and Disability; Education, Skills and Training Deprivation; Geographical Access to Services.* Those indices, in turn, were aggregated into one Multiple Index. The most prosperous communities scored in low single figures against the index, the most deprived, over 70.

SECTION VI
A Broad and Diverse Land

20

Cosmopolitan Scotland?

SALLY DAGHLIAN

FOR MANY, THE PREVAILING view of Scotland is of a monolingual, monocultural country. This is seen in much of the commentary that accompanied the recent arrival of asylum seekers as part of the Government's 'dispersal scheme'. While the Scottish press has never been quite as vitriolic as some of their sister papers south of the border, there has still been a detectable subtext that seems to query why there are any asylum seekers or refugees in Scotland at all. Many commentators and the public at large seem to have forgotten that Scotland has welcomed and benefited from the arrival of refugees throughout its history. Indeed the term 'melting pot' so often applied to the ethnic diversity of the USA could as easily be applied to historic Scotland.

Scotland is, and has always been, a multiracial and multicultural society. From ancient times when the country was made up of a mixture of tribes, right through to today. Until the late 1700s three languages were spoken here; Lallans (the language of the Lowland Scots akin to English), Gaelic, and pockets of a form of Welsh that survived in the southwest. Even today the northern isles of Orkney and Shetland would claim not to speak English at all but rather a dialect with affinity to ancient Norse. Our language is a rich stew of ingredients drawn from all the peoples who have come to Scotland. You wouldn't be able to sweep *stoor* under the carpet or *skelp* a behind without the Vikings. And where would our grannies be without their *bonny baffies* if it wasn't for the French? The Auld Ally France also gave us some of our most distinctive Scots clans; Robert the Bruce was a French descendent after all!

Pictland, the land of the painted people, was a troubled and hostile area when it was first encountered by the Romans. Although the Romans fought various battles in *Caledonia*, they all but gave up hope and built various walls to keep the marauding natives in place.

The original Scots arrived as refugees from a war-torn Ireland of the 5th Century. There is no record of exactly what the locals made of these new arrivals but since it was the Scots that introduced the written word this is perhaps not surprising. Since then the country has always accommodated refugees and newcomers of one kind or another. As the Romans moved north, defeated British tribes fled before them towards the shelter of Caledonia where they were tolerated by the locals – albeit reluctantly. With the collapse of the Empire, the Romanised Britons in their turn found sanctuary in Scotland from the marauding Saxons.

In the 7th Century St Columba fled Ireland to escape war and political instability and established his monastery at Iona where literacy and civilisation were kept alive during the dark ages. He was afforded sanctuary by the local Scots king as a refugee from his homeland. Iona's monks contributed enormously to the level of education in Dalriada (as the original Scots kingdom was then known), bringing skills the Scots lacked, strengthening the country and bringing lasting peace and eventual political unification with the neighbouring Picts.

Following the Norman Conquest large numbers of Saxons, whose ancestors had overrun Britain, now fled north in their turn to find refuge in Scotland, in the Borders and Lothian. The triumphant Normans were not far behind them with a significant number of wealthy French landowners settling in the fertile parts of Scotland at the behest of the Scottish King. Many of the great Scots clans are more properly French families such as Graham and Jardine as well as several of the Royal families of Scotland such as Bruce, Balliol and Stewart. These 'economic migrants' brought with them their religion as well as their language.

In the middle ages, refugees from religious persecution fled to Scotland for safety and these again contributed to the economic life of the country. The mercantile class was dominated by Dutch settlers, particularly in the wool and cloth trade (Fleming and Taylor are both Dutch Scots names) and helped develop the economy of the Burghs. This also helped Scotland forge links in Europe with trade taking place with countries as far away as Russia.

Around the same time the Scots began their dispersal around the globe. Some left of their own volition, others were driven out in the great clearance of the Highlands that followed the Jacobite uprisings of the 18th Century. There is barely a corner of the English-speaking world and beyond where the influence of Scots migrants was not felt. From the American Declaration of Independence through to the train system of India, to the administration of the Cape Colony, Scots made their mark.

In the 19th Century hundreds of thousands of Irish migrants sought shelter in Scotland from the effects of the potato famine, while many thousands of Jews arrived in Glasgow fleeing from the pogroms in Russia, Eastern Europe and the Baltic. Their descendants established a thriving community in the Gorbals, where Yiddish was widely spoken and they contributed to the garment trade and later to the economic and political life of the city and beyond. These include the late economist and broadcaster Ralph Glasser and Tory grandee Malcolm Rifkind.

In the twentieth century Scotland did her share of providing a home for eastern European refugees from the Second World War and the cold war, and in the 1970s we provided sanctuary for east African Asians fleeing Uganda and Chileans fleeing the brutal regime of General Pinochet. Between 1979 and 1981 over a thousand Vietnamese 'boat people' were resettled, followed by Bosnians and Kosovars all on government sponsored refugee programmes.

The past has often been called a foreign country and it is true that it is seldom visited. Most people have forgotten how Scotland developed, and that what was once viewed as foreign is now familiar and 'Scottish'. For example, you couldn't get a more Scottish name than Dougal. Yet, as you begin to investigate, you uncover the fact that Dougal or *Dubh Gall*, that is the black foreigner, originally referred to Danes or more colloquially 'pirate' – although the original meaning could well be closer to 'thieving foreigner'! It is also worth remembering that the dark and peaty lands of Sutherland were given the name because the land itself represented the most southerly outpost of the Viking Empire. The traditional first footing ceremony having to be done by a dark haired man reflects an ancient fear of the outsider with red or blond hair. The red hair associated today with Scotland abroad was brought by invaders, yet is now seen as almost an emblem of the country, as witnessed at any Scottish away game.

So what are the prospects for Scotland's new migrant and refugee communities? Integration, assimilation or alienation appear to be the options. Assimilation is a discredited notion which requires individuals to somehow relinquish their existing cultural identity and language and adopt solely those of the host country. In effect, to deny their ethnic cultural and linguistic heritage in favour of some mythical homogenous host society identity. Assimilation is neither realistic nor desirable. On the other hand, integration is a two way interactive and multifaceted process. It supports and enables migrants to become a valued and contributing part of the host community whilst respecting and accommodating cultural and other differences. The integration process allows refugees and other migrants to develop their potential and participate fully in the cultural and economic life of the country. In many respects it is the key to the development of harmonious communities and a society that supports and values all of its members. Integration is based on mutual rights and responsibilities. The migrant adapts to new obligations and circumstances and respects the laws of the land. The host community in its turn must also adjust and ensure full access to legal rights and services and enable full participation in social and economic life.

The alternative to integration is alienation. Today Scotland is confronted with a choice. It can either embrace change and support integration or it can preside over the growth of deep intractable divisions, hostility and poverty, borne of exclusion.

An inclusive, safe and welcoming society is key for the successful integration of refugees, migrants and other minorities. Integration requires social networks and bonds within and across communities and is facilitated by such features as language and cultural knowledge, security and a feeling of safety. Refugees themselves have sometimes simply described integration as 'feeling accepted'.

The new UK citizenship rules, as set out in the Nationality Immigration and Asylum Act 2002, require those who would become naturalised British citizens to demonstrate competence in the English language (and therefore tacitly acknowledges the key importance of language as a tool of integration), as well as a basic knowledge of British society, history and social norms, though the latter is somewhat difficult to define. To meet these requirements requires a significant commitment, and not just from the would be citizen. In the case of refugees the government itself must provide adequate resources to facilitate access to high quality accessible language classes and orientation sessions, as well as mentoring and support. Employers of migrants should also be encouraged to facilitate language and other orientation support, this is essential particularly where employers are actively bringing workers to the UK or targeting migrants to fill vacancies.

We need innovative social welfare policies and the necessary underpinning resources to tackle the problems of social, emotional and financial poverty and disadvantage in the wider community which breed violence, prejudice and resentment. Fear of strangers and hostility towards those perceived as different are symptoms of underlying insecurity and lack of confidence. Support for citizenship should not just be for new citizens.

Professor Ager of Queen Margaret University College Edinburgh, in collaboration with partners including refugee experts, has established a series of key markers of integration relating to employment, housing, education and health, and against which progress can be clearly measured. The development of this approach has been supported by the Home Office. We now have the tools to understand the processes of integration and monitor our success in Scotland. For example, employment is a critical area and barometer of integration. As well as the economic benefits, employment fosters self esteem and helps to build social networks. Refugees are often highly qualified and skilled, yet rarely find employment commensurate with their skills. Access to employment must be facilitated. Practical assistance is required in both verification and conversion of qualification, as well as to provide job shadowing and placement opportunities. The continuing problem of discrimination and prejudice which prevents some people from ethnic minority backgrounds accessing jobs or progressing must be addressed. Race equality must be tackled vigorously using both legislation and persuasion. Housing policy is of particular importance to ensure that we support integrated communities rather than creating ghettos which lead to the social segregation witnessed in other countries such as France where those of North African descent are clustered in vast suburbs physically and socially isolated.

Scotland has the opportunity to benefit from and harness the skills, energies and talents of migrants, but to do this it must address the fears and prejudices which inhibit integration. We require a zero tolerance approach to racist discrimination and attacks backed by strong enforcement. But this alone is not enough. We need to address xenophobia, not by preaching or haranguing people but by education, engaging in honest debate, and actively building bonds, bridges and links between hosts communities and new migrants.

So how can we do this? There are many positive examples using arts, culture and sport. Demonstrate this approach. For example in 2003 the Gallery of Modern Art hosted, in partnership with the Scottish Refugee Council and Amnesty International, a major contemporary exhibition on the theme of exile. This was an astounding success bringing an unprecedented number of visitors, some new to modern art and some new to human rights issues. The power of art to change views and challenge perceptions was evident in the visitors' comments. Running in parallel was a programme of work in local communities bringing together refugees, local people and artists. Some of this work is continuing in Sanctuary, a new Glasgow based project supporting artists in exile. The Scottish Refugee Council's drama project has toured Glasgow schools with a play that brings alive the experiences of refugees in a way that is accessible to young people. This has been well-received, stimulating debate and understanding. Our most recent project, carried out in partnership with the National Museums of Scotland and the RSNO, is 'Stuff'. Stuff is a multi-media arts project that encourages refugees and their neighbours to come together in creating something positive for their communities. The participants focus on their most treasured possession (their 'stuff') – a locket, a photo-graph, anything they feel is precious – then we ask them to make a piece of art about it. Through exploring these objects in a safe and constructive environment we hope to form bonds and stimulate debate between refugees and their host communities whilst creating innovative and exciting expressions of integration and solidarity in some of Glasgow's most diverse communities.

Projects which bring people together for leisure or to work for their geographic communities (whether planting trees or playing football) are invaluable in the creation of friendships and under-standing, as well as breaking down perceived barriers. Schools, sports associations, arts and cultural organisations all have a role to play, not just in the areas with significant migrant populations but throughout Scotland. Opinion polls and the evidence of the letter-s' pages of Scotland's newspapers indicate that those with the great-est fears of immigration are often those least likely to have contact with migrants.

Although there is much that can done at the level of individual refugees and those groups which would help them find their feet there is a real need for political leadership. Too often our politicians at Westminster (less so at Holyrood) are indifferent to the needs of asylum seekers and refugees and not infrequently are guilty of stoking the flames of intolerance. Several Home Secretaries have pandered to public fears, reaching for restrictive legislation rather than attempting to provide moral leadership.

Hostile tabloid headlines about asylum seekers 'eating our don-keys' and 'roasting the Queen's swans' do not help either. Most peo-ple in Britain have never met an asylum seeker or a refugee, yet current opinion polls now consistently put asylum as an issue high on the public agenda. The constant repetition of half-truths and assertions by some sections of the press has demonised a whole community. Yet there is hope. 65% of those surveyed in Scotland in a Mori Poll for Oxfam believe Scotland should offer a safe haven for refugees. Some 46% however think the number of asy-lum seekers living in Scotland is a problem. It is hard to reconcile such discrepancies. The common notion would appear to suggest that sympathy is the order of the day for refugees near their home-land but that it varies inversely with proximity of these refugees to the British Isles. The UK has long been recognised as a nation of charitable donors particularly supporting overseas disaster relief. However, such support does not always manifest itself in the same way for refugees who arrive on our doorstep.

Frequent legislation and reference to getting tough and stamping out abuse have fostered a climate where immigration and asylum are perceived as major threats to our social order and the public good. This in turn legitimises and encourages attacks, both physical and verbal, on asylum seekers and refugees. The truth is that the UK hosts only a tiny fraction of the world's refugees and, as one of the world's wealthiest nations we can readily afford to do so. Those countries in the developing world who support more than three-quarters of the world's refugees are often all but bankrupt and struggle to provide even the most basic levels of support. Yet with the limited support of UNHCR and other humanitarian aid agencies, they do. However, this would be threatened if wealthy countries are seen to shirk their responsibilities and close the door on refugees.

As a nation, we have international moral, legal and humani-tarian obligations. We should be proud to contribute to resolving global problems. Those for whom moral, legal or humanitarian arguments hold no sway should consider that Scotland also needs migrants for its common good and wellbeing. We need people to work in our industries and operate in our surgeries and pay taxes and send their children to school. These are the things that a society depends upon. We have a responsibility to ensure that those who come here, for whatever reason, are not bullied, harassed or made to feel unwelcome.

Amongst the refugees who come to Scotland are journalists, former government ministers, politicians, teachers and other pro-fessionals. Their reasons for coming to the UK in particular often include a belief in our justice and democratic systems. A faith that they will be treated fairly and will be safe. Many will (willingly) return to their countries of origin when it is possible. Do we want them to return and broadcast views of Scotland as an inhospitable nation where foreigners are derided and abused when they could return as ambassadors for Scotland?

The Scottish diaspora stretches to every corner of the world. Scots have assumed the right to travel and settle wherever they choose whether for economic or other reasons. In the past flight was often of necessity, forced by poverty or persecution, or the sharp end of a redcoat bayonet. Migration to and from Scotland is not new. Today Scotland has a unique opportunity to invest in and support the development of an integration framework harnessing the human potential of all its citizens.

So what will Scotland be like in 2020? Scotland does not stand still, nor should it. We are not the same as we were in 1920, even less so than in 1820, yet there is continuity. We don't have to say 'out with the old' when we welcome the new. Identity and culture are not relics in a museum, nor are they monoliths. Education, class, geography, gender, religion, family background, political beliefs and individual foibles and philosophies are some of the elements which inform and contribute to our personal identities and cultures. Scotland must embrace cosmopolitanism. This means tackling prejudice and racism, promoting human rights and respect for difference, whether arising from culture, creed or ability.

The best known symbol of Scotland (love it or hate it) is her tartan, head on to the world wide web and search for the word 'tartan' and you will find some 1,620,000 sites listed with some reference or other to the plaid of Scotland. There is even now a celebration of all things Scottish in New York that bears the title 'Tartan Day'. In many ways Scotland's ethnic diversity is like the tartan, with strands of many colours, just as there are many ethnic groups in Scotland; some bold and dominant, others feint and narrow, but each band and stripe criss-crossing each other to create a pattern recognised the world over as distinctly Scottish.

The Scots are drawn from many lands, from Ireland and England, from Scandinavia and France, from the East Indies and the West Indies, from the ancient lands of Eastern Europe and the new-drawn lands of Africa. Some arrived wearing horned helmets and pillaging as they went. Others descended the steps from an aeroplane carrying with them all that was left of their worldly possessions. Our identity is a tapestry, the threads of which come from many sources, some older, some very new, but all part of the whole and continuing to grow and blend. The new threads do not destroy the old but throw them into sharper relief, adding new depth and meaning to existing patterns. One does not focus on a single theme, or even on a few. The pattern must be enjoyed as a whole. Wherever refugees came from, whenever they arrived, they are now all threads in that rich tapestry we know as Scotland.

21

North of Shettleston

JEAN URQUHART

THE HIGHLANDS. That'll be the area north of Perth then? Glencoe, that's the Highlands. Some say the Highlands don't begin until you are north of Inverness – but no Munro bagger could possibly agree. The Highland Council boundary defines the highlands for the purpose of this paper. The Highland Council area with a population of just over 200,000 and covering 10,000 square miles – our local government serves an area the size of Belgium. It is obvious that there is little that is 'local' about Thurso in Lochaber and little that is 'local' about Lochaber in Thurso. There is 175 miles between these communities yet they have a common council comprising 80 councillors. (Now that the freedom of information act has become law anyone, at any time, can check how many council miles are travelled by these same 80 councillors in the course of local governance). Erosion of local government and the centralisation of service delivery are much talked about. Core funding for the council is reduced year on year and new money comes ring-fenced to fund new directives of the Scottish Executive.

Many of our problems are a result of so much land and so few people. Supersparsity it's called. Our greatest strength is often our greatest problem. A real problem when the discussion is about the school transport budget and a real asset when encouraging folk to live here. A real problem when we try to introduce new Scottish Executive initiatives like Community Planning but a real asset when we promote ourselves in Europe and elsewhere.

The land is our greatest asset and it is fantastic. Little travelled as I am, I happily accept the plaudits heaped upon our landscape by the many thousands of visitors met during more than thirty years of working in Ullapool. People from all over the world who find their way here declare that there is nowhere like it on earth. I have never challenged their opinion. And anyone who has ever driven from Durness to Ullapool (via Drumbeg), or stood on Big Sand in Gairloch looking towards Skye and the Hebrides on a clear day or climbed Bein Ghoblach for a winter view of An Teallach wouldn't either.

It is easy to get passionate about this land; it is easy to get romantic about it too. Community buy-outs could be the beginning, the very beginning, of a necessary revolution. Absentee land owners have hindered much and for too long; many have abused their power by restricting developments, by denying land for housing, and by denying competition if they own local shops or petrol stations.

For generations young people have been encouraged in education as the 'way out' of the highlands. Historically children brought up in the highlands have left to seek better opportunities elsewhere, never to return to work or live in the area again. Given that excelling academically was seen to deliver a passport to success, conversely, not leaving was akin to failure. In recent years this has fundamentally changed. There are a growing number of young people who are choosing to live here. The establishment of a University of the Highlands and Islands (UHI) is already making a difference. It currently has fourteen colleges and fifty learning centres across the Highlands, Perthshire, Argyll and the islands. This is not intended to keep our young folk here when they have a desire to leave but rather it delivers higher education to those who wish to study here and may offer opportunities for employment for returning graduates. It also attracts students into the highlands to study. Sabhal Mor Ostaig, the gaelic college in Skye has an enviable reputation and its presence declares a new confidence in the language and culture. Creating new job opportunities in learning and teaching and changing communities in a positive way.

Lack of affordable housing is the biggest barrier to development and the main reason for the predicted depressing demographic. Regeneration is the name of the game and the depopulation trend will not be reversed until we address the housing problem. We need to change planning law and be much more creative in housing design. Some energy, enthusiasm and political leadership are essential to inspire new and different ways of building houses in the 21st Century. The problem is nationwide I know and the most unimaginative and depressing housing estates are spreading across Scotland like a rash. Nothing distinguishes one estate from another, whatever part of our country they are built in. Why are we allowing this to happen? I want to believe that we could design houses for the locale, homes designed for and special to that place. One design does not fit all and what might be right for Watford is rarely right for Inverness. The Highlands, with an abundance of land should have so much to offer. Could we not use new materials? First person to recycle old tyres, old plastic and old cars into house building materials will become a national hero (if we were good at recognising national heroes that is). Recycling in rural Scotland is another challenge, but little sign of rising to it. Why, when we declare that we want our rubbish separated into plastic, paper, textiles, aluminium/tin, garden and food waste, are we still building homes with space for only one bin? If we don't make it practical to collect and recycle waste, we wont make it work. But we can make it work and that has to be the message delivered.

Sustainable development. Two words that became ubiquitous. Will the industrialisation of wind energy prove sustainable – or economically viable? Developing renewable sources of energy is essential; involving local communities in the process is admirable and local communities developing their own renewable energy is desirable.

But what, apart from money, will the Western Isles get from 230 large wind turbines? Who will really foot the bill for the safe transmission of energy via pylons, sub-sea cable across the Minch and more pylons across the highlands at a cost of more than £600m? Small is beautiful and development of this natural resource, wind, could benefit the area where it is produced. That's value added. What about the islands and other parts of the highlands where wind energy is being produced actually benefiting by way of cheaper electricity? It would be a real incentive to re-locate or start up a new venture in an area where energy, now a considerable cost of any business balance sheet, would cost less. If, as has been said, the

Western Isles have the equivalent of striking oil, then let there be some benefit to all of the islanders. A global company offering to pay the council compensation money, even if it is a few million, has to be less attractive in the long term. There are other arguments about pylons and landscape that are well reported elsewhere and I believe to be the least interesting aspect of these developments in a way. If we compare with the oil industry then there is a perfect example of why we must manage this differently; the country must reap the reward of exploiting our natural resources. The country must decide whether the investment in the infrastructure is desirable for social, cultural or economic reasons. This is not about heavier taxation but rather the potential of local involvement and invest-ment. The high-handed manner in which wind-farm developments are introduced to local communities is unacceptable. Equal opportu-nity, early discussion in the planning process, clarity of purpose and real local benefit are not impossible. Political determination is not enough and a strategy for wind and tidal power generation is miss-ing. At a time when this development should be exciting everyone it is tearing communities apart, the debate is ill-informed and there is no political leadership or sharing of political vision if it exists.

Tourism plays an important part in the highland economy. I am not of the opinion that we should offer a chocolate box image of the highlands and there should be no pretence. It is my experi-ence that visitors enjoy their discovery of a new place and all of its industry. Mostly they want to join in and share a bit of our way of life, feel welcomed and included. Clean and comfortable accom-modation that meets basic standards should be a given and after that there are individual interests and needs that may or may not be satisfied. When we start to think that there is such a person as a tourist, some homogenised being who can be interpreted and serviced because the research has been done that tells us 'what the tourist wants', then we will fail.

Scotland can and does welcome people and I believe we instinctively know what to do and how to offer hospitality. We may lack knowledge of our country and we may lack confidence, but we must not interpret this as being unable to look after visitors. It is important to note that getting good service in bars and restaurants and hotels is not the whole story. If we keep people ignorant of their own country and its history, geography and culture then we are less able hosts. If we lack confidence we hide behind a corporate slogan and feel inferior in our service to others. The highlands of Scotland must resist the mundane, the pedantic and the boring interpretation awarded by our failed lead body, VisitScotland. Why, in a country well endowed with writers, artists and musicians, don't we use them? Why doesn't Alasdair Gray write visitor information leaflets for Glasgow or George Gunn for Caithness or Ali Smith for Inverness.

And perhaps this is the nub of what I would like to say about the highlands. Why are we so reluctant to invest in what we have? Why is Irish tweed on every catwalk in Rome, Milan, Paris and New York and the Harris tweed industry failing? Why can we not distribute local produce when we are producing some of the worlds finest? Why do we find it so difficult to invest in ourselves? Why do we find it so difficult to celebrate difference?

Jim Hunter, the recently retired Chairman of Highlands and Islands Enterprise (HIE) delivered a speech where he talks about the Celtic Tiger and talks up the highlands for being progressive. Sites the growth in population in parts of the highlands, against the falling figures outside the highlands. New industries, new technologies, better communications, better way of life, better health, better roads, less crime and active citizens. I'd endorse most of that and feel part of it in a small and sustainable kind of way.

The A9 is still shorter going south though. For too many people in Scotland the highlands are unknown, a dark secret, backward, uncivilised, unimportant. Until they come here. And they would if we only had houses. There can be no smart, successful Scotland as long as folk are sleeping on the street or emigrating to get a roof over their head. Housing is the key to the further regeneration of the highlands and the regeneration of the highlands will make smart successful Scotland united and inclusive.

The highlands and islands in the 21st Century should and could become far more important to the nation than in the past. It is a place full of potential where opportunity abounds. A place where the landscape itself has influence and makes us more respectful of the environment and the power of nature. Like much of Scotland, it is truly admired and enjoyed by thousands from other parts of the UK and abroad but is often disregarded and undervalued by us ourselves.

22

Capital City 2020

DONALD ANDERSON

OUR VISION FOR EDINBURGH is ambitious. By 2020 we want it to be the most successful and sustainable city in Northern Europe.

Already Edinburgh is a success. What was once a sleepy provincial city has been consciously and carefully transformed into a dynamic modern capital for the 21st Century. In Scotland this presents the country with a problem. Culturally Scotland is much more comfortable with the politics of failure than the politics of success.

Politicians, and what are conventionally described as the chattering classes, have spent a generation fighting cuts, protesting at mass unemployment and campaigning for home rule. Across Scotland wealth and work are more readily available than for any time in the last forty years. Despite this, in the words of Edwyn Collins, there are 'too many protest singers, not enough protest songs.'

The problems of Glasgow not only generate more debate and discussion than the success of Edinburgh; they produce more debate than the successes of Glasgow. Glasgow has seen record job growth and, between 1994-2004, a massive 62% reduction in unemployment, 82% reduction in long-term unemployed and 98% reduction in long-term youth unemployment (at present only 75 youngsters are classified as long-term unemployed). At the same time it has delivered a year-round tourism industry and become the UK's third tourism destination, but still it finds itself at the centre of fierce debate about its failures. Liverpool, by comparison, is only just pulling itself up to the level of success Glasgow has achieved for many years. But, in Scotland, it is always the negatives that catch the attention and the headlines.

Understanding Edinburgh's success and, more importantly, supporting Edinburgh's success is vital not just for the city, but for

Scotland. Flourishing economies around the world are now built on thriving cities. We need to make sure that what Edinburgh has achieved, by and large on its own, now gains the support of the public, politics and resources of the nation. Such investment in Edinburgh and in Glasgow will pay off not just for our cities, but is the only means of ensuring the success of the whole of Scotland.

So, why is Edinburgh a success, what has been achieved and how do we ensure that in 2020 we realise our vision?

It is worth reflecting, for a moment, on our feats. We are a major financial centre and home to the world's sixth largest bank. Independent analysis shows that Edinburgh is forecast to be the fastest growing UK city over the period 1999-2005."[1]

Unemployment has stayed below 3% for the last four years, probably for the first time in history and there are now three jobs for every jobseeker.

We are the UK's second most important tourist destination and with 9 Best City Awards from the *Guardian/Observer* newspaper and Conde Nast travellers' bible in the last 6 years, we have a trophy cabinet that would be envy of Manchester United Football Club.

Our tourism infrastructure is well developed and accommodation for major companies in the city is modern and well served.

Our people are well skilled and highly qualified. Quality of life has never been better and is now arguably the best in the UK. Our cosmopolitan city – 24% of people in Edinburgh are born outside the city – is attracting talented people who want to share and contribute to our success.

That is the story so far. What of our future? We cannot just sit back, bask in our success and naively assume the capital will continue on its bountiful path.

To achieve our vision, we need to be ambitious and invest for success. If we are to really take our capital and nation up a level, multi-layered policies need to be implemented consistently over a long period of time. For those that see politics simply as a popularity contest, the easy way out is to take short-term decisions and make quick hits. This will do us all an injustice though in the longer-term. The route to reaping real and long-lasting rewards for ourselves and our children is to accept the long-term nature of investment and establish incentives that re-inforce these long-term decisions.

Such ambition is needed when you consider the increasingly tough and competitive world we inhabit. Many other cities in Europe and around the world are raising their game and we are all jockeying for position. Edinburgh and Scotland are not alone in wanting to be seen as a prime tourist destination, a location to do business and a place where you can enjoy a high quality of life.

Our competitor cities are investing heavily in infrastructure and the public realm, in service delivery and in marketing and promotion. Already we see fledgling festivals emerging in other parts of the UK, overseas countries developing their financial services sector and other cities overtaking us with their public transport offering. We need to continue to evolve, to pioneer and offer a unique package that will attract businesses, residents, tourists and investors.

Perhaps the most recent and obvious example of this phenomenon that directly affects the city region is the move to 'offshore' financial services and 'call centre' type jobs. This sector now accounts for some 200,000 direct and indirect jobs in Scotland – 10% of the country's workforce

Given the importance of financial and business services to Edinburgh, the wider city region and indeed the rest of Scotland – the offshoring phenomenon has potentially massive implications for us.

In recent months there have been a series of announcements of job transfers from the UK to locations abroad. Scottish Widows, Lloyds TSB's specialist provider of life assurance, pensions and investments products, currently employs 5,000 people and is headquartered in Edinburgh. It is undertaking a pilot exercise in 2004 involving up to 50 roles being carried out in India.

A recent report by consultants Bain & Co estimated that the offshoring market in India would increase by 57% by 2006 and the market in Russia by 45% over the same period. Accentuate, a firm of IT consultants, expects there to be particularly strong growth in offshoring finance and accounting functions, jobs that not long ago had to be within the purview of head office.

In a broader context, Deloitte & Touche estimate that as many as 730,000 European financial services jobs will migrate offshore by the end of 2008. They highlight that the cost saving of around 39% puts enormous pressure on companies to move some operations offshore.

To maintain a strong financial sector, Edinburgh will have to show that quality, not cost, is a real competitive advantage. Edinburgh is not short of strengths with which to sell itself – a well-educated population, expanding airport, world-class cultural facilities, a reputation for being dynamic and innovative, excellent universities and schools and an improving and expanding integrated transport network.

But we need to keep on our toes, pursue a diverse economy and make sure that Edinburgh's package remains attractive. We must plan and act now to sustain future economic success for the benefit of not just Edinburgh and the surrounding region, but for the whole of Scotland. We can only do this if we understand these issues and, importantly, agree what to do about them.

Recognising this, and in an attempt to stimulate a wide ranging debate on the strategic issues and longer term challenges facing the Edinburgh City Region, the Council together with key public sector partners and the private sector initiated a major scenario planning exercise. The resulting scenarios trace two possible futures for the Edinburgh City Region between now and 2020. (information can be found at www.edinburgh.gov.uk/capitalreview – click on 'links/research')

If you have not read these scenarios I would encourage you to do so, but briefly, 'Capital Punishment' features a cushioned, almost 'genteel' decline. In this we are all subject to a deteriorating quality of life, conservative views, gridlock and poor public transport, lack of social housing, disjointed and timid vision, infrastructure decay, business becoming detached, government spending focuses on the west of Scotland, exodus of head offices and a general feel bad factor.

'Capital Gains' illustrates the impact of a continuing boom in the financial services sector, population growth, the introduction of an integrated solution to the transport challenges, desirable quality of life, women increasingly in leadership positions, bold vision, burgeoning civic pride, big events hosted in the city, immigration and a feel good factor.

The reality is that neither scenario will prevail in its entirety in 2020 – although, interestingly, already we can see elements in both beginning to emerge and become issues for consideration. That is exactly the point of the exercise – to highlight the key strategic challenges, the choices that we have to make and the consequences of these choices.

Transport emerged as the single most important issue that we need to tackle as we move forward. Put another way, failure to resolve the city's transport problems was considered to be the most likely impediment to future economic success.

A majority of the employers we consulted with indicated that congestion and the general lack of predictability in the network was beginning to cause them major concerns. It was making business less effective and efficient. The problem is exacerbated by some of our other big challenges – the availability of affordable housing and the continuing tight labour market in the region – which we are also tackling.

Business leaders are becoming increasingly aware that many of their employees have to make long and frustrating journeys to work. This is because workers either live well out of the city, experience greater congestion on their route or a combination of both. This has serious implications for productivity – employees often turn up for work tired and stressed – and for companies' ability to attract and retain additional staff of the right calibre.

There is also a view that we need to invest heavily in public transport to bring ourselves up to the minimum standard of our key competitor cities. Business leaders talked in terms of the need to deliver a 'step change' in the quality of our public transport system. The re-introduction of trams and greater connectivity that exists in cities like Marseilles, Strasbourg, Amsterdam, Barcelona and Nantes were seen as key to this.

We are working towards such a step change. The Council now

has plans and funding for two tram lines. Research has shown that trams designed simply to meet transport needs will not improve a city's competitiveness though[2]. To be effective a tram system needs to be designed to change the ways in which people perceive and connect with the city. It is for this reason that our integrated transport policy, of which the trams are a core element, includes the congestion-charging component. The logic is simple. Car usage in the city continues to grow at a rate that is not sustainable. The road space in the city is finite. We therefore need a means of rationing its usage. The congestion charge will do this but it will also encourage the 'modal shift' necessary to free up the network at peak times.

The congestion charge would generate a significant amount of revenue – an estimated £760 million over 20 years that would be used to deliver and improve a wide range of transport projects across the region. This would include a third tram line. In addition, it would fundamentally change our concept of mobility, accessibility and connectivity in the city.

In February 2005, the people of Edinburgh will have the opportunity to vote in a referendum on our preferred transport strategy, which includes congestion charging. I hope that they take a moment to consider carefully this important crossroads in the history of the capital. They will have the chance to vote for a transport system fit for the 21st Century. This would deliver enormous benefits to the people in the city region but, crucially, it would give our businesses the platform they need to compete and take maximum return from the city's core strengths.

As well as investing in success, we need to get better at telling the rest of the world about it. We are not inclined to shout our success from the rooftops, but this is essential if we are to compete on the world stage. It will help us attract investment, businesses and tourists.

A brand is currently being developed which will promote Edinburgh and the Lothians. This will be launched in Spring 2005. Research conducted by the project team has shown that beyond the UK, awareness of Edinburgh is low as a place to visit and do business.

They have identified many qualities which are well worth

making a fuss about though. Interviewees, who can be described as knowing Edinburgh well, viewed Edinburgh as a city that is inspiring, magical and beautiful, with a distinctive atmosphere and dramatic physicality. They also identified the city's character as being intelligent and sophisticated, but in an understated way. Our strengths were identified as being accessible and compact, quality of life, education, innovation and safety.

We, of course, cannot do all of this alone. Cities are recognising the benefits of developing closer working relationships with other cities. Scotland is fortunate to have two world-class cities within 40 miles of each other. By combining our joint weight, pioneering innovative joint projects and facing the wider world together, I believe our two small cities and Scotland stand a much better chance of success economically, culturally and politically.

The benefits of collaboration between cities are beginning to be much more clearly understood and it is a policy that is being actively pursued by a growing number of cities such as Malmo and Copenhagen, Milan and Turin and Liverpool and Manchester. Collaboration between cities can provide a mechanism to better utilise resources, physical assets and human capital in such a way that their combined position in the global economy is improved. It's about working smarter and more effectively together on areas of common interest – or to use the jargon 'collaborating to compete'.

I am a strong believer in partnership between Edinburgh and Glasgow. It is a commitment that is shared by my counterpart in Glasgow, Councillor Charlie Gordon. The reality is that we have been working closely with Glasgow on a number of fronts for some time, but perhaps the most visible example to date was the joint promotion of Scotland by the Lord Provosts of Edinburgh and Glasgow at the Tartan Day celebrations in New York last year. The time is now ripe for our two cities to build on and formalise our relationship to help us pack an even better punch.

Areas of potential collaboration between Edinburgh and Glasgow are being explored. These could include tourism marketing, trade development, joint lobbying, securing new international events and joint promotion of city growth sectors such as financial services, biotechnology and the creative industries. It is proposed that monies from the City Growth Fund could be used to fund collaborative projects.

Relationships and networks between the public and private sectors also need to be improved. Edinburgh has been very successful to date in engaging the private sector, especially with delivery of key projects in the city. We have broken new ground for local authorities by the innovative way we have established joint venture companies to deliver our large projects.

The focus to date though has largely been on project delivery. However, some of our European rivals have much better, long-standing networks and forums for engaging with local businesses on an on-going basis. These are used to discuss and agree a whole range of issues of importance to the city from governance to future strategy and direction.

Such an arrangement would put Edinburgh in a good position to tackle the challenges en-route to 2020. As a means of starting this process, I have invited some prominent members of the local business community to join a Business Assembly. The purpose of the assembly will be to establish a meaningful on-going dialogue with representatives of the private sector, to provide a forum for discussion, to share ideas and to exchange information. I hope that over time the assembly can add real value and an extra dimension in our effort to ensure the city continues to prosper.

To continue with this progressive and forward-thinking agenda, the City of Edinburgh Council needs to continue to benefit from strong leadership, the ability to make big decisions and have efficient practices. It must also win the support, rather than the resentment, of the nation. We must work to change our economic factions and our culture. The culture of doom and gloom must be placed firmly to one side. Edinburgh and Scotland can and must be confident about our success. We must build a relationship with the rest of the UK and with Europe that sees Edinburgh as *the* location to live in, invest in and visit. Our quality of life and the quality of our people must be mobilised and supported to achieve their full potential.

This is one of the most beautiful cities in the world, located in one of the most beautiful countries in the world. We have some of the sharpest minds in academia and in business. We have a strong reputation as straight-talkers and straight-doers. Our education system is producing increasingly highly qualified young people. We are cosmopolitan rather than metropolitan in our approach. We not only welcome the huge component of English and other nationalities who choose to be Edinburgh's citizens; they are an essential ingredient in our future success.

Our small, beautiful and successful city can be the catalyst for a small, beautiful and successful country. This is a world class city – now is not the time to put down what we have, but raise our game. Scotland, with the vital ingredients of a strong Edinburgh and Glasgow, can become the strongest and most sustainable economy in Northern Europe.

This generation of Scots, particularly politicians who have protested so much and so well in the past, need to move into the role of thinkers and doers for the future. Having confronted and defeated the forces of centralisation in the 80s and 90s we must rise to the challenge of delivering from our success. This is Edinburgh and Scotland at the dawn of the 21st Century and we can, must and will do it.

[1] On first page: Extract from Edwin Morgan poem 'Open the Doors!' reproduced by kind permission of the Scottish Parliamentary Corporate Body

[2] Docherty, I. (2004) 'Connecting Edinburgh to itself and to the world', presentation to the City of Edinburgh Council / Scottish Enterprise / Centre for Scottish Public Policy conference on 'The Edinburgh City Region in the 21st Century', 11 May, Edinburgh. P 224

23

Scotland: Organising for Peace

LINDA FABIANI

SCOTLAND'S PARLIAMENT RECONVENED IN 1999, reclaiming some measure of democratic determination after a period of almost 300 years. Few institutions can have had a gap in their activities that spans such a change in international context.

In 1707, the biggest factor in Scotland's decision to enter the United Kingdom was an economic one; the right to access England's American colonies. Seventy years later this decision was rendered obsolete when America secured its independence. By this time Scotland was playing a major role in the subjugation and governance of the largest empire the modern world has seen. That empire collapsed in the middle years of the 20th Century, and from the 1950s onwards, through the Cold War and the nuclear age, the USA has increasingly come to dominate international relations, with all of the former European colonial powers struggling to find an alternative to the destructive competition that saw Europe decimated by a seemingly endless series of conflicts. By the time our parliament reconvened in 1999, most former colonies had been freed from direct external control and had processes established for self-government, some democratic, some not.

However, despite the process of decolonisation, globalisation combined with the growth in US military, economic and political might, means that populations of the former colonies see effective control of their economy and resources as much in the hands of the West as ever. Looked at from the perspective of underdeveloped countries, the West's domination of the global economy can be seen as no more than commercial and cultural neo-colonialism.

Whether we acknowledge it or not, our historic development is seen as an expression of a set of beliefs and an approach to society that do not necessarily accord with those of the populations of many of the recently (in historical terms) liberated countries. While the process of decolonisation has seen a growth in the number of countries in which an alternative set of values hold sway, the power of the corporate West to broadcast and disseminate the West's values has increased and continues to increase daily. Also, the post-colonial settlement in many areas reflects more of the relative success of the colonial powers than a natural resolution of local disputes over land and resources, or development of governance arrangements among people with perceived mutual interests.

Situations ripe for disputes abound across the world: ethnic and religious strife in the Kosovo/Albanian/Macedonian region; the splitting of Kurdish groups amongst Iran, Iraq, Turkey; division of the island of Timor between the animist/Roman Catholic community in the former Portuguese colony East Timor and Muslim domi-nated former Dutch colony West Timor. In some countries there is internal division, perhaps reflecting continued political or economic dominance by a colonial elite, without the clear consent of a majority of the population. In some cases, no effective governance has been established and competing private interests have led to continuing instability and in some cases, chaos and genocide.

The example of Zimbabwe is stark, the backlash from an oppressed population leading to similar abuses of human rights as under the old regime. Where we proselytised a 'superior culture' and sought to impose our own values, we left instead a legacy of dis-possession and resentment which has become the perverse justifi-cation for an undermining of society in that former colony.

Prior to the incorporating Union in 1707 Scots were reputed diplomats to many European courts and Scots soldiers of fortune were sought after additions to many European armies. Since 1707, both of these strands of Scottish expertise continued to develop in the context of the growth and decline of the British Empire and subse-quent international developments. Between now and 2020 Scotland faces new challenges in a changing world. The recent decision by the UK government to destroy the Scottish regimental system was a clear signal that there is no 'no change' option available.

The Scotland re-emerging from the shadows of its larger

neighbour into this new world has to stake its place in the world. It has to set its own goals, establish new relationships, participate in the international arena, and decide how to deploy its resources to best effect. Some might suggest that this lack of a clear definition of Scotland's place in the world is evidence of our immaturity as a nation, yet another reason why we should stay where we are in international terms, a stateless, invisible nation. Yet, is there any evidence that the UK is much clearer about its place in the world than Scotland?

It is over 40 years since US Secretary of State Dean Acheson issued his famous challenge that 'Great Britain has lost an empire and not yet found a role.' That this question has yet to be fully answered by the British Government has been acknowledged as recently as January 2002, when Tony Blair said 'We are not a super-power, but we can act as a pivotal partner... a force for good... I believe we have found a modern foreign policy role for Britain'.

Of course, events since then have made clearer just how Tony Blair sees that role being played out. The UK's Prime Minister sees Britain's role post-Empire as providing a bridge between Europe and the US; a link between the old imperialists of Europe, with their cultural diversity and inherited divides, and the new imperialism of American and Western global economic, cultural and moral dominance. This is evidenced perhaps most strongly in the willingness to comply with the USA over the Iraq issue, to use the office of Prime Minister of the UK to preach the gospel according to George W. Bush to the rest of Europe, rather than acting in concert with European partners. On the streets and in the oil fields of Iraq, it is the forces of global corporations that are seen to be as much part of the occupying forces as the US Marines, their military allies and increasingly, civilian aid workers.

Bush and Blair have made plain their vision of the future. The West will protect its global dominance, with less direct control than in the past, but more subtle methods of subjugating the interests of the developing countries. This is being done, and will continue to be done, through international bodies such as the World Trade Organisation, World Bank and the International Monetary Fund, in some of whose critical deliberations the global corporations have secured direct participation. The US has made it clear that it will choose to be bound by the work of such organisations only when it perceives this to be in its direct interests, and will disregard any requirements with which it disagrees. A similar approach to how the US deals with international institutions and concordats – the United Nations, the Geneva Conventions, the International Criminal Court.

The 'do as I say, not as I do' approach, the addition of a justification of the need for 'regime change' to the basis for aggressive action, internationally sanctioned or unilateral, is seen in under-developed countries as an erosion of their own freedom to choose their own future, the views and wishes of the West always to the fore. Even Tony Blair's much vaunted Commission for Africa is regarded with suspicion by many Africans, whilst at the time of writing his Middle East Conference initiative flounders in the face of Bush's refusal to endorse even-handed aims for Israeli and Palestinian participation. So, other than as a cat's paw for US defined strategies, has Mr. Blair really found a modern foreign policy role for Britain or is Dean Acheson's question still open?

If this is the context in which Scotland is beginning to operate, first as a significant regional government and in future as a fully independent participant in international affairs, what should be the drivers of a nascent Scottish foreign policy? The Scottish Executive has already published an International Strategy, which is a start, albeit a pale and insubstantial shadow of a fully developed strategy to reclaim Scotland's place. The big issues of International Development, Peace, and the Global Economy are left to West-minster. The document demonstrates a narrow and introspective focus missing Scotland's potential benefit from taking a wider view and a more outward-looking perspective. In particular, in emphasising issues of international trade and the primacy of direct Scottish advantage it overlooks Scotland's possible contribution to tackling deep-seated international tensions, and addressing the increasing gap between standards of living in the West and those in the under-developed countries.

So what can Scotland's contribution be? This will be determined in great part by who we are – so who are we? We are a small nation with some sense of identity and community. When Scottish character is at peace it is generous of spirit with a strong sense of natural justice. Scotland historically is international – the auld alliances, our universities, the international exchange tradition and of course our massive Diaspora. We are perceived as trustworthy, we are known for our work ethic and although we have a strong military tradition we are not necessarily seen as an imperialist nation. We have a long tradition in voluntary work overseas, often in times of conflict as a counter-balance to being militarily active, a desire to help people caught in the crossfire – the Scottish Women's Ambulance Corps in the 19/20th Century Balkan Wars, Scottish hospitals in war-torn France and revolutionary St. Petersburg, Red Cross in Scotland activism raising money for hospitals in Poland during ww2, and currently Scottish aid workers and volunteers in Palestine and Iraq.

We are also a small nation in the process of re-establishing self-government which has secured significant constitutional change in a totally peaceful, democratic fashion. In today's world that is important, in fact in a world that today is a much more dangerous place than ever before, with wars between countries, amongst countries and within countries, it is to be lauded and applauded. Scotland does have something unique to offer; we have specific experience and expertise in the field of governance and in the voluntary sector, a vibrant civic society in Scotland which probably doesn't have an equal elsewhere in the uk. Scotland's parliament is already the focus for others seeking to strengthen the rights and influence of civic society within their own governmental and parliamentary structures – Eastern Europe, Latin America, South East Asia, and Africa. Significantly, Scotland's Parliament has already endorsed a visit by the Palestinian Legislative Council and agreed to share good practice.

Our peaceful, democratic transition from centralised uk Government to devolution, and the acceptance by all that ultimately it is our own electorate that will decide whether the step to nation-statehood will be taken, allows Scotland, or Scots, to act as natural and neutral hosts or mediators for those in regional conflict situations who need assistance in resolving their difficulties in their own ways.

In his final address to the European parliament Nobel Peace Prize Laureate John Hume called for the creation of a peace and reconciliation department, serviced by an EU Commissioner who would be dedicated to the task of conflict resolution. A worthy call certainly, but also a pragmatic and eminently sensible call to which Scotland should give a very positive response.

Too often in recent times we have seen the military option as the only option, trying to make peace by first making war. Not only are potential opportunities for making peace without resorting to violence lost, but war is then followed by the paradox of those in the front line of waging it suddenly being transformed into the role of peacekeepers. In 2001, Javier Solana, High Representative of the EU for Common, Foreign and Security Policy stated 'Troops cannot be expected to carry out civilian duties. That is why we need to focus on developing resources such as police, prosecutors, judges, legal experts, monitors, human rights experts, administrators and civil protection teams'.

Some in Europe have already recognised the benefits of peaceful conflict intervention and resolution by civilians rather than by the military. This is not a pacifist stance, nor is it to say that there is no place for the military option to respond proportionately in particular circumstances; rather it is an acknowledgement that it is possible to have different kinds of organisations and forces that can complement each other in conflict situations, as noted by Snr. Solana. Austria has had a civilian peace service since 1993, Germany since 1999; Norway has established such a service, others such as Sweden and Italy are in the process. Funding is potentially available from the European Union for member states and the European Initiative for Democracy and Human Rights expanded this year to include conflict prevention within its remit.

Unfortunately the UK is lagging behind in terms of establishing and funding such a national service despite the vast experience of Non-Governmental Agencies (NGOs) in Northern Ireland working in the areas of community relations, human rights, policing issues, ex-paramilitaries, and others which would have direct relevance to overseas conflicts. The UK does participate in conflict resolution initiatives of course. The Foreign Office, Department for International Development (DFID) and the British Council do fund capacity building, conflict resolution, governance and democratisation work through NGOs active in the field, but in general funding is piecemeal and limited and much depends on charity and private donations.

Many civilians in Scotland and the UK already work in conflict resolution, professionally or voluntarily, through NGOs, religious institutions or activist groups. This can be problematic though, with precarious funding dictating timescales of involvement and lack of status beyond that merely of the individual, charity or group making it difficult to obtain the right to remain. Government has yet to recognise the value and potential of such contributions. In purely financial terms it is obvious that civilian conflict resolution is cheaper than the costs of military intervention. In humanitarian terms every option should be explored before resorting to violence, with war itself avoided at all costs in a world where, according to Kofi Annan, General Secretary of the United Nations, 'it is now conventional to put the proportion of civilian casualties some-where in the region of 75%'.

If Britain has indeed not yet found a role on the world stage other than assistant to the US, there is no reason why Scotland cannot carve itself a unique role. The First Minister, following the launch of the International Strategy, announced a sum of £3.5m for international development, so there is cross-party consensus that it is acceptable to promote and fund projects which technically come under the remit of 'reserved matters'. There have already been many calls of course for the use of the first year's £3.5m, the most recent being to assist the victims of the Indian Ocean Tsunami. But if Scotland is to assert its identity, by use of a comparatively small amount of development funding direct from its Government, then targeted use of the resource is crucial. Consideration must be given to initiatives that can be steadily built upon to show concrete results towards a redefined international strategy for Scotland. To paraphrase an American President; it's not just about how the world can benefit Scotland, but about how Scotland can benefit the world.

The creation of a European Centre for Peace and the establishment and promotion of a well-trained corps of people who can be called upon to assist in conflict prevention and peace building worldwide would be legitimate ventures for the Parliament and the Executive to undertake. Such an initiative could act as a catalyst for action to tackle some of Scotland's acknowledged weaknesses; the development of language skills, increased national self confidence and an improved international profile. This could tie in with the Parliament's and Executive's existing strategies on volunteering and citizenship, the Fresh Talent initiative and developing a greater international perspective in Scottish companies.

The foundations are there – Scotland already has its Centre for Non-Violence based in Dunblane, and this has provided training to civilian peace workers operating in Israel and Palestine. The Scottish Network for Civilian Peace Service is already active, working closely with the Steering Group for a UK Civilian Peace Service. Conflict Resolution courses are available in Scottish Universities. The location in East Kilbride of the main operating centre for the UK's Department for International Development also provides a local source of talent and expertise on which to build.

Small nations can play an important role in building peaceful and stable international relations for the 21st Century, Norway for example kick-started the Middle East peace process a decade ago. Scotland can be one of these nations and act as an honest broker. This in fact happened at the close of 2003 when, on the initiative of Angus Robertson MP, talks took place in his Speyside Constituency amongst 30 parliamentarians from Armenia, Azerbaijan and Georgia over the disputed territory of Nagorny Karabakh.

Scotland can stake its place in Europe and the world by having the vision to promote peace and stability. Our reputation for democratic and peaceful constitutional change means that we could be established as a force in aiding conflict resolution, even within our current regional status. We can invite people here from overseas and provide a peaceful setting for mediation and negotiation, and we can send Scots outward in the spirit of international co-operation and world stability.

The aim of this piece is to sketch out a vision for Scotland in 2020 and to set an agenda for action. Too often in the field of international development targets are negotiated, announced in triumph, quietly forgotten for a while, and then rehashed when the target date looms closer. Witness for example, the response to the recognition that on current progress in lots of countries many of the United Nations' Millennium Development Goals won't be achieved by 2015. Continuing conflict and instability in many regions of the world is one of the key factors cited in mitigation for countries failing to meet these goals; poverty continues because conflict destroys infrastructure and institutions.

A 15 year span of attention can be either helpful in raising sights beyond the problems of the day or counter-productive in providing scope for prevarication and inaction. If the Scottish Parliament, working through the Scottish Government, truly has the will to effect change, then establishing Scotland as a new force for peace by the year 2020 is both an achievable and a worthy aim. The challenge is to come out of the shadows and stake Scotland's claim.

A Sporting and Cultural Renaissance

24

Scottish Football: Grassroots to Glory

TONY HIGGINS

THE YEAR IS 2020, the country Scotland, the game, Scotland v Italy at Hampden Park in the finals of the Euro championship. The score is 1 – 1 and in the dying seconds, a Scot scores a wonderful goal to take Scotland through to the second stage of the tournament. The nation unites in triumph, at last we are there: we have qualified for the second phase of a major tournament.

Is this possible? Of course it is but we all need, including those of us in football, to bang our heads together for the sake of our national sport and with the financial assistance of the Executive to get back onto the football rails heading for qualification again for major championships as an initial goal.

For a small country like Scotland, football is so important in promoting our national identity; the team and the Tartan Army have over the years played a major part in developing a positive attitude towards Scotland throughout the world.

At the time of writing, Scotland are ranked 86th in the world, our lowest ever ranking. I think it is useful to establish some of the reasons behind our demise, where we are currently and where we hope to be in 2020. We have to be realistic here, Scotland has never achieved the type of success of a Denmark (with a similar population to Scotland) for instance at international level but our club sides have had players who were highly respected throughout the world. Scottish footballers were sought after particularly in England, and provided the nucleus for many of the great English sides of the past.

In the post war years probably up until the 1970s kids played football for endless hours in parks and streets thereby learning their trade informally. Twenty a side, two a side and 'heidy fitba' (as we called it in Glasgow) were played depending on the number of willing participants; there was always something going on involving a ball particularly in working class areas.

The competition between clubs was also more intense partly due to the fact that resources were much more equally shared. Clubs shared their home gates, which meant that although in financial terms the Old Firm were still dominant, the gap between them and the rest was not so evident. Good players were spread between the clubs and of course the number of foreign players in the Scottish game was negligible.

Demographics were also different, the post war baby boom resulted in families having five, six or seven children; again producing many young boys to play our national game and pursue the dream of becoming a full time professional footballer.

Today the game has made giant strides commercially, and income generated from sources other than gate money has brought a tremendous wealth to the game unrecognisable from the 1960s, 1970s or 1980s. But at what price?

Following the Bosman case in 1995, for whatever reason, clubs lost all sense of fiscal sensibility, paying wages way beyond what they could afford and in some cases paying over 100% of their turnover. This short term thinking unfortunately resulted in the development of young players been given a low priority and with expensive foreign acquisitions being the fashion. The policy of spend now, think later, put almost all our full time clubs in an financial mess. The only positive aspect to emerge from this is the belief that rearing your own players is not only better in the playing sense but also financially.

Youth development, whilst much talked about as an aspiration, lost its focus of being a major objective within the club strategy; the quick fix solution was paramount, resulting in us being at least ten years behind our major competitors in the development of players.

Competition has also suffered. The Old Firm have always dominated Scottish football and will continue to do so but as mentioned earlier the gap between them and the rest is getting wider and wider. In the past a number of clubs have successfully challenged

Rangers and Celtic and from time to time would win the League Championship, creating good competition and stimulating spectator interest. Indeed a number of clubs would also win the League and Scottish Cups on a regular basis.

However the domination of the Old Firm in recent times now means that fans at many of our other top clubs are not attending in such vast numbers as they do not think they have any realistic chance of beating them, while Celtic and Rangers fans are not excited by the prospect of playing non-old firm clubs because they see little evidence of real competition. That is why they flock in such numbers to see European teams. Uncertainty of outcome is what keeps football alive; predictability in any sport creates boredom.

By 2020 what do we have to do to ensure that we restore our credibility in the world of football? I think there are three main areas that we have to concentrate on:

1   The structure of the Governing Bodies.

I believe that Scottish football cannot afford two separate bodies running the professional clubs at senior level. I feel that from the SPL and the SFL a new body has to emerge so we have one rationalised body running the professional game in Scotland with more resources going into more clubs. For whatever reason the current system has not delivered what it set out to do. Football should be brave enough to admit that the current structure has failed and therefore, we should look to create a new structure.

Along with a new professional league being run under the auspices of the SFA other sections could be created as well; women's football, youth football, recreational football, junior football could all operate as entities under the control of the SFA but not managed by them on a day-to-day basis. Hopefully this would allow all bodies to work more closely to develop a shared vision for our national sport.

Anyone who has watched our national game over the last few years will recognise the tremendous amount of bickering that has been going on between the Governing Bodies. This has not provided the ideal backdrop for developing changes in the structure which most informed commentators have agreed is required. By

2020 I would like to see a structure which involves people who have expertise and knowledge of the game on the various SFA and League Committees. Why should it only be Directors who serve on these committees? If this sport is called the People's Game, why is it so few of the stakeholders have any say? Other countries and even FIFA and UEFA have former players and coaches involved in the administrative side of the game. In an effort to challenge the orthodoxy that prevails in football, why can't Scotland do this?

2 The role of the Scottish Executive.

Whatever the success or otherwise of devolution, I do feel strongly that in the area of sport devolution has worked and has many potential spin-offs for Scottish sport in general and football in particular. Speaking as someone who frequently met the various Ministers of Sport in London, their lack of interest in Scottish football was obvious maybe understandably given that their eye was on the ball of English football where greater headlines and better publicity could be obtained.

Having the Executive in Edinburgh has resulted in more contact between politicians, civil servants and football bodies. The members of the Scottish Executive and other politicians don't have to be told about the state of Scottish football; they see it themselves. There has always been a mutual mistrust between politicians and football, and given the state of our national game we need to engage the Executive in a real debate about the future of football and its role within Scottish society.

The two largest budgets the Executive administers are Health and Education. A closer relationship between football and the Executive working on a joint strategy could provide many benefits. The nation's health and childhood obesity has been widely reported; exercise is one of the main solutions to the problem. Football is a very simple game to play with little requirement in terms of finance for equipment, not a costly sport like some others. It is also the sport that most of our national sporting heroes emerge from.

Using former players and coaches positively in discussion with school children emphasising the need for exercise and proper diet will ensure the nation gets a clear message from the football industry.

One has only to look at the Ross County model as something that other clubs could aspire to; the funding for this was largely obtained from public bodies. The Chairman (Roy McGregor), the Manager (Alex Smith), and the very able Board have managed to develop a facility which is the envy of many not only in Scotland but throughout the UK. An indoor playing facility, floodlight training areas and outdoor quality grass training pitches are all part of this magnificent scheme. This facility allows Ross County and Inverness Caley the two local senior teams direct access to good training even when inclement weather would have stopped previous development plans. They can get on with ensuring their young players can be trained and coached properly without fear of disruption due to bad weather or other factors. This type of facility is sadly lacking throughout Scotland although I understand there is work in the pipeline which may help to rectify this.

Many clubs in Scotland are what is known as community clubs but they haven't thought out properly what this means in practice. To their credit Ross County have not only delivered football and development to the area but also work with schools, colleges and local businesses in other service delivery strategies which are mainly located at the football ground. This model is certainly one for other clubs and communities to follow.

3. Youth Development.

In the mid nineties I had the great honour of working with the legendary Dutch Coach, Rimus Michels to whom the renaissance of Dutch football was largely attributed. Although he was a successful senior coach at club and international level he had a great interest in the development of young players. He recalled how one afternoon when he was driving into his office in Amsterdam he noticed that kids weren't playing football in the street. From that initial observation, he developed a series of imaginative coaching principles and, by working with other forward thinking coaches, ensured that they were eventually adopted by the Dutch Football Federation.

If kids are not playing football in the street how do we get them to play?

Because modern living means that the street has been taken

over by the car, Rimus felt he had to help create new structures to deal with this. Coaches who understand the mentality of young children and adolescents had to be trained and they had to be convinced that the most important element in any young players development following their coaching session was their commitment to practice away from the training ground. He also felt that indoor facilities were also important as well as good practice areas for young players to perform on.

If you think back to the great players who were born after the war, they played endless hours of football in the park or in the street and therefore learned the game the hard way learning skills and techniques informally. Michels felt that we had to create systems that instil in the player the need to practice away from the coaching session following the demonstration of a skill or technique. Practice, practice, practice was the key phrase used in Holland. In Scotland we know it as homework and we all know what that meant. He also convinced the Football Federation and the Government in Holland that they had to work together to create better facilities which not only benefit football and other sports, but the community as well.

Thinking this way is simple and logical. Young boys in Scotland very often only attend one or two training sessions a week and play their weekend game which could result in only three or four hours contact with the ball each week. More contact with the ball is required and we need good coaches who instil the ethic of practice with good facilities to promote this.

The SFA Technical Department has made immense progress in this area in the last few years and is now producing many coaches with real ability to work in the areas of children and youth coaching. They will obviously assist our future development. But good coaches require good facilities and this is one area where sports and politics have to mix.

Scottish football is not wealthy enough to do it on its own so we need the financial assistance of the Executive. It is time for politicians and football administrators to work together for the right result for Scottish football.

A People's Arts

ELAINE C SMITH

WHAT A YEAR!! Six years into our Independence as a nation, the confidence and self-esteem of our country has grown and grown. There have been hiccups, stumbling blocks and a few resignations along the way, but for the last couple of years our standing in Europe and the world has grown at a steady pace, with Scotland's measured approach as a full member of the Council of Europe allowing our country to flourish.

As we hit our major public holiday on St Andrews Day... now a major tourist event in Scotland like St Patrick's Day in Ireland or Thanksgiving in the US of A... we can look back on a terrific year in the Arts, Film and Television in Scotland.

The fact that we now have control over our broadcasting has been a major boon to the arts, culture, sport and current affairs. Our news programmes are now no longer bound by the old Scottish parochial agenda. We are now able to report from all over the world, from every troublespot with an outward looking view of the world as opposed to the intense navel gazing that used to go on. We still have a great input of local and Scottish viewpoints but stories about the last kestrel to be seen in Sauchiehall Street or the ingredients of the best fish supper are no longer seen as headline news!!! With excellent journalists now able to live and work in their own country without having to go to London to allow their careers to develop, our current affairs, political and investigative programmes are winning awards all over the world.

Our Television screens are no longer dominated by London or the US... though the excellent comedies, dramas and films made in those countries are still a big part of the TV output. But fortunately, thanks to the investment in film and television from the Government and their belief that Scotland has all the skills and expertise to make quality product, our own comedies and dramas are matching anything from outside. Our investment in creative writing in schools, communities and universities (particularly the new universities in Possil, Kelso and Ullapool) have tapped into a seam of creative writing and talent that was smothered by poverty and hopelessness before. Damp, cold, squalid housing has been eradicated in the cities and in our rural communities by demolishing inadequate houses. Building warm centrally heated homes with gardens has had a huge impact on the lives of ordinary people.

The fact that our schools are now state of the art (with visitors from all over Europe coming to Scotland to see how we have increased our educational standards so quickly allowing us to reach the top five best educated countries in the world)) has helped our young people to excel; particularly in the creative arts which for decades was viewed by the educational establishment as unimportant!! With a free nutritious meal served in schools across the country, bottled water and fruit available in every class, new sports facilities with tennis, squash, football, athletics and more all available as a core part of the curriculum, our children are now fitter and healthier than ever before. All of this has had a huge knock on effect on the behaviour, attention and enthusiasm of children in state schools. These educational standards (which had only been evident in children from private schools, which are of course a thing of the past, as the need for these schools for the privileged and rich are no longer necessary!!) are now prevalent throughout our education system.

The investment in the Health Service is paying off at last with nurses and doctors working as hard as ever but finally being paid what they truly deserve and relishing the fact that they have enough staff to allow them all to work a 38 hour week. Their delight at working in spotlessly clean hospitals is evident and the dark days of the MRSA bug that blighted the service 15 years ago is a thing of the past! Changes in diet and lifestyle have taken much of the pressure off the Health Service – thanks also to research in Glasgow and Dundee – and have made deaths from cancer and heart disease amongst the lowest in the world.

All of these facts have helped create an atmosphere where our arts and cultural life can flourish. The divide between supposed high and low art is now very blurred with people from Motherwell as likely to be at a thriving Scottish Ballet as a pantomime at the newly refurbished Kings Theatre in Edinburgh or a pop concert in the new National Arena in the grounds of the old Hampden.

The fight for years to ensure that the Culture Minister would fund a new National Theatre Building in Easterhouse finally came to fruition. The National Theatre now has fantastic rehearsal spaces... available for all theatre, dance, opera companies to use. It contains fitness facilities, recording studios, bar/café, small studio theatres, and orchestra facilities allowing people from all different areas of the arts to have a place to meet and work for the first time in our history. Our new National Auditorium in Strathclyde Park has proved a huge success. Holding 1,500 people, with excellent new transport links by rail and road, it has become a landmark for all of the arts, as has the Highland Auditorium on the banks of the River Ness in Inverness. This, along with the Scottish National Orchestra base and facilities in Stirling run by composer James MacMillan and his team and the new Centre for Painting and the Visual Arts in Dundee headed by Alison Watt and Ken Currie, has ensured that the artistic and cultural base in Scotland is solid and thriving.

The ability to finally accept that as a nation we are not better, but different from our close friends and neighbours in England, has proved a huge turning point in our theatres. At last we can celebrate the style of performing, so derided a generation ago by the artistic snobs and apologists who cringed at the fact that as artists we were not the same as Metropolitan London. Those cringers who branded anything working class or 'variety based' as kailyard rubbish, are now a thing of the past.

The style of acting so loved by audiences in popular culture... from TV to theatre... is now accepted as highly skilled and as important to our cultural life as the acting styles of Shakespeare and contemporary drama using 'the Method'. It is hard to believe now, but for decades the stars of popular culture, particularly within comedy, were seen as lesser talents among the then arts establishment and broadsheet critics. This of course was based on a lack of knowledge or experience and a divide between the mass audience and the critics.

A great deal of this was due to the fact that a university education consisting of regurgitating received teaching and wisdom was the norm and instead of a desire to 'better' ourselves, a cringe mentality developed. This occurred when dealing with our own culture... particularly mass popular culture... resulting in a deriding of the heightened, talking to the audience, anarchic, front cloth style of acting... loved from the days of the Italian Comedia d'el Arte to present day Pantomime. This style of acting and performing would be given rave reviews and cash at the Edinburgh Fringe if done by a Polish, French or Italian company but our own star performers couldn't get house room! From the legendary Jack Milroy and Ricki Fulton to Billy Connolly and Dorothy Paul who received grudging responses on every level and for too many years... except, of course, from the audiences who turned up in their thousands!

The reasons for this self-loathing were, I believe, class based; i.e. the working class love this broad, no pretending that there is a fourth wall sort of stuff. The educated believed that they were above all that. There existed a lack of acceptance that this was part of their culture and one that was intrinsic to who we are as a nation. The self-loathing that developed was as destructive to them as it was to the rest of the culture.

This new thinking has been aided by the fact that the Scottish Arts Council (apart from having guaranteed funding due to the fact that our Government believes that a rich cultural life leads to a richer nation at all levels) is now democratically elected. Every theatre in Scotland now nominates people for elections voted on by all the union members of Equity, the MU, BECTU and working theatre staff. Once elected these MACs (Members of the Arts Council) can appoint experts or public figures to various boards to help distribute money, but they are no longer the Quango that used to exist. The fight over scraps of funding no longer applies.

The critics and snobs have been silenced by the developments in all of the arts throughout the world and by the fact that so many of our performers are out there in the world doing so well. No longer are we asked by our fellow countrymen, when another of our films wins an award in the US or Italy or France or Australia 'How do they understand your accent?' Because the answer is that they hear it so often now, that they make the same effort as we always did to understand a cockney, a Geordie or a New Yorker.

The best thing is that the very word 'entertain' is no longer a dirty word in artistic terms, but seen as the ultimate aim of any artist... as well as to move, to educate and motivate!

What a cultural shift!!!

So far this year we have had the Touring pantomime, visiting the main theatres in all our major cities. Written by veterans Bob Black, Tony Roper, Alex Norton and many others, starring our current comedy stars, this lavish production toured by the Scottish National Theatre company for the last 10 years has been hugely successful and a tonic for audiences in the winter months,

The international award winning Celtic Connections Festival now runs for a month in Glasgow and then tours around various cities and to Canada, Australia, Europe and the USA. All these touring shows take exhibitions of pottery, sculpture, painting and installations with them.

Scottish Opera, Scottish Ballet and all our six Orchestras have been enjoying the freedom gained by full and adequate funding and are performing to huge audiences both at home and abroad, the new training facilities proving a breeding ground for dance and classical music.

The Edinburgh Festival has consolidated its position as the biggest International Arts Festival in the world and with more of our own companies able to participate we are now seeing more Scots than ever before attending and feeling that the Festival belongs as much to them as to anyone else. Changed days from the time that the majority of Scots felt that the Festival and Fringe was for everyone else but them!

The studio built in Perth by the now almost 90 year old Sean Connery is working so well we are able to encourage filmmakers from all over the world to use our facilities here which has had a knock on effect on our indigenous film and TV industry and to the economy in general. The fact that Sean returned after we became Independent was a great boost to the Film Industry. These facilities and the general growth in cultural confidence have resulted in our first significant haul of Oscars, beating previous major winners like Titanic.

The new Edwin Morgan Centre for Poetry and Creative Writing is thriving in Wigtown. After years of building up their Book Festival, Des Dillon and Jackie Kay now head up this state of the art building with students from all over Britain heading for the border area. Visits from Maya Angelou, Alice Walker, Liz Lochhead, Tom Leonard, Aonghas MacNeacail and many others have helped put this dynamic centre on the map of writing worldwide.

Our first Best Picture Oscar went to Richard Jobson last year with his romantic comedy 'A Pie and a Pint' set in Dunfermline; it also won Best Cinematography and a Best Actor for Dougray Scott. But this year, Lynne Ramsay's political thriller 'The Blair Identity', has swept the boards. Ewan MacGregor and Billy Boyd are superb and deserve their actor gongs and Denise Mina's sceenplay well worthy of her Oscar as well as Lynne Ramsay for directing, and to Sir Sean as Producer of the Best Picture. As well as the awards for production and Cinematography it is wonderful to finally see a female from Scotland win an Oscar for her acting and newcomer Hannah Morton deserves it... what a fab actress.

With our Television dramas winning Emmys, our musicians picking up Grammys and Country Music Awards too, we are finally reaching the status of being a grown up nation... its been a long haul. But don't it feel good?!

Books Don't Crash;

How digital, corporate and cultural shifts will change publishing in Scotland by 2020

LORRAINE FANNIN

'This collection of books and manuscripts... may be considered as the Nation's memory'

The late Donald Dewar MSP, celebrating the National Library of Scotland

PUBLICATION IS THE INTERFACE between the writer and the reader, the issuing and distribution of information, commentary, opinions and ideas, fiction and verse. It uses newsprint, magazines, and now electronic formats, as well as the book. Each medium uses content in a different way; writing for a newspaper is not the same as writing a book. The book, however, is the one which endures, remaining available limitlessly, unlike the more impermanent media, although perhaps the endurance of electronic formats has yet to be tested. For the purposes of this discussion, however, book publishing has the greater long-term cultural significance. Recording the spirit of the times is what books do well, as the quotation above from the late Donald Dewar identified. Books have retained intrinsically the same form for 500 years, yet the harnessing of new technology to change how they are produced and delivered has resulted in unprecedented development in the publishing sector in the last fifteen years. In the next fifteen years, to 2020, the change may well be in reader habits, as human behaviour catches up with technology.

This technology, and the occasional assumption that it can work miracles, brings two kinds of debate to the fore: the first, are publishers needed? And secondly, what does it matter where publishers are based? If creative writing as well as information can be made available on the web, will the role of publisher as interface between writer and reader become unnecessary? If the web serves as the means of communication, then might not the publisher in London, New York or Paris define what is produced for readers in Glasgow or Argyll by 2020? Should that happen? Should we permit it to happen, if market forces so dictate?

In the pre-digital era, Scotland's publishing had an uneven history. Some of the great names in English language publishing emerged from its major cities in the 19th Century, names like Collins, Chambers, Thomas Nelson and Blackie. Then in the 20th Century business decisions and globalisation of the industry reduced the sector dramatically, though in the new millennium, growth has come from creative independents. This is a growth driven by people with a passion for books, but in a society which is increasingly fed a diet of consumer goods, homogenised to suit the maximum number of buyers, they must ensure there is an appetite for what they offer, if they are to survive.

Writing and reading as activities are valued, respected and enjoyed by a significant part of Scottish society. Yet the process which joins writer to reader may be overlooked: publishing is the delivery mechanism between them. An obvious fact is that if books are not published, literature does not flourish. Creative writing is not easily read on screen, not a comfortable way to relate to such work (though children brought up on screen-based entertainment today may not agree in the future). The I-Pod, must-have gadget of today, is unlikely ever to provide a comfortable reading experience. The process of bringing writing to print is highly skilled, creative, makes a vital contribution to the integrity and quality of what the writer offers the reader, and offers a delivery mechanism for education, imagination and ideas.

'There is... a sense that what [the publishers] do helps sustain a sense of community and core values and promotes cultural vibrancy. In contrast, therefore, if a solely commercial imperative

drove the publishers then such Scottish content might be lost, and with it, diversity, pluralism, heritage and creativity.'

'Publishing as a process is a set of skills and core competences consisting of the acquisition, selection, editing, project management, marketing and sale of content. Although traditionally publishing has been linked with the production of printed material, it is too limiting to think of it solely in those terms. Although the death of print has been greatly exaggerated, the medium in which content reaches its end user can take a number of different forms including digital media such as CD-Rom or DVD. Publishing is a cultural and educational industry. Literature represents only one, albeit the most glamorous, sector of publishing. If culture is given a more inclusive definition, perhaps along the lines of UNESCO's 'all distinctive spiritual and material, intellectual and emotional features which characterise a society or group', then publishing as a cultural industry can be seen to encompass a wider range, including educational, than just creative writing. Its outputs are part of the cultural life and education system of the nation...'

'...Publishing as a 'cultural industry' enjoys a particular public esteem... a recognition of the cultural worth of publishing in carrying Scottish values, representations of its communities, past and present, to audiences here and in the other nations of the world must be accompanied by an acknowledgement of its economic and employment impact that includes its role as a source and a training ground for other 'high profile' media such as film and broadcasting.'

From the *Review of Publishing in Scotland*, by PriceWaterhouseCooper, Commissioned by the SAC in 2003

The processes of publishing add value to writers' work and often shape it. In Scotland some 70% of work published in books is commissioned by the publisher, and the concept of a book, as well as the nurturing process, makes a profound difference to what reaches the reader. Scotland publishes mainly in the English language but this is not necessarily the advantage it first seems. In countries whose boundaries define their language, publishing requires little infrastructure support as the indigenous industry delivers foreign literature, bestsellers and educational resources as well as work from its own writers. In English-language territories, which border a larger neighbour, such as Scotland, Ireland, Wales and even Canada, there is a danger that indigenous publishing may in future be squeezed out of existence by the more powerful US and UK-wide companies. They may have a view that Scotland is a reasonable 'local' market and may publish for it, but it is not a priority for a global corporate publishing entity. Does this matter?

There are many ways to argue that it does, and will matter profoundly. If book publishing is part of the process of recording the nation's intellectual life, then Scottish publishing is crucial. Book publishing in the UK now is dominated by large companies, whose owners are based in London, New York, and Germany. Over 80% of UK book sales come from six of them, two of which are UK-owned. Predictions suggest that this percentage will not decrease. Scottish bookselling is now dominated by chains managed from the South of England. Huge expansion in Scotland by these stores has brought a homogeneous, sophisticated range to the market, but it has in many cases also altered the national cultural identity of the books on offer, even in libraries.

It is claimed that this makes little difference to good Scottish writers, who may in any case depart for the large, richer global companies once they are established (often thanks to their first small publisher). But global companies are notoriously risk-averse and hesitate about untested writers' new work. It is to be welcomed that Scottish writers are enjoying unprecedented popularity; but if there were a threat to the infrastructure of publishing in Scotland and if the global preferences moved on, new writers could find fewer outlets for their work. Scotland cannot forever rely on having its writers published elsewhere, nor should Scotland's cultural commentaries be filtered through an external publishing or political lens.

Another argument is that publishing in Scotland must support its indigenous languages. The report, *A Fresh Start for Gaelic*, argued that Gaelic publishing be supported to be the carrier of Gaelic written tradition, without which the language may ultimately die.

The responsibility to keep in print the languages of Scotland lies within Scotland and depends on the knowledge and skills of its publishing sector. Scots language survival also needs the publication of major language dictionaries, and books which use it, particularly for the young. This development also rests within a strong and healthy publishing sector in Scotland.

Output from Scotland's 80-plus publishers covers the whole spectrum of books: fiction and poetry, biography, academic, educational, children's, photography, maps, business and self-help, art, music, history, reference, medical. Many publishers in Scotland are independent organisations; they believe strongly that what they publish matters. Could it be done differently? In 2020 could we have creative teams, as in other media industries, who come together for a specific project or book and then disband to re-form elsewhere? Could bookshop chains become the commissioners of consumer books, driven by what they can sell well? Given the skills-set needed, it is perhaps unlikely. More probable is that ideas will be formatted across a range of media simultaneously: audio, animation, interactive electronic formats. Printed books will probably remain the staple. They are – as a young publisher described – 'the most effective, and user-friendly format for text, and they never crash.' The population moves about a great deal, and on journeys, books remain an easily portable form of stimulation and entertainment.

How will book publishing in Scotland compete in future? Now they try to make a collaborative voice heard when individually it might not be possible. Publishers join forces to sell books into various markets, including export. They can avail themselves of the services of a collectively-owned distribution company which received (modest) public funding in its early days. Currently an e-commerce website for Scottish books is in discussion making it possible for a world-wide diaspora of Scots to find a link to their family's past or present. New technology may hold the key to competitiveness, either through its use in the conventional publishing processes, in the supply chain, or in offering wider choices and channels. Hitting on some bestsellers also helps.

To quote again from the *Review of Publishing in Scotland*

*'The use of web technology, both internet and intranet, by distribu-
tors is still in its infancy but may have potential in offering portals
for Scottish books and other cultural products ... The Welsh Books
Council, for example, run a site, Gwales.com, which offers information on over 17,500 Welsh titles. The impact of one well-designed
site with e-commerce facilities can be seen to be greater than a fragmented set of websites from each publisher though of course it
doesn't preclude the publisher having their own site.'*

What of the future? Will there be a Doomsday scenario, in which
books are no longer read? Will publishing become a partnership
between new technologies and new media, exploiting 'content' in
every form? There is pressure on time spent reading, especially for
children. Readers are, and will become, increasingly highly selective. The *Harry Potter* phenomenon, however, shows that it only
takes a really good story to beat off the competition, but shorter
books, however simplistic that idea, may be in demand to alleviate
the pressures of daily life. A gap may grow between easy 'dispos-
able' fiction and more literary work; markets are already differentiated. Web 'content' providers will need conventional publishers'
skills to provide what is sought. In academic and reference publishing more will be available on-line. At present journals publishers
are nervous of government's 'Open Access' policy which threatens
the income stream from their subscription base. There is an expectation at large that information on the Web is or should be free,
with the consequent threat to Copyright law, a development, which
has to date, undermined the profitability of the music industry.

However, the idea that the internet will kill off the printed word
is not realistic. Commentators have concentrated on the changes
likely to be made by publishing directly on the Web, but in fact
technological changes in the publishing industry are happening
constantly as print methods alter, television and home entertainment
transforms leisure habits and the cinema devours stories (often
prompting consequent increased sales of the books). Even more
profound are the changes which offer a wider range of production

methods, costs and processes. Short-run print technology allows minority-interest work to be produced economically, and digital technology is able to offer a range of print-on-demand facilities that are revolutionising the publishing supply chain. Customised books may be the norm in fifteen years, not from the desktop printer, where a messy pile of A4 sheets is not an attractive reading option, but instead a pre-sampled, self-defined collection of essays or information could be ordered on-line from a print-on-demand resource and received by post within days.

Scottish publishing needs to keep abreast of these changes to maintain its place in this new technology. Its size and independence may allow it to lead and innovate as has already happened with Canongate's use of short-film on its website to build a keen young readership community. In this respect, public investment in the sector's infrastructure and resources will be vital, just as it is in the development of creative writing.

The media, critics, libraries and readers all help keep available Scotland's published output, through their belief in the value and importance of what is produced and created here. In future the sector must engage with the media in all its forms to ensure that it retains the attention and commitment of the public which is increasingly bombarded with the sophisticated consumer marketing which has successfully turned shopping into the most popular leisure activity for much of the population.

Public funding support for publishing will help the framework for creative writing and literature just as support for theatres, galleries and concert halls provides for an interface between creative artist and audience. Literary publishing is high-risk and needs capital expenditure; as reading faces greater competition, there is a need to support the infrastructure of the sector as a whole. There is a need to ensure that new technology is developed within the sector to allow access and delivery to keep pace with social and commercial change and expectation. That there is a strong appetite for books in Scotland is very clear; it is important that the identity of Scotland is maintained within the book world of the country, and carried abroad with the work of the country's creative writers.

About the Contributors

JOHN ALDERSEY-WILLIAMS graduated in Geology from Cambridge in 1984. Starting as a geologist with Britoil and Sun Oil, he completed an MBA and worked at Schroders, a leading UK investment bank, before returning to the oil industry in a commercial role with British-Borneo. He then moved to Texaco, where he took the role of Finance Director for its North Sea Producing Business Unit in Aberdeen in 1999. In 2001, he left the oil industry to establish Redfield Consulting, a strategic, commercial and economic consultancy working in the renewables sector. Redfield counts the Carbon Trust, Talisman Energy, the European Marine Energy Centre and Camcal among its clients.

DONALD ANDERSON has been Leader of the City of Edinburgh Council since 1999 and represents the Kaimes ward of the capital. He was elected to Lothian Regional Council in 1986 and had responsibility for economic development between 1992-1999. He was educated at Liberton High School and Napier College in Edinburgh. Before becoming Leader of the Council, he was employed as a Medical Laboratory Scientific Officer for the Scottish National Blood Transfusion Service until February 1998. He is married with two children.

ALEX BELL is a journalist and broadcaster. He currently contributes columns and the occasional leader article to the Herald, he presents a variety of programmes on BBC Radio Scotland and he co-runs the country's only media web site, allmediascotland.com. A BBC Trainee, he has reported from North America, Africa and the Far East as well as spending a lot of time in Ireland. He is a husband and a father.

SARAH BOYACK MA Hons Dip Town Planning is the Labour MSP for Edinburgh Central. She worked as a town planner in the London Borough of Brent (1986-88), with Central Regional Council (1988-92), then as a Lecturer at Edinburgh College of Art/Heriot Watt University (1992-1999). Sarah served in the first Scottish Cabinet as Minister for Transport and the Environment, from May 1999 to November 2001. She then served as a member of the European and Audit Committees. Since 2003 she has been Convenor of the Environment and Rural Development Committee. In November 2004 she was awarded the RSPB Centenary Goldcrest award for the person who had made the most significant contribution to the development of environment policy since the reopening of the Scottish Parliament in 1999.

PROFESSOR SIR DAVID CARTER MD FRCSE FRSE is currently Chairman of the Health Foundation and Queens Nursing Institute Scotland, and is a Trustee of Cancer Research UK. He was formerly St Mungo Professor of Surgery, Glasgow (1979-1988), Regius Professor of Clinical Surgery, Edinburgh (1988-1996), Chief Medical Officer Scotland (1996-2000) and Vice Principal of Edinburgh University (until 2002). His surgical interests lay in pancreatic and hepato-biliary surgery. He is a past President of the Association of Surgeons of Great Britain and Ireland, Surgical Research Society and British Medical Association, and a former Vice President of the Royal Society of Edinburgh.

DR CAROL CRAIG is author of *The Scots' Crisis of Confidence*. Since its publication in February 2003 the book has attracted a large amount of publicity and favourable comment in the press and is having considerable impact on policy-makers in Scotland. At the beginning of January 2005 she became Chief Executive of the Centre for Confidence and Well-being, a new Glasgow based organisation which she helped to set up. Prior to taking up this post Carol had fifteen years experience of running her own training and development business. Before this she worked for BBC Scotland. She has a BA in politics from the University of Strathclyde and a PHD in politics from the University of Edinburgh.

ROBERT CRAWFORD is presently director of strategy and corporate development at the Wood Group (Gas Turbine Services) based in Aberdeen. Prior to that he was CEO at Scottish Enterprise, where he led a significant restructuring of the organisation and introduced a series of major initiatives directed towards increasing support for productivity, R&D and internationalisation of Scottish companies, including 'Globalscots', 'the co-investment scheme' and the 'intermediate technology institutes'. Prior to joining Scottish Enterprise he was a partner at Ernst and Young. Crawford worked at the World Bank in Washington DC for two years where he was a senior specialist in trade and investment. This followed a highly successful three tenure as Director of the then inward investment agency for Scotland, 'Locate in Scotland'.

DR ANDREW CUBIE CBE FRSE LLD WS is a Consultant to the laws firm Fyfe Ireland WS also sitting on the boards of public and private companies. He was the Chairman of Governors of George Watson's College and is currently Chairman of the Court of Napier University. He is also the Chairman of the Scottish Credit and Qualification Framework. He is a former Chairman of the CBI in Scotland, and was a member of the Consultative Steering Group, which developed the working arrangements of the Scottish Parliament. He was Convenor of the Independent Committee of Inquiry into Student Finance in Scotland ('the Cubie Committee') which brought about the abolition of tuition fees in Scotland. He is the Chairman of Quality Scotland, serves as a member of the Management Board of HMIE and is a Commissioner of the Northern Lighthouse Board. He is also Chairman in Scotland of the RNLI, British Council, British Executive Service Overseas, Scotland's Health at Work and Scotland's Garden Trust.

SALLY DAGHLIAN is the Chief Executive of the Scottish Refugee Council. She was born in the UK of Armenian descent and graduated from Glasgow University in 1981. Sally has over 10 years experience in the refugee field and is a member of a variety of UK and European refugee policy fora and networks. She was a member of the Board of Trustees of the British Refugee Council until 2004. Sally has recently been appointed to the independent Advisory Board on Naturalisation and Integration, under the chairmanship of Sir Bernard Crick, to advise on the government's integration and citizenship programme.

SUSAN DEACON is Labour MSP for Edinburgh East and Musselburgh. She was appointed by Donald Dewar as Minister for Health and Community Care in the first Scottish Cabinet in May 1999 and served in that role until November 2001. Prior to becoming an MSP, Susan worked in local government, management consultancy and in higher education. An enthusiastic campaigner for devolution, Susan has always been a passionate advocate of high quality public services and has a particular interest in the management of change. Her proudest achievement is her two children Clare (7) and Jamie (2) – who keep her feet firmly on the ground.

DR IAIN DOCHERTY is Senior Lecturer at the School of Business and Management, University of Glasgow. Iain is one of the leading researchers and commentators on transport issues in Scotland, working in both academia and consultancy. In addition to his regular columns for the professional media, he has published widely on transport and related public policy areas, including *A New Deal for Transport?* (Blackwell, 2003), the first detailed critique of New Labour's record on transport. Iain has also acted as academic advisor to a variety of organisations and individuals, including the Commission for Integrated Transport, Scottish Enterprise, and members of the Holyrood Shadow Cabinet. In 2003, he stood for the SNP in Dumbarton at the Scottish Parliament elections.

DAVID DONNISON, long retired from Glasgow University, still does some teaching and research in their Department of Urban Studies. He was previously Chair of the Supplementary Benefits Commission, Director of the Centre for Environmental Studies, and Professor of Social Administration at the London School of Economics.

OWEN DUDLEY EDWARDS BA, FRHist, FSA (Scot) has been a Reader in the Department of History of Edinburgh University since 1979 and his main areas of research are the social history and culture of modern Ireland, Britain and North America. A member of the editorial committee for *Drouth* and has been a contributor to *The Irish Times, The Scotsman, Scottish Affairs* and the BBC. He has worked as a lecturer across North America, Wales and Scotland. As well as producing a number of published works, including biographies of James Connolly and Eamon de Valera, he has achieved distinction as a literary critic. He has also written widely on Arthur Conan Doyle and his annotated Sherlock Holmes is considered definitive. His chapter in *The Red Paper on Scotland* (EUSPB, 1975) was entitled 'Scotland: Lessons from Ireland'.

LINDA FABIANI was elected to Holyrood in 1999 and represents Central Scotland for the SNP. Linda was a UN Observer at the East Timor independence ballot in 1999 and has maintained links with that developing nation. In 2000 she took part in an Electoral Assessment Study in Peru, and visited again as Keynote Speaker at an International Women's Conference following the democratic election in 2001. In November 2004, she spent a week in Tanzania participating in the British Council's UK/Tanzania initiative. She is a Trustee of Just World Partners, a charity working in the Pacific region, Central America, Asia and Africa, and is a founding member of the Scottish Network for a Civilian Peace Service.

LORRAINE FANNIN is the Director of the Scottish Publishers Association (SPA).The SPA represents publishers in Scotland. It aims to provide advice and training facilities, to foster high standards, and to assist publishers to market their books widely. The SPA is committed to advising small and developing publishers, to assisting those working in remote areas, and to ensuring that creative writing, literary work, educational material and cultural studies are developed fully. Members must adopt a Code of Practice in dealings with authors. Scotland's publishing industry is relatively small but it has a high level of cultural influence; its output records the country's historical, social and political life. The SPA believes that books provide a window on Scotland to the world.

TONY HIGGINS is the Senior Organiser of the Scottish Professional Footballers' Association. Tony has been involved in Professional Football for 34 years of which 17 were spent as a player. He played for various clubs including 9 seasons at Hibernian FC and 3 seasons at Partick Thistle FC. He was a Community Development Officer with Strathclyde Regional Council for 5 years prior to hisappointment as full-time leader of the Scottish Professional Footballers' Association, 14 years ago. Tony was a member of the Independent Review Commission on the way forward for Scottish Football, the Football League's Transfer Tribunal and the Government's Football Taskforce. He is an executive member of the Institute of Professional Sport and the Scottish representative on FIFPRO the international players' organisation, where he works on UEFA committees representing the views of players.

ROGER HOUCHIN was for 29 years a prison governor, latterly as Governor of Barlinnie Prison, now working in Glasgow Caledonian University, where he is Co-Director of the Centre for the Study of Violence. Has specialised expert knowledge in the area of human rights in prisons and the public supervision of prisons. Was for 5 years Head of Training and Development for the Scottish Prison Service. Has authored internal management development texts on prison management and prison law. Is an associate of the International Centre for Prison Studies, Kings College, London. Has worked in the recent past In Turkey, the Russian Federation, Armenia, Libya and Bosnia and Herzegovina advising on the management of prisons in accordance with international human rights standards, the development of training and development for prison administrators and staff, the management of life sentenced and high-risk prisoners, the use of clemency and independent investigation of complaints and allegations. Now divides his time between teaching and research in the University and working as an expert advisor on prison reform for the Council of Europe.

ALLAN MacASKILL was educated at Linlithgow Academy, Heriot Watt University and Edinburgh University. On graduation he joined the BP Group where he worked in a variety of positions in Operations and Production in the UK and North America. In 1998 he joined Talisman Energy, a leading independent producer, where he has worked on oilfield developments and renewable projects. Allan has been an active member of the SNP and is currently Treasurer of Ellon Branch.

KENNY MacASKILL has been a Lothians MSP since 1999. A senior member of the Shadow Cabinet since its inception in 1999, Kenny has held portfolios covering enterprise, transport, tourism, telecommunications and Justice. He is a long standing member of the SNP's NEC and has been National Treasurer and Vice Convener of Policy. Kenny was also the SNP's Poll Tax spokesperson, leading the party's popular 'Can Pay, Won't Pay' campaign. Kenny was educated at Linlithgow Academy and Edinburgh University and was a senior partner in a law firm until becoming an MSP. He is married with two sons.

DUNCAN MACAULAY is currently Director of Social Work with the City of Edinburgh Council. Since graduating from Stirling University in 1975, Duncan has held a number of social work management positions. He became Head of Operations at Edinburgh Council following local government reorganisation and has been interim Director since May 2004. Duncan was adviser in Social Work to the British Institute for Learning Difficulties for 6 years during the 1980's and advised on child care project development for the Social Welfare Department of Moscow City Council from 1993 – 2001. He became involved with ADSW in the 1990's and has chaired the Mental Health Group and served as an Executive member. He was elected President of the Association of Directors of Social Work in May 2003, a position he held for 1 year.

RT HON HENRY MCLEISH was First Minister of Scotland from 2000-2001. Minister for Enterprise and Lifelong Learning in the first Scottish Parliament 1999-2000. A member of the UK parliament from 1987-2001 and Minister for Devolution and Home Affairs in the labour government from 1997-1999. An elected member in local government from 1974 to 1987 and the Leader of Fife Regional Council for five years. A Privy Councillor. Resigned from politics in 2003. Recent work includes acting as an adviser and consultant, writing, seminars, conferences and lecturing in the USA on a variety of topics.

SHONAIG MACPHERSON practised as an intellectual property lawyer for over 20 years. Recognised as a leader in her field Shonaig retired from the law in September 2004 when she was Senior Partner of McGrigors, one of the United Kingdom's top 45 law firms. Shonaig holds a variety of non-executive positions including ITI Scotland Limited, BT Scotland and with the Management Group of The Scottish Executive. In addition she is deputy president of British Chambers of Commerce and Chairman of Scottish Council for Development and Industry. She is married with 2 sons and a stepson.

JIM MATHER was elected to the Scottish Parliament in 2003 representing the Highlands and Islands and is currently the SNP's spokesperson on Enterprise and the Economy. Previously a chartered accountant, he spent most of his career in the computer industry, working initially for IBM and then latterly running the ComputerLand Franchise in Scotland. He subsequently ran a business that helped young technology companies get off the ground. In recent years, he founded and ran Business for Scotland, an organisation that built bridges between the Scottish National Party and the Scottish business community.

JAMES MCCALLUM is Chief Executive of the Energy Services company Senergy. Senergy has subsidiary companies in both the oil and gas and renewable energy sector. James, who is 44 graduated in 1980 with an honours degree in Mechanical Engineering and Drama from Aston University, Birmingham. He is an esteemed fellow of the Institute of Civil Engineering. A well-known speaker for charity on the poetry of Robert Burns, James lives with his wife Gemma and his two sons James-Lachlan and Finlay-Broch at Worminsoune in Fife, a 16th Century merchants house which they restored over 10 years

JAMES MITCHELL is Professor of Politics at the University of Strathclyde. A graduate of Aberdeen and Oxford Universities, he held a chair in the University of Sheffield before his return to Strathclyde in 2000. He is the author of numerous articles in academic and other journals and is author or co-author of six books. His most recent book is *Governing Scotland*, Palgrave 2003. He is currently completing a book on 'Devolution in the United Kingdom'.

LINDSAY PATERSON is Professor of Educational Policy at Edinburgh University. He has written on many aspects of Scottish education, politics and culture. He is editor of the quarterly journal *Scottish Affairs*. His most recent book, *Scottish Education in the Twentieth Century*, is published by Edinburgh University Press.

RT HON GEORGE REID Presiding is Officer of the Scottish Parliament. Deputy Presiding Officer 1999-2003. SNP MSP since 1999 and in 2004 was made a Privy Councillor. SNP Member of the House of Commons (1974-79), member of the Parliamentary Assemblies of the Council of Europe, the Western European Union and was also a member of the Government Steering Group for the Scottish Parliament in 1997. From 1965 he worked in broadcast journalism including working as a correspondent for the BBC (1979-84) and as Head of News and Current Affairs for Scottish Television (1969-74). He is also the producer of over 200 television documentaries, including the Emmy prize-winner Contract 736. From 1984 until 1994 he was Director of Public Affairs of the International Red Cross and served in Armenia, Ethiopia, Mexico, Mozambique, Pakistan, Russia, Sudan, South Africa and Zimbabwe. For his work in Armenia he was awarded the Pirogov Gold Medal of the USSR and the Gold Medal of the Supreme Soviet of Armenia.

DR DOUGLAS ROBERTSON is Director of the Housing Policy and Practice Unit, at the University of Stirling, Scotland's premier centre for vocational housing education. He is also an accomplished policy researcher with a long standing interest in urban living, especially tenements, the buying and selling of private housing and the role of housing associations in neighbourhood renewal. He has previously worked on Scottish planning history and community planning. His voluntary work for the housing association movement enhanced a long lasting interest in the community dimension in both regeneration and local politics.

ELAINE C SMITH is one of Scotland's most popular performers having worked successfully in radio, television, film and theatre for over 20 years. She started in TV in landmark shows like Laugh I Nearly Paid My Licence Fee, City Lights, Naked Video and of course played the long-suffering Mary doll in the cult series Rab C Nesbitt. With her partner, she has also helped form and run the production company RPM Arts Ltd that has produced her own national solo tours plus 3 series of her TV series Elaine for BBC Scotland. Elaine has also been the only woman to headline the hugely successful yearly panto at the Kings Theatre, Glasgow for the last 7 years. She is a tireless political campaigner and charity worker, an ardent supporter of the Scottish Parliament. Her book, *Elaine's World* was published in 1998; she is a regular contributor to Scotland's newspapers and magazines. At present she is a regular columnist for *The Sunday Mail*. She is married with two children and lives in the East End of Glasgow.

JEAN URQUHART has lived and worked in Ullapool since 1973. She runs (after) The Ceilidh Place, a small hotel/cafe/bar/venue/bookshop and is the local councillor (SNP) on Highland Council. Her particular bag is tourism, small sustainable businesses, and the arts in all their forms. She is the founder of the Commercial Christmas Resistance Movement – whose purpose is to raise awareness of real need in this country and around the world. She is convinced she lives in the best bit of Scotland and loves both her jobs. Her greatest ambition is to live in an independent country, preferably this one.

Some other books published by **LUATH** PRESS

published from Scotland, read around the world

Building a Nation

Post Devolution Nationalism in Scotland
Viewpoints [series]
Kenny MacAskill
ISBN 1 84282 081 8 PB £4.99

'Where stands Scotland post Devolution and what is the future for Nationalism in a devolved Parliament? Is the Scottish Parliament a Unionist dead end or a Nationalist Highway to Independence? Has Devolution killed the SNP stone dead or given it a platform to build from? These are questions that need answered as Scotland begins to come to terms with Devolution and decides where and whether to go next'.
KENNY MacASKILL

In this book, Kenny MacAskill searches for the answers to these questions, vital to the future of 'the best small nation in the world'. He makes the case for a distinctive Scottish version of social democracy that can balance a vibrant economy with quality public services, and believes that Post Devolution Nationalism is about Building a Nation to be proud of.

This book is an important, possibly seminal, contribution to a debate that reflects on the meaning of independence, not just in terms of its constitutional-legal meanings but its wider meanings. It is challenging and provocative in the very best sense. There is an underlying and powerful message of optimism, a quiet self-confidence which challenges what Kenny MacAskill calls the 'outward swagger but huge inner self-doubt'. The book may be primarily addressed to a Nationalist audience but should be read well beyond supporters of constitutional independence.
PROFESSOR JAMES MITCHELL, DEPARTMENT OF GOVERNMENT, UNIVERSITY OF STRATHCLYDE

A timely intervention for a party entering a critical phase in its history... a manifesto to inspire and infuriate; pacey, intelligent and accessible. Like all good political pamphlets it is best enjoyed when read out loud.
SCOTTISH REVIEW OF BOOKS

Scotlands of the Mind

Angus Calder
ISBN 1 84282 008 7 PB £9.99

Does Scotland as a 'nation' have any real existence? In Britain, in Europe, in the World? Or are there a multitude of multiform 'Scotlands of the Mind'?

These soul-searching questions are probed in this timely book by prize-winning author and journalist, Angus Calder. Informed and intelligent, this new volume presents the author at his thought-provoking best. The absorbing journey through many possible Scotlands – fictionalised, idealised, and politicised – is sure to fascinate.

This perceptive and often highly personal writing shows the breathtaking scope of Calder's analytical power. Fact or fiction, individual or international, politics or poetry, statistics or statehood, no subject is taboo in a volume that offers an overview of the vicissitudes and changing nature of Scottishness.

Through mythical times to manufactured histories, from Empire and Diaspora, from John Knox to Home Rule and beyond, Calder shatters literary, historical and cultural misconceptions and provides invaluable insights into the Scottish psyche. Offering a fresh understanding of an ever-evolving Scotland, *Scotlands of the Mind* contributes to what Calder himself has called 'the needful getting of a new act together'.

Thoughtful and provocative, Calder is among the best essayists of today.
Bernard Crick, THE GUARDIAN

Angus Calder has proved himself one of the most sophisticated thinkers and writers on the gleaming new Scotland.
THE SCOTSMAN

A Long Stride Shortens the Road

Donald Smith

ISBN 1 84282 073 7 PB £8.99

Ranging from a celebration of the Holyrood parliament to a dialogue between Jamie Saxt and a skull, from a proposed national anthem to an autobiographical journey through pre-history, *A Long Stride Shortens the Road* traverses a Scotland that is irrevocably independent of spirit, yet universal in outlook.

The poems in this collection chart the main staging posts in Scotland's recent history. As writer, theatre director, storyteller and political foot soldier, Donald Smith has been at the centre of the cultural action. The poems, however, also reveal a personal narrative of exile and attachment, an intimate engagement with Scottish landscape, and a sense of the spiritual in all things.

This book is for anyone interested in the crucible out of which Scotland emerged, and where it might be going. Donald Smith writes poems to reflect on in the early days of a new nation.

Donald Smith's is a voice we need to hear in Scotland. He has a story to tell, a vision to shape, a song to declare.

TESSA RANSFORD

Scotlands of the Future: sustainability in a small nation

Introduced and edited by Eurig Scandrett

ISBN 1 84282 035 4 PB £7.99

What sorts of futures are possible for Scotland?

How can citizens of a small nation at the periphery of the global economy make a difference?

Can Scotland's economy be sustainable?

How do we build a good quality of life without damaging others'?

Could there be an economy that is good for people and the environment?

And if so, how do we get there without damaging people's livelihoods?

What can the Scottish Parliament do?

What difference can we make in our organisations, our trade unions, and our businesses?

Scotlands of the Future looks at where we've got to, where we can go next, and where we might want to get to – essential reading for those who think about and want to take action for a sustainable Scotland, and anyone else who cares about the future.

The anti-slavery campaigners succeeded. Politicians and civil society must rise to this new challenge, which is just today's version of the same injustice. We must show imagination, courage and leadership and champion a sustainable economy – for Scotland and the world.

OSBERT LANCASTER, EXECUTIVE DIRECTOR, CENTRE FOR HUMAN ECOLOGY

Eurovision or American Dream? Britain, the Euro and the Future of Europe

David Purdy

ISBN 1 84282 036 2 PB £3.99

Should Britain join the euro?

Where is the European Union going?

Must America rule the world?

Eurovision or American Dream? assesses New Labour's prevarications over the euro and the EU's deliberations about its future against the background of transatlantic discord. Highlighting the contrasts between European social capitalism and American free market individualism, David Purdy shows how Old Europe's welfare states can be renewed in the age of the global market. This, he argues, is essential if European governments are to reconnect with their citizens and revive enthusiasm for the European project. It would also enable the EU to challenge US hegemony, not by transforming itself into a rival superpower, but by championing an alternative model of social development and changing the rules of the global game.

In this timely and important book David Purdy explains why joining the euro is not just a question of economics, but a question about the future political direction of Britain and its place in Europe. PROFESSOR ANDREW GAMBLE, DIRECTOR, POLITICAL ECONOMY RESEARCH CENTRE, DEPARTMENT OF POLITICS, UNIVERSITY OF SHEFFIELD

Scotland – Land and Power
the agenda for land reform

Andy Wightman
in association with
Democratic Left Scotland
foreword by Lesley Riddoch
ISBN 0 946487 70 7 PB £5.00

What is land reform?
Why is it needed?
Will the Scottish Parliament really make a difference?

Scotland – Land and Power argues passionately that nothing less than a radical, comprehensive programme of land reform can make the difference that is needed. Now is no time for palliative solutions which treat the symptoms and not the causes.

Scotland – Land and Power is a controversial and provocative book that clarifies the complexities of landownership in Scotland. Andy Wightman explodes the myth that land issues are relevant only to the far flung fringes of rural Scotland, and questions mainstream political commitment to land reform. He presents his own far-reaching programme for change and a pragmatic, inspiring vision of how Scotland can move from outmoded, unjust power structures towards a more equitable landowning democracy.

Writers like Andy Wightman are determined to make sure that the hurt of the last century is not compounded by a rushed solution in the next. This accessible, comprehensive but passionately argued book is quite simply essential reading and perfectly timed – here's hoping Scotland's legislators agree.
LESLEY RIDDOCH

Old Scotland New Scotland

Jeff Fallow
ISBN 0 946487 40 5 PB £6.99

Together we can build a new Scotland based on Labour's values. DONALD DEWAR, Party Political Broadcast

Despite the efforts of decent Mr Dewar, the voters may yet conclude they are looking at the same old hacks in brand new suits. IAN BELL, *The Independent*

At times like this you suddenly realise how dangerous the neglect of Scottish history in our schools and universities may turn out to be.
MICHAEL FRY, *The Herald*

... one of the things I hope will go is our chip on the shoulder about the English... The SNP has a huge responsibility to articulate Scottish independence in a way that is pro-Scottish and not anti-English.
ALEX SALMOND, *The Scotsman*

Scottish politics have never been more exciting. In *Old Scotland New Scotland* Jeff Fallow takes us on a graphic voyage through Scotland's turbulent history, from earliest times through to the present day and beyond. This fast-track guide is the quick way to learn what your history teacher didn't tell you, essential reading for all who seek an understanding of Scotland and its history.

Eschewing the romanticisation of his country's past, Fallow offers a new perspective on an old nation.

Too many people associate Scottish history with tartan trivia or outworn romantic myth. This book aims to blast that stubborn idea.
JEFF FALLOW

A Passion for Scotland

David R. Ross
ISBN 1 84282 019 2 PB £5.99

David R. Ross is passionate about Scotland's past. And its future. In this heartfelt journey through Scotland's story, he shares his passion for what it means to be a Scot.

Eschewing xenophobia, his deep understanding of how Scotland's history touches her people shines through. All over Scotland, into England and Europe, over to Canada, and the United States – the people and the places that bring Scotland's story to life and death, are here. Included are the:

- Early Scots
- Wallace and Bruce
- The Union
- Montrose
- The Jacobites
- John MacLean
- Tartan Day USA

and, revealed for the first time, the burial places of all Scotland's monarchs.

This is not a history book, but it covers history.

This is not a travel guide, but some places mentioned might be worth a visit.

This is not a political manifesto, but a personal one.

Read this book to discover your roots and your passion for Scotland.

The biker-historian's unique combination of unabashed romanticism and easy irreverence make him the ideal guide to historical subjects all too easily swallowed up in maudlin sentiment or 'demythologised' by academic studies.
THE SCOTSMAN

Ross's patriotism is straightforward and unquestioning, albeit relieved by a pawky sense of humour.
THE HERALD

Blind Harry's Wallace
William Hamilton of Gilbertfield
Introduced by Elspeth King
Illustrations by Owain Kirby
ISBN 0 946487 33 2   PB   £8.99

The original story of the real braveheart, Sir William Wallace. Racy, blood on every page, violently anglophobic, grossly embellished, vulgar and disgusting, clumsy and stilted, a literary failure, a great epic.

Whatever the verdict on BLIND HARRY, this is the book which has done more than any other to frame the notion of Scotland's national identity. Despite its numerous 'historical inaccuracies', it remains the principal source for what we now know about the life of Wallace.

The novel and film *Braveheart* were based on the 1722 Hamilton edition of this epic poem. Burns, Wordsworth, Byron and others were greatly influenced by this version 'wherein the old obsolete words are rendered more intelligible', which is said to be the book, next to the Bible, most commonly found in Scottish households in the eighteenth century. Burns even admits to having 'borrowed... a couplet worthy of Homer' directly from Hamilton's version of BLIND HARRY to include in 'Scots wha hae'.

Elspeth King, in her introduction to this, the first accessible edition of BLIND HARRY in verse form since 1859, draws parallels between the situation in Scotland at the time of Wallace and that in Bosnia and Chechnya in the 1990s. Seven hundred years to the day after the Battle of Stirling Bridge, the 'Settled Will of the Scottish People' was expressed in the devolution referendum of 11 September 1997. She describes this as a landmark opportunity for mature reflection on how the nation has been shaped, and sees BLIND HARRY'S WALLACE as an essential and compelling text for this purpose.

A true bard of the people.
TOM SCOTT, THE PENGUIN BOOK OF SCOTTISH VERSE, on Blind Harry.

A more inventive writer than Shakespeare.
RANDALL WALLACE

The story of Wallace poured a Scottish prejudice in my veins which will boil along until the floodgates of life shut in eternal rest.
ROBERT BURNS

Hamilton's couplets are not the best poetry you will ever read, but they rattle along at a fair pace. In re-issuing this work, the publishers have re-opened the spring from which most of our conceptions of the Wallace legend come.
SCOTLAND ON SUNDAY

The return of Blind Harry's Wallace, a man who makes Mel look like a wimp.
THE SCOTSMAN

Notes from the North incorporating a brief history of the Scots and the English
Emma Wood
ISBN 1 84282 048 6   PB   £7.99

Notes on being English
Notes on being in Scotland
Learning from a shared past

Sickened by the English jingoism that surfaced in rampant form during the 1982 Falklands War, Emma Wood started to dream of moving from her home in East Anglia to the Highlands of Scotland.

She felt increasingly frustrated and marginalised as Thatcherism got a grip on the southern English psyche. The Scots she met on frequent holidays in the Highlands had no truck with Thatcherism, and she felt at home with grass-roots Scottish anti-authoritarianism. The decision was made. She uprooted and headed for a new life in the north of Scotland.

She was to discover that she had crossed a border in more than the geographical sense. In this book she sets a study of Scots-English conflicts alongside personal experiences of contemporary incomers' lives in the Highlands. Her own approach has been thoughtful and creative. *Notes from the North* is a pragmatic, positive and forward-looking contribution to cultural and political debate within Scotland.

... her enlightenment is evident on every page of this perceptive, provocative book.
MAIL ON SUNDAY

An intelligent and perceptive book... calm, reflective, witty and sensitive. It should certainly be read by all English visitors to Scotland, be they tourists or incomers. And it should certainly be read by all Scots concerned about what kind of nation we live in.
THE HERALD

public pressure governments will not abide by the Advisory Opinion nor implement their international agreements to abolish nuclear weapons.

This fine book should be read by everyone, especially those who have the slightest doubt that the world will one day be rid of nuclear weapons.
JOHN PILGER

Reading this book will help you play your part in keeping human life human.
REV DR ANDREW MacLELLAN,
MODERATOR OF THE GENERAL
ASSEMBLY OF THE CHURCH OF
SCOTLAND 2000/2001

Trident on Trial: the case for people's disarmament

Angie Zelter
ISBN 1 84282 004 4 PB £9.99

On a beautiful summer's evening in 1999, three women – Ellen Moxley, Ulla Roder and Angie Zelter – boarded a barge moored on a Scottish loch and threw some computer equipment overboard. Sheriff Margaret Gimblett acquitted 'The Trident Three' on the basis that they were acting as global citizens preventing nuclear crime. This led to what is thought to be the world's first High Court examination of the legality of an individual state's deployment of nuclear weapons...

Is Trident inherently unlawful and immoral?

When can a state use or threaten to use nuclear weapons?

Should international law take precedence over a sovereign government's?

Can a government be held accountable for ownership of weapons of mass destruction?

When is a citizen justified in acting against what she reasonably believes to be Government crime?

Is whose name does the UK government deploy 144 nuclear warheads, each around 10 times the power of that dropped on Hiroshima killing some 150,000 people?

This is Angie's personal account of the campaign. It also includes profiles of and contributions by some of the people and groups who have pledged to prevent nuclear crime in peaceful and practical ways. Without such

[Un]comfortably Numb: A Prison Requiem

Maureen Maguire
ISBN 1 84282 001 X PB £8.99

People may think I've taken the easy way out but please believe me this is the hardest thing I've ever had to do.

It was Christmas Eve, the atmosphere in Cornton Vale prison was festive, the girls in high spirits as they were locked up for the night. One of their favourite songs, Pink Floyd's *Comfortably Numb*, played loudly from a nearby cell as Yvonne Gilmour wrote her suicide note. She was the sixth of eight inmates to take their own lives in Cornton Vale prison over a short period of time.

[Un]comfortably Numb follows Yvonne through a difficult childhood, a chaotic adolescence and drug addiction to life and death behind bars. Her story is representative of many women in our prisons today. They are not criminals (only one per cent are convicted for violent crimes) and two-thirds are between the ages of 15 and 30. Suicide rates among them are rising dramatically. Do these vulnerable young girls really belong in prison?

This is a powerful and moving story told in the words of those involved: Yvonne and her family, fellow prisoners, prison officers, social workers, drug workers. It challenges us with questions which demand answers if more deaths are to be avoided.

Uncomfortably Numb is not a legal textbook or a jurisprudential treatise... it is an investigation into something our sophisticated society can't easily face. AUSTIN LAFFERTY

Reportage Scotland: History in the Making

Louise Yeoman
Foreword by Professor David Stevenson
ISBN 1 84282 051 6 PBK £6.99

Events – both major and minor – as seen and recorded by Scots throughout history.

Which king was murdered in a sewer?

What was Dr Fian's love magic?

Who was the half-roasted abbot?

Which cardinal was salted and put in a barrel?

Why did Lord Kitchener's niece try to blow up Burns's cottage?

The answers can all be found in this eclectic mix covering nearly 2,000 years of Scottish history. Historian Louise Yeoman's rummage through the manuscript, book and newspaper archives of the National Library of Scotland has yielded an astonishing range of material from a letter to the king of the Picts to Mary Queen of Scots' own account of the murder of David Riccio; from the execution of William Wallace to accounts of anti-poll tax actions and the opening of the new Scottish Parliament. The book takes pieces from the original French, Latin, Gaelic and Scots and makes them accessible to the general reader, often for the first time.

The result is compelling reading for anyone interested in the history that has made Scotland what it is today.

... a marvellously illuminating and wonderfully readable book telling 'the story of Scotland' ... I find this almost intolerably moving. Yet many extracts made me laugh aloud.

ANGUS CALDER, *Scotland On Sunday*

Absolutely inspired – a splendid selection of the quirky and the quintessential from Scotland's rumbustious history.

MAGNUS MAGNUSSON KBE

A monumental achievement in drawing together such a rich historical harvest.

CHRIS HOLME, *The Herald*

NATURAL WORLD

The Hydro Boys: pioneers of renewable energy
Emma Wood
ISBN 1 84282 047 8 PB £8.99

Wild Scotland
James McCarthy
photographs by Laurie Campbell
ISBN 1 842820 96 6 PB £8.99

Wild Lives: Otters – On the Swirl of the Tide
Bridget MacCaskill
ISBN 0 946487 67 7 PB £9.99

Wild Lives: Foxes – The Blood is Wild
Bridget MacCaskill
ISBN 0 946487 71 5 PB £9.99

Scotland – Land & People: An Inhabited Solitude
James McCarthy
ISBN 0 946487 57 X PB £7.99

The Highland Geology Trail
John L Roberts
ISBN 0 946487 36 7 PB £5.99

Red Sky at Night
John Barrington
ISBN 0 946487 60 X PB £8.99

Listen to the Trees
Don MacCaskill
ISBN 0 946487 65 0 PB £9.99

THE QUEST FOR

The Quest for the Celtic Key
Karen Ralls-MacLeod and
Ian Robertson
ISBN 1 84282 084 2 PB £7.99

The Quest for Robert Louis Stevenson
John Cairney
ISBN 1 84282 085 0 PB £8.99

The Quest for the Original Horse Whisperers
Russell Lyon
ISBN 1 84282 020 6 HB £16.99

The Quest for Arthur
Stuart McHardy
ISBN 1 84282 012 5 HB £16.99

The Quest for the Nine Maidens
Stuart McHardy
ISBN 0 946487 66 9 HB £16.99

The Quest for Charles Rennie Mackintosh
John Cairney
ISBN 1 905222 43 2 PB £8.99

ON THE TRAIL OF

On the Trail of the Pilgrim Fathers
J. Keith Cheetham
ISBN 0 946487 83 9 PB £7.99

On the Trail of Mary Queen of Scots
J. Keith Cheetham
ISBN 0 946487 50 2 PB £7.99

On the Trail of John Wesley
J. Keith Cheetham
ISBN 1 84282 023 0 PB £7.99

On the Trail of William Wallace
David R. Ross
ISBN 0 946487 47 2 PB £7.99

On the Trail of Robert the Bruce
David R. Ross
ISBN 0 946487 52 9 PB £7.99

On the Trail of Robert Service
GW Lockhart
ISBN 0 946487 24 3 PB £7.99

On the Trail of John Muir
Cherry Good
ISBN 0 946487 62 6 PB £7.99

On the Trail of Robert Burns
John Cairney
ISBN 0 946487 51 0 PB £7.99

On the Trail of Bonnie Prince Charlie
David R Ross
ISBN 0 946487 68 5 PB £7.99

On the Trail of Queen Victoria in the Highlands
Ian R Mitchell
ISBN 0 946487 79 0 PB £7.99

ISLANDS

The Islands that Roofed the World: Easdale, Belnahua, Luing & Seil:
Mary Withall
ISBN 0 946487 76 6 PB £4.99

Rum: Nature's Island
Magnus Magnusson
ISBN 0 946487 32 4 PB £7.95

LUATH GUIDES TO SCOTLAND

The North West Highlands: Roads to the Isles
Tom Atkinson
ISBN 1 842820 86 9 PB £6.99

Mull and Iona: Highways and Byways
Peter Macnab
ISBN 1 842820 89 3 PB £5.99

The Northern Highlands: The Empty Lands
Tom Atkinson
ISBN 1 842820 87 7 PB £6.99

The West Highlands: The Lonely Lands
Tom Atkinson
ISBN 1 842820 88 5 PB £6.99

South West Scotland
Tom Atkinson
ISBN 1 905222 15 7 PB £6.99

TRAVEL & LEISURE

Die Kleine Schottlandfibel [Scotland Guide in German]
Hans-Walter Arends
ISBN 1 842820 98 2 PB £8.99

Let's Explore Berwick-upon-Tweed
Anne Bruce English
ISBN 1 84282 029 X PB £4.99

Let's Explore Edinburgh Old Town
Anne Bruce English
ISBN 0 946487 98 7 PB £4.99

Edinburgh's Historic Mile
Duncan Priddle
ISBN 0 946487 97 9 PB £2.99

Pilgrims in the Rough: St Andrews beyond the 19th hole
Michael Tobert
ISBN 0 946487 74 X PB £7.99

FOOD & DRINK

The Whisky Muse: Scotch whisky in poem & song
various, compiled and edited by Robin Laing
ISBN 1 906307 44 X PB £9.99

First Foods Fast: how to prepare delicious simple meals for your baby, from first tastes to one year
Lara Boyd
ISBN 1 905222 46 7 PB £4.99

Edinburgh and Leith Pub Guide
Stuart McHardy
ISBN 0 946487 80 4 PB £4.95

WALK WITH LUATH

Skye 360: walking the coastline of Skye
Andrew Dempster
ISBN 0 946487 85 5 PB £8.99

Hill Walks in the Cairngorms
Ernest Cross
ISBN 1 842820 92 3 PB £4.99

Easy Walks in Monarch of the Glen Country: Badenoch and Strathspey
Ernest Cross
ISBN 1 842820 93 1 PB £4.99

The Joy of Hillwalking
Ralph Storer
ISBN 1 842820 69 9 PB £7.50

Scotland's Mountains before the Mountaineers
Ian R Mitchell
ISBN 0 946487 39 1 PB £9.99

Mountain Days & Bothy Nights
Dave Brown & Ian R Mitchell
ISBN 0 946487 15 4 PB £7.50

Of Big Hills and Wee Men
Peter Kemp
ISBN 1 84282 052 4 PB £7.99

BIOGRAPHY

The Last Lighthouse
Sharma Krauskopf
ISBN 0 946487 96 0 PB £7.99

Tobermory Teuchter
Peter Macnab
ISBN 0 946487 41 3 PB £7.99

Bare Feet & Tackety Boots
Archie Cameron
ISBN 0 946487 17 0 PB £7.95

Come Dungeons Dark
John Taylor Caldwell
ISBN 0 946487 19 7 PB £6.95

SOCIAL HISTORY

Pumpherston: the story of a shale oil village
Sybil Cavanagh
ISBN 1 84282 015 X PB £10.99

Shale Voices
Alistair Findlay
ISBN 1 906307 11 3 PB £10.99

A Word for Scotland
Jack Campbell
ISBN 0 946487 48 0 PB £12.99

Crofting Years
Francis Thompson
ISBN 0 946487 06 5 PB £6.95

Hail Philpstoun's Queen
Barbara and Marie Pattullo
ISBN 1 84282 095 8 PB £6.99

HISTORY

Desire Lines: A Scottish Odyssey
David R Ross
ISBN 1 84282 033 8 PB £9.99

Civil Warrior: extraordinary life & poems of Montrose
Robin Bell
ISBN 1 84282 013 3 HB £10.99

FOLKLORE

Luath Storyteller: Highland Myths & Legends
George W Macpherson
ISBN 1 84282 003 6 PB £5.00

Tales of the North Coast
Alan Temperley
ISBN 0 946487 18 9 PB £8.99

Tall Tales from an Island
Peter Macnab
ISBN 0 946487 07 3 PB £8.99

The Supernatural Highlands
Francis Thompson
ISBN 0 946487 31 6 PB £8.99

GENEALOGY

Scottish Roots: step-by-step guide for ancestor hunters
Alwyn James
ISBN 1 842820 90 7 PB £6.99

SPORT

Over the Top with the Tartan Army
Andy McArthur
ISBN 0 946487 45 6 PB £7.99

Ski & Snowboard Scotland
Hilary Parke
ISBN 0 946487 35 9 PB £6.99

FICTION

Torch
Lin Anderson
ISBN 1 84282 042 7 PB £9.99

Heartland
John MacKay
ISBN 1 84282 059 1 PB £9.99

The Blue Moon Book
Anne MacLeod
ISBN 1 84282 061 3 PB £9.99

The Glasgow Dragon
Des Dillon
ISBN 1 84282 056 7 PB £9.99

Driftnet
Lin Anderson
ISBN 1 84282 034 6 PB £9.99

The Fundamentals of New Caledonia
David Nicol
ISBN 1 84282 93 6 HB £16.99

Milk Treading
Nick Smith
ISBN 1 84282 037 0 PB £6.99

The Road Dance
John MacKay
ISBN 1 84282 024 9 PB £6.99

The Strange Case of RL Stevenson
Richard Woodhead
ISBN 0 946487 86 3 HB £16.99

But n Ben A-Go-Go
Matthew Fitt
ISBN 1 905222 04 1 PB £7.99

The Bannockburn Years
William Scott
ISBN 0 946487 34 0 PB £7.95

Outlandish Affairs: An Anthology of Amorous Encounters
Edited and introduced by Evan Rosenthal and Amanda Robinson
ISBN 1 84282 055 9 PB £9.99

Six Black Candles
Des Dillon
ISBN 1 84282 053 2 PB £6.99

Me and Ma Gal
Des Dillon
ISBN 1 84282 054 0 PB £5.99

The Kitty Killer Cult
Nick Smith
ISBN 1 84282 039 7 PB £9.99

POETRY

Burning Whins
Liz Niven
ISBN 1 84282 074 5 PB £8.99

Drink the Green Fairy
Brian Whittingham
ISBN 1 84282 020 6 PB £8.99

Tartan & Turban
Bashabi Fraser
ISBN 1 84282 044 3 PB £8.99

The Ruba'iyat of Omar Khayyam, in Scots
Rab Wilson
ISBN 1 84282 046 X PB £8.99

Talking with Tongues
Brian D. Finch
ISBN 1 84282 006 0 PB £8.99

Kate o Shanter's Tale and other poems [book]
Matthew Fitt
ISBN 1 84282 028 1 PB £6.99

Kate o Shanter's Tale and other poems [audio CD]
Matthew Fitt
ISBN 1 84282 043 5 PB £9.99

Bad Ass Raindrop
Kokumo Rocks
ISBN 1 84282 018 4 PB £6.99

Madame Fifi's Farewell and other poems
Gerry Cambridge
ISBN 1 84282 005 2 PB £8.99

Poems to be Read Aloud
introduced by Tom Atkinson
ISBN 0 946487 00 6 PB £5.00

Scots Poems to be Read Aloud
introduced by Stuart McHardy
ISBN 0 946487 81 2 PB £5.00

Picking Brambles
Des Dillon
ISBN 1 84282 021 4 PB £6.99

Sex, Death & Football
Alistair Findlay
ISBN 1 84282 022 2 PB £6.99

The Luath Burns Companion
John Cairney
ISBN 1 906307 29 6 PB £7.99

Immortal Memories: A Compilation of Toasts to the Memory of Burns as delivered at Burns Suppers, 1801-2001
John Cairney
ISBN 1 84282 009 5 HB £20.00

Into the Blue Wavelengths
Roderick Watson
ISBN 1 84282 075 3 PB £8.99

The Souls of the Dead are Taking the Best Seats: 50 World Poets on War
Compiled by Angus Calder and Beth Junor
ISBN 1 84282 032 X PB £7.99

Sun Behind the Castle
Angus Calder
ISBN 1 84282 078 8 PB £8.99

LANGUAGE

Luath Scots Language Learner [Book]
L Colin Wilson
ISBN 0 946487 91 X PB £9.99

Luath Scots Language Learner [Double Audio CD Set]
L Colin Wilson
ISBN 1 84282 026 5 CD £16.99

Luath Press Limited
committed to publishing well written books worth reading

LUATH PRESS takes its name from Robert Burns, whose little collie Luath (*Gael.*, swift or nimble) tripped up Jean Armour at a wedding and gave him the chance to speak to the woman who was to be his wife and the abiding love of his life. Burns called one of 'The Twa Dogs' Luath after Cuchullin's hunting dog in Ossian's *Fingal*. Luath Press was established in 1981 in the heart of Burns country, and now resides a few steps up the road from Burns' first lodgings on Edinburgh's Royal Mile.

Luath offers you distinctive writing with a hint of unexpected pleasures.

Most bookshops in the UK, the US, Canada, Australia, New Zealand and parts of Europe either carry our books in stock or can order them for you. To order direct from us, please send a £sterling cheque, postal order, international money order or your credit card details (number, address of cardholder and expiry date) to us at the address below. Please add post and packing as follows: UK – £1.00 per delivery address; overseas surface mail – £2.50 per delivery address; overseas airmail – £3.50 for the first book to each delivery address, plus £1.00 for each additional book by airmail to the same address. If your order is a gift, we will happily enclose your card or message at no extra charge.

Luath Press Limited
543/2 Castlehill
The Royal Mile
Edinburgh EH1 2ND
Scotland
Telephone: 0131 225 4326 (24 hours)
Fax: 0131 225 4324
email: sales@luath.co.uk
Website: www.luath.co.uk